```
    Iowa
    323.4
A153   Allen
         Freedom in Iowa
                                    780511
```

DATE DUE

Fe 15 '90			

Learning Resources Center

Marshalltown Community College

Marshalltown, Iowa 50158

OEMCO

FREEDOM IN IOWA:

The Role of the Iowa Civil Liberties Union

FREEDOM IN IOWA:

The Role of the Iowa Civil Liberties Union

EDWARD S. ALLEN

The Iowa State University Press / Ames

EDWARD S. ALLEN, professor of mathematics at Iowa State University, holds A.B., A.M., and Ph.D. degrees from Harvard. He has written, edited, and translated several books in mathematics and physics. One of the founders of the Iowa Civil Liberties Union and three times its president, he has received a number of awards for his long and devoted service to civil liberties.

© 1977 The Iowa State University Press
Ames, Iowa 50010. All rights reserved

Composed and printed by The Iowa State University Press

First edition, 1977

Library of Congress Cataloging in Publication Data

Allen, Edward Switzer, 1887-
    Freedom in Iowa.

    Includes bibliographical references and index.
    1. Civil rights—Iowa—History. 2. Iowa Civil Liberties Union.
I. Title.
KFI4611.A94   323.4'09777   76-47009
ISBN 0-8138-0700-X

TO MINNE

CONTENTS

	Foreword	ix
	Preface	xi
	Introduction	xiii
1	Civil Liberties in Iowa prior to 1935	3
2	Criminal Syndicalism	13
3	State Legislation	22
4	The Iowa Civil Liberties Union and the American Civil Liberties Union	28
5	Freedom in the Universities	40
6	Rights of Teachers	50
7	Censorship	55
8	Police Practices	60
9	Clothing Controversies in Schools	65
10	Child Custody	73
11	Miscellaneous Litigation	79
	Suspicion of Sodomy	79
	Protesting Pacifist	81
	Swift and Careless "Justice"	81
	Clerk's Transcript	82
	Lèse Majesté	83
	Segregation of Migrants	84
	Priority Projects	84
	Management of War Memorials	85
12	Religion and the State	86
13	The Disadvantaged	96
	The Mentally Ill	96
	Minority Races	99
	Conscientious Objectors	104
	Welfare Recipients	109
	Women	111
14	German Visitors	116
15	Chapter Activities	118
	Quad Cities	118
	Hawkeye Area	119

	Grinnell	122
	Northeast Iowa	123
	Northwest Iowa	124
	Sioux City	124
	Cardinal Area	125
	Des Moines Area Committee	129
16	Organization	130
	Awards	130
	Publications	132
	Finances	134
	Presidents and Staff	135
	Appendix 1. Correspondence Relating to the 1940 Resolution	138
	Appendix 2. Three Statements of ACLU Concerning the 1940 Resolution	141
	Appendix 3. Statement of ICLU Relating to the 1940 Resolution	146
	Appendix 4. Statement from the State Board of Regents, July 1970	149
	ICLU Statement on Regents' Uniform Rules of Personal Conduct	152
	Appendix 5. Resolution Urging Return of Japanese-Americans Studying in Iowa Colleges to Their Relocation Centers	155
	Appendix 6. ICLU Statement on Governmental Data Banks and Civil Liberties	157
	Abbreviations	161
	Notes	163
	Name Index	175

FOREWORD

WHEN I became president of the Iowa Civil Liberties Union in 1964, I made a search for material relating to the history of the Iowa affiliate. I could find none, either in the scanty ICLU files or in the Des Moines or state libraries. So I asked Edward Allen, an ICLU founder who had remained a faithful board member all through the years, if he would be willing to write a history of the organization. He generously agreed to do so.

By a happy coincidence, he was able to make extensive use of the ACLU files on deposit at Princeton University during several summers that he and his wife, Minne, spent with their daughter who lived in the area. From this source he has been able to retrieve a good deal of information about the ICLU which has helped him in developing this work.

All who have been associated with the ICLU have great affection and respect for Edward Allen for his long and devoted service to the cause of civil liberties. This history is added testament to this devotion.

LOUISE NOUN

PREFACE

NOT long after Louise Noun became president of the Iowa Civil Liberties Union, she suggested I be named its historian. After that came the idea that I write a history of the organization. For this idea there were good reasons: I had met Roger Baldwin in 1917 when he was placed in charge of a forerunner of the American Civil Liberties Union and had had much correspondence with him from then on; I had had three terms as president (including the first after the founding of ICLU); I had been one of the editors of its Bulletin during the years it was produced in Ames. What she did not realize was the small store of documents I had kept—partly through carelessness, partly because of moving from place to place, above all because I had no thought that a history of this affiliate of ACLU would some day be written.

The fact that the archives of the American Civil Liberties Union are in the library of Princeton University, together with the fact that the material I had was scanty and not systematically selected, made a prolonged stay in Princeton absolutely necessary. Very fortunately our daughter, Rosemarie Lechner, lived with her family near Princeton and later in that community. Even more important was the hospitality of Dr. Joseph Rampona and his wife, Ruth, whose home became the home of my wife and me for three summers.

Gathering material from the archives of ACLU, I soon realized that a story of ICLU alone would be but a fragment of a possible history of the realization and nonrealization in the state of the ideals of ACLU—freedom and equality—an account that would cover years both before and during the existence of ICLU. The broader scope of the narrative made it possible, indeed imperative, to mention occasions when this affiliate of ACLU had failed to act on situations in its own field of interest.

Let me now speak briefly of the main sources on which I have relied.

The American Civil Liberties Union Archives constitute by far the most important source of material for this account of freedom in Iowa. Documents of the most recent five years are retained in the New York office of ACLU; then they are transferred in annual installments to the library of Princeton University. The papers of the earlier years of the ACLU were collected in scrapbook volumes; the older volumes (through 1930) are for the most part so fragile that they cannot be handled either for reading or for photoduplication. A microfilm of the archives from their beginning through 1952 was made at the New York Public Library which was the repository prior to the archives' being acquired by Princeton. Other institutions holding copies of the complete or nearly complete microfilm are the New York Public Library, Brandeis University Library, and the University of Wisconsin.

I wish to express warm thanks to Alexander P. Clark, the librarian in charge of the ACLU Archives, and to the members of his staff for their most friendly and efficient help in fulfilling every request.

The records of the American Union against Militarism, out of which ACLU eventually grew, are kept in the Peace Collection of Swarthmore College Library. I studied them there.

The Immer Papers were given me by Esther Immer, who had for a time been secretary of ICLU. They cover not only her term of office but records she inherited from predecessors.

The Ransom Papers are material (largely newspaper clippings) I was able to examine in the office of Charles F. Ransom (once president of ICLU) in his office (Des Moines Register and Tribune).

Thanks are due to many who have given me information, encouragement, and advice. First of course is Louise Noun, who proposed the project of such a history of ICLU. Both information and editorial advice came from Herbert Kelly while he was executive secretary of ICLU. Important counsel has been given by Will C. Jumper, professor of English at Iowa State University and for a time president of the Cardinal Area Chapter of ICLU. Many officers of the various chapters have been truly helpful. Nearly all of the typing was done by Vera Markt, whose resourceful and efficient work I wish to acknowledge with warm thanks.

The interest, encouragement, and cooperation of my wife, Minne E. Allen, have been heartening—indeed essential—to the progress of the work.

It is certain that we will always have civil liberties problems in Iowa—some of natures we cannot yet guess. I have hope and confidence that ICLU will continue to work vigorously and with growing effectiveness; it should be the best embodiment of the state's motto: OUR LIBERTIES WE PRIZE; OUR RIGHTS WE WILL MAINTAIN.

INTRODUCTION

"WHO I am and why I came to Harvard"; writing on this theme was the first task set a student in his beginning English course at that college. Now that I have been asked to write about the history of the Iowa Civil Liberties Union (and find it important to expand the topic to cover the general condition of freedom in the state), I put the question to myself: "What is the civil liberties portion of complex me; how did it fit me for this assignment?"

From 1902 to 1905 I attended the Atlantic City High School. Since the old Athenian Literary Society seemed to some of us too anemic, we founded the Webster-Hayne Debating Society. It had frequent meetings and a dwindling membership, resulting in ever-growing demands on the remaining faithful. When a debate on divorce was announced, the principal let it be known that he would not favor our talking on this subject. However, he did not use "proper channels" in reaching us, so we ignored the warning. The debate took place, with the principal in the audience. No more was said.

At graduation time I gave the valedictory address; in it I thanked the faculty for teaching us never to fear the truth, wherever it might lead. The main subject of my talk was "American Diplomacy." My elders persuaded me to make it milder in its treatment of our government than I had intended.

My memories of five subsequent years in Cambridge contain hardly a hint of devotion to the principles of the Civil Liberties Union. The nearest that I can come to such a concern is a brief inactive membership in the Harvard Socialist Club. Perhaps I joined because my dormitory neighbor, Walter Lippmann, was its president. Neither do I find in my two years of study in Italy any relevant memories. I accepted the Italian version of the Libyan war almost uncritically, as I had accepted the American version of the war against Spain.

Dartmouth was the scene of my first college teaching of mathematics. There I rediscovered my classmate Roy Wilson Follett (as author he later dropped the Roy), who was teaching English. We had many congenial hours together, especially when he played the piano, I the violin. He had been persuaded to stay at Dartmouth, even though Washington University invited him to go to St. Louis, by a promise of advancement at the end of the year—the year we shared in Hanover. During that time, however, he fell from favor; the device used for ousting him was revealing.

Roy taught a course in advanced composition. One student, in spite of the warning that he seemed unqualified, insisted on enrolling. The warning was justified. The student took to writing a theme by putting down whatever words came into his head. Roy wrote on a paper returned to the boy: "If you continue in this way you will land in the mad house."

The student, wishing to drop the course, called on the president's closest assistant and showed him the paper with comment. The administrator said, "You may drop the course if you will write what I dictate to you." What he dictated was a statement that Follett had insulted and humiliated him and owed him an apology.

Armed with this letter "from a student," the president told Roy that only this apology would give him a chance for retention at Dartmouth; there was no longer a question of that advancement he had been promised a year before.

When I was invited that spring to an instructorship at Brown, I accepted. I reported to the head of my department that the treatment of Roy Follett was the reason for my leaving. He said I could have stayed, had I wished; however, I also was under a cloud because of close association with four critics of the college—Follett and three boardinghouse table-mates—even though I was accused of no unseemly attitude. Thus I came to know guilt by association.

The summer of 1914 I spent in Germany. That season, disastrous for the world in general, was a time of great good fortune for me. Minne Müller-Liebenwalde and I met and became engaged. Our common devotion to the ideals of equality, freedom, and peace became clear during those months; sharing in them has had much to do with our happiness in our connection with the Civil Liberties Union.

In September I returned to America and found that Follett had also gone to Brown; indeed, he and his wife had reserved a room for me in their home.

Back in Germany in the summer of 1915, I married Minne in August. I had accepted an instructorship at the University of Michigan, and we reached Ann Arbor just in time for my first faculty meeting.

When the war between Germany and the United States began, we had the fear of total isolation—fear that the people of one nation would not think of those of an opposing nation as persons. Minne and I hoped that we could do a little to prevent this estrangement. We thought of going to Denmark, there receiving human interest news from both America and Germany and passing it on to sympathetic journals in Germany and America. Alexander Ziwet, head of my department, thought the plan would almost surely fail and advised against it. By disregarding his advice and persisting in our at-

Introduction

tempt, we brought him to a closer friendship than ever before. Such a man was he!

Minne already knew Jane Addams, director of Hull House, the renowned Chicago settlement house. When her peace-seeking group visited Berlin in 1915, Minne had served as interpreter for them. We told Miss Addams of our Danish scheme, and she thought well of it. She did what she could for us in Chicago and recommended other possible helpers, among them Lillian Wald in New York. When I went there to see her, she was just leaving for a luncheon meeting and asked me to accompany her. It turned out to be a session of the American Union against Militarism—that meeting (June 25, 1917) at which the name of National Civil Liberties Bureau was accepted for the section devoted to work for conscientious objectors. Roger Baldwin, its director, was among those present. So came my early initiation into the movement.

Naturally we never came near to embarkation for Denmark but lived on in Ann Arbor. When conscription was proposed in Congress, a peace organization asked those who were opposed to it to sign a petition. I wrote a letter to the newspaper in favor of the petition. I expressed regret, however, that the sponsor was an organization specifically for peace—all lovers of freedom, whatever their views on the war, ought to wish military service to be voluntary. (The petition was stolen from the drugstore where it lay open and so never reached Congress.)

The war needed money—"voluntary" money. Another mathematician called our whole department together to get us to buy war bonds. I alone did not respond; I said truthfully that I could not afford to. But I wrote him that I also had other reasons: specifically, war is so destructive that it may claim voluntary support only if one's own cause is much better than that of the adversary. That, I believed, was not the case in 1917. I said that I wrote this out of esteem for him, for his eyes only. But other eyes saw the letter, and it had consequences.

Then there was the day when all Washtenaw County men of military age but not in military service were summoned to Hill Auditorium. After mass singing and atrocity propaganda had dulled the critical faculties, we learned what the summons was about. Our county had done well by the Liberty Bonds, but the minibonds—War Savings Stamps—had not been sold in the desired quantities. Each of us was expected to promise to buy or sell these stamps in the amount of $50.00 and to indicate willingness by standing. Ushers went up and down the aisles, noting the sitters. In my row there were a Chinese student and I; I found it senseless to insist on small-scale lending in an area where so much had already been gathered in the large.

The war ended. But in the summer of 1919, when all other teachers had long-delayed increases in salary, the increase Alexander Ziwet had recommended for me was denied—because of "disloyalty." I could stay on for a year only, but with no raise. I had a conversation with the dean of Engineering (I taught in his college), who stated it to be the duties of my German wife and me to hold contrary views. What a marriage did he envisage! Thereafter came a formal hearing with the president. My restoration to equal standing might take place, he said, if I would promise to support every future war of the United States in all ways—even those not demanded by law.

Professor Ziwet did all he could for me; in Michigan nothing was possible, but his efforts secured me a post at West Virginia University. During our two years at Morgantown I showed little active concern for freedom or equality. Just before leaving for Iowa, however, I sent a letter to the <u>Old Dominion</u>, giving reasons for not accepting a recent invitation in its pages to join the Ku Klux Klan. The journal never printed my letter; but a copy, sent to Roger Baldwin, was a further link with the ACLU.

This, then, was my preparation for that growing interest and involvement in Iowa's civil liberties which followed my coming to this state in 1921.

FREEDOM IN IOWA:

The Role of the Iowa Civil Liberties Union

CHAPTER 1

Civil Liberties in Iowa prior to 1935

FOR the ancestry of the ACLU we must go back to November 1915. The war in Europe had a strong influence in the United States, still neutral. Then an Anti-Militarism Committee was formed, with Lillian Wald (director of the Henry Street Settlement in New York) as its chairman. She and Alice Lewisohn were among the chief contributors. A few weeks later the name was changed to Anti-Preparedness Committee. In April 1916 the organization became the American Union against Militarism.

On November 12, 1917, preference for the word "for" instead of "against" led to reorganization as the American Union for a Democratic Peace; this change, however, seems to have been short-lived, for we find the title American Union against Militarism in use again thereafter.[1]

Early in 1916 the Union distributed copies of testimony given by General Nelson A. Miles in the Senate: against unusual expenditure for armaments, for more efficiency, for removal of private profit, for levying of income and inheritance taxes to meet new costs, for creation of a Pan-American Congress, for study of relations with the Orient.

By September 1916 AUAM had developed its own program: opposition to conscription, promotion of an international tribunal, work for the people's direct action against war. The influence of popular opinion in preventing war with Mexico was cited as an example. After America entered the war, the Union changed its emphasis.

In 1917 Norman Thomas of New York was already active in the Socialist Party and in resistance to war. On April 12, he, Jane Addams, and Lillian Wald sent Newton Baker (Secretary of War) a memorandum on exemption from that compulsory military service whose enactment they expected. They urged that exemption be granted to individuals on the ground of their own beliefs and that authority to grant such exemption be in a civil tribunal. They named the degrees of conscientious objection to be expected and ended with a note: "In offering this memorandum we do not imply support of the principle of selective draft, which we are obliged to oppose as in itself dangerous to democracy."

Baker answered at once, addressing a letter to Jane Addams. He would bring the suggestions to the attention of chairmen of the Senate and House Committees, and he thanked her for the clarity of the statement.

On May 2, 1917, Roger Baldwin—who had come from St. Louis to begin his long service in the cause of freedom—wrote to the conferees on the Army bill. He objected strongly to the limitation of recognized conscientious objection to "well-recognized sects whose creeds oppose participation in war." Insisting that conscience is nothing if not individual, he gave cogent reasons for his position. Four days later Charles T. Hallinan, who was to work in this cause for some years, also wrote to the conferees, questioning the constitutionality of the draft. By July the draft law had been ruled constitutional,[2] and the AUAM had to give up hopes of opposing it as a whole.

The Union then gave much attention to the kind of peace that would follow the war against Germany and Austria. It urged a settlement in a spirit of reconciliation—such as one ought to hope for on the basis of Woodrow Wilson's earlier praise of "peace without victory" (Jan. 22, 1917); such as the German Reichstag, by a strong majority, had urged in the summer of 1917; such as Russia (the Kerensky Russia which followed the revolution of March 1917) desired. In brief, there should be no forcible annexation, no crippling indemnities.

Emily Greene Balch was a professor of economics at Wellesley College—a position she would lose in 1918 because of her pacifism. A strong supporter of AUAM, she was urged by that Union to write a book that would further its purpose. It was hoped that the work could be issued by October 1917; actually the Author's Note, which serves as a preface, was dated January 1918. The book, published by B. W. Huebsch, is entitled Approaches to the Great Settlement. The introduction is by Norman Angell, British author of The Great Illusion and many other books, who would receive the Nobel Peace Prize in 1933. The Balch work published for the AUAM is a "brief objective account of the successive steps in approaching a settlement of the war," beginning with an entry from President Wilson's Peace Note of December 1916 and continuing to the various replies to the Note which Pope Benedict XV published in August 1917. It contains 165 pages of text, 150 pages of documents, and 40 pages of bibliography—a work of thorough scholarship which had, sad to say, less influence than it deserved. One may regret its covering an interval that ended before the October revolution in Russia. However, its value is great in that it tells of the Russia between the two revolutions of 1917.

The book seems to have been undeservedly ignored. A search in the book review columns of six journals (Independent, New York Times, Nation, New Republic, Outlook, Survey) revealed mention in only one—a single descriptive sentence in the Independent. The silence of the Survey is especially strange, since that periodical

frequently printed reviews by Miss Balch of other books.
  Although its emphasis was always contrary to the government's program, AUAM emphasized its "lack of intention or desire to interfere with the government's plans for prosecuting the war."[3] Having failed to prevent conscription during the war, AUAM lent its energy to opposing plans for permanent compulsory military service or training.
  This Union had supporters in Iowa. On September 24, 1919, the secretary reported that James M. Pierce, in addition to giving $500 worth of printing free, had offered the Union free publicity in his periodicals—Iowa Homestead, Wisconsin Farmer, and others.
  The Iowa Homestead was later merged with Wallaces Farmer. Donald R. Murphy, since 1935 both an editor of this journal and an important supporter of ICLU, wrote me in 1967 when I had told him of this generous act:

> One of the fine things about Jim Pierce was his attitude during World War I on "pro-German areas." As you recall, there were unhappy incidents involving people of German ancestry. Pierce protested against high pressure methods used to sell Liberty Bonds to farmers. He fought vigorously against the wartime tendency to pin disloyalty charges on farmers of German descent. . . . I didn't know about the AUAM record on Pierce, but I am not surprised.

  The Palimpsest for September 1956, an issue written by Donald Murphy, celebrates the century of agricultural journalism of which these two papers are a part and shows in particular the role played by James Pierce from 1885 until his death in 1920.
  Closely associated with the opposition to conscription as an institution was the solicitude of AUAM for conscientious objectors. Early in the war it decided to have a special branch for counseling and defending such young men; this was named the Bureau for Conscientious Objectors. At the Board session of June 25, 1917, it was renamed the Civil Liberties Bureau. Under the direction of Roger Baldwin, the Bureau was concerned with much more than conscription and those who resisted it. A memorandum of September 11, 1917, tells of invasions of constitutional rights:

> 1. Free speech and assemblage. There had been eight indictments. In Philadelphia thirteen were arrested and charged with treason; they had distributed "Long Live the Constitution of the United States," which dealt in a lawful way with the constitutionality of conscription.
> 2. Unlawful arrest, search, and seizure. "Gross violation of law in making arrests for opposition to war policies."
> 3. Assumption of power by the military.
> 4. Activities of overzealous district attorneys in cases of unlawful arrest.
> 5. Arbitrary action by the Post Office Department. Twenty issues of a bulletin were held and declared unmailable under the Es-

pionage Act, even though the Department of Justice asked no indictment of the publishers. Private, sealed first-class mail was held six weeks without notice. (On July 24, 1917, Roger Baldwin had reported that copies of a bulletin on freedom of the press and on the creation of the Civil Liberties Bureau had been mailed ten days earlier to 2500 contributing members but not delivered to them.)

The Civil Liberties Bureau, created by the AUAM, declared its independence within four months and added the adjective National to its title. On October 17, 1917, it was announced that, "owing to the rapid expansion of its work, requiring additional funds and a supervisory committee of its own, it has severed connection with the parent organization."

In September A. A. Berle (who served Tufts College as professor of Applied Christianity) had written to Crystal Eastman (author of Work Accidents and the Law) an interesting prediction: "The American Union against Militarism is comprehensive and inclusive. The Civil Liberties Bureau will naturally disappear with the war."[4] It turned out quite the contrary; the AUAM dwindled in membership and activity, expiring officially on February 1, 1922.[5]

The National Civil Liberties Bureau, reorganized and renamed the American Civil Liberties Union in 1920, has been aiding freedom ever since, with growing support and influence. That growth, to be sure, has had its setbacks, its flaws, its disappointments—as the reader of these pages will learn. The greatest disappointment is the slow rate at which the ideals of freedom and equality permeate the American people.

Roger Baldwin was so opposed to conscription and to war that he could not obey the Selective Service Law. He resigned from the directorship of the Civil Liberties Bureau in the summer of 1918. He was arraigned on October 10 and tried on the 30th. Although a prisoner, in the intervening twenty days he restored order to the papers of NCLB, which the investigation of that body had put in disarray. In his trial he made an eloquent statement of his personal principles, making it clear that he was not speaking for the organization. He spoke of his

> uncompromising opposition to the principle of conscription of life by the State for any purpose whatever, in time of war or peace. . . . I regard the principle of conscription of life as a flat contradiction of all our cherished ideals of individual freedom, democratic liberty and Christian teaching. . . . I am opposed to this and all other wars. . . . My opposition is not only to direct military service but to any service whatever designed to help prosecute the war.

His sentence of a year in prison was expected—almost invited. For himself he made no complaint about the days he spent in the Tombs (New York), Essex County Jail (Newark, N.J.), and Caldwell Prison Farm.

Albert DeSilver replaced Baldwin faithfully and efficiently

until the latter returned to the directorship of NCLB in December 1919; even after that DeSilver helped in the direction of the organization, both before and after its reorganization.

The American Civil Liberties Union, with its home in New York, was concerned with problems of the whole nation. A nationwide organization was needed. It is still in the process of formation, in the sense that there are still states with no "affiliates" (as regional branches are now called), and some in which only a fraction of the territory is covered. In Iowa, for instance, there was no branch until 1935; yet the Iowa Civil Liberties Union is one of the affiliates with the longest continuous history.

From the outset, however, ACLU sought the help of correspondents and cooperating lawyers everywhere and found a few in Iowa. What we can record of the years before 1935 is threefold: what was done (or attempted) in cooperation with Iowans; what was done by direct contact between New York and individuals; and what, for lack of an effective state body, was left undone though it should not have been neglected.

The Civil Liberties Bureau, growing out of concern for conscientious objectors, shows that emphasis in its reports relating to Iowa. Its Bulletin Six[6] lists men who had been court-martialed and sentenced; "conscientious objection seems the motive for resisting orders." In this single bulletin we read of cases handled at Camp Dodge, Iowa: seven men had 25-year sentences, and one was to serve 20 years.

An Iowan seeking advice from the New York office was H. E. Campbell of West Branch, Iowa. As a conscientious objector who did not belong to a pacifist sect—one who was needed on the farm—he was in correspondence with AUAM from August 1917 until February 1918. On February 2 Roger Baldwin advised him as to the best time for refusing to go further—when military training would be required. This apparently was on the assumption that the board was unanimous in refusing exemption.[7]

In March 1918 Laetitia Moon Conard of Grinnell (later one of the founders and zealous workers for the Iowa Civil Liberties Union) wrote to NCLB about conscientious objectors, not Quakers, who were spiritually lonely in prison. She was in contact with three at Fort Leavenworth, one of whom called her the spiritual "mother" of the group. She hoped through this letter to stir others to give like help. Baldwin cautioned her that the War Department had warned against encouragement of such correspondence; it could have results disastrous to sender and recipient.[8]

During the war Iowa was in the area of concern for NCLB, partly because of the conscientious objectors held at Camp Dodge. About a dozen of them were in correspondence with the New York office—men mostly from states other than Iowa. One of them was Otto Wangerin. T. E. Latimer wrote Baldwin that Wangerin was willing to do any noncombatant work but refused to put on a uniform or to drill. He received a 15-year sentence. This sentence was affirmed, with numerous others, by the Supreme Court of the United States, when that court found the Selective Draft Law constitutional, January 7,

1918. Walter Nelles had presented a brief amicus curiae.[9] Latimer wrote: "It appears that the attitude of the officers of the various cantonments is extremely hostile to the conscientious objector, especially if he happens to be a Socialist."[10]

About this time Baldwin wrote, perhaps too trustingly: "The officials at Washington are still displaying the most liberal and sympathetic attitude, but of course we have trouble in many of the cantonments."[11]

A letter from Mrs. David T. Blodgett in Des Moines to Roger Baldwin[12] started a rather long correspondence. She reported that her husband was in Fort Leavenworth, sentenced to 20 years' imprisonment for violating the Espionage Act. He had, she said, bitter enemies whose corruption he had exposed. Could NCLB help an appeal?

As a candidate for Congress, Blodgett had called for conscription of both men and property—all capital above $200,000 and all income above $4000. He was convicted mainly for a pamphlet advocating the defeat of legislators who had voted for compulsory military service. Addressed "To Voters of Iowa," it had been mailed to several thousand men of draft age.[13]

Nelles replied that the case was not a hopeful one. He personally felt that Blodgett was a victim of a wrong construction of a bad law. The NCLB had no money to spare but might help an attorney with advice.[14]

Later NCLB tried to find a lawyer in Des Moines who would help the prisoner, but with no success. Hubert Utterback wrote: "Blodgett's conduct has forfeited my sympathy and good will." E. R. Mason said that he had been charged with an "attempt to cause insubordination and resistance to the law." Common report had it that the severity of the sentence and the excessive bail required were the result of Blodgett's general reputation.[15]

Certainly Blodgett was a man who won enemies easily. He wrote President Woodrow Wilson, complaining that postage for mail which had not been delivered was not refunded to him. A later letter of complaints to the President was five pages long. In an appeal that his trial be reported fairly, he called the publisher of the Daily Capital "an influential, wealthy, and vulturous criminal."[16]

The difficulty in finding an attorney to defend Blodgett came both from his personality and from wartime bias in the people. Thus E. R. Mason wrote that C. O. Holly, a candidate for mayor of Des Moines, was attacked as pro-German because he espoused the cause of Blodgett. He got a very small vote.[17]

The Des Moines law firm of Brammer, Lehman, and Seevers, after voicing strong disapproval of Blodgett himself, added: "Our entire lack of sympathy with such cases is probably partially due to the fact that we believe that the activities of such men have a direct tendency to prolong the war."[18]

Yet more outspoken was H. C. Horack of Iowa City, secretary of the Iowa State Bar Association. "I am extremely suspicious of any organization which is making it its business to worry about free speech in times like these."[19]

Blodgett was freed on Christmas 1921 through commutation of

Civil Liberties in Iowa prior to 1935

his sentence. This was the same time Eugene Debs was released from prison. Debs had been imprisoned, first for his part in a railway strike, later because he made a speech condemning government prosecutions for sedition. He was Socialist candidate for President four times, once receiving a million votes while he was in prison.

Another man who gained freedom then was the Reverend Wilhelm Schumann, minister of the German Lutheran Church at Pomeroy. He had been convicted of preaching a disloyal sermon and had served two years of his sentence when released.[20]

Strikes often involve civil liberties issues. Defenders of civil liberties will insist that strikers have every opportunity to make their case heard but that they not use violence against their opponents. Following are a few such cases occurring before the foundation of the Iowa Civil Liberties Union in 1935.

In the autumn of 1921 the Amalgamated Meat Cutters and Butcher Workers of North America struck against the Ottumwa plant of John Morrell and Co. Governor Nathan E. Kendall ordered troops to duty there, "not on strike duty but for law and order."[21] Not concerned with the issues of the strike but anxious that workers not be deprived of their rights, ACLU sought an Iowan who would conduct an impartial investigation. Clarence N. Case of Iowa City replied to the appeal:

> Conditions are such that it is not only impossible for a teacher in a state institution to take a hand in such a matter as that at Ottumwa, but it is not even advisable to say much about it in a public way. . . . I believe that to take hold of this would lead to such a sacrifice (of position), not because of any lack of desire on the part of our University administration to maintain academic freedom, for they are not remiss in that respect, but because conditions are just what they are, and because the University has to operate in the face of these conditions.[22]

Receiving a similar request, I (having just come to Iowa State College) said I could go to Ottumwa on Saturday and Sunday only; I did not think this would give time enough for the study that would be needed. Lucille B. Milner, who had become field secretary of ACLU on its creation, wrote a little later that they thought they could get the facts without my going.[23]

Of the conditions at Ottumwa, J. Hillgardner, director of the strike, reported in early December that the troops were gone but replaced by 200 deputies and that they were worse than the soldiers. There were 73 injunctions against as many union members. Three officers of the local were forbidden to go down one street; some business people were not allowed to stand in front of their places of business.[24]

In connection with picketing by union barbers in a shop with lower pay and longer hours, the Supreme Court of Iowa stated: "There is a fair field of persuasion; but where such statement injures business, the union's act becomes conspiracy and intimidation." One may ask whether this opinion would permit any picketing at all; surely picketing that does not injure business would usually be pointless.[25]

At Cedar Rapids Judge F. L. Anderson was willing to permit iron molders to speak singly to strikebreakers at the Holland Furnace Company, but "a striker must have his drawing room manners with him."[26]

A labor dispute of much interest to ACLU was that involving the United States Gypsum Plaster Company at Fort Dodge. Since 1921 the company had been fighting for an open shop. The form of application for employment used in 1929 is revealing. One applied for a job at a certain rate—subject to revision at the option of the company. If the employee were to leave, he must allow time for replacement to be found; the company might discharge him at any time. The applicant promised not to strike nor to unite with other employees for a change of hours, wages, or working conditions. He had to state that he was not and would not become a member of IWW, the Communist Party, or a like organization. He promised to obey all rules.

After John Heslop of the Gypsum Mill Workers Union had denounced this "yellow dog contract," Judge George C. Scott issued an injunction against him and others, forbidding them to:

1. conspire to injure the complainant's business, trade, and good will, to prevent its operation on an open shop basis, to coerce him to have a closed shop;
2. say that the company was unfair to organized labor or advocate a boycott;
3. say that the strike of 1921 or any strike existed or was endorsed by the Fort Dodge Labor Assembly;
4. say that the company employed convict laborers paroled to it.[27]

This injunction, issued July 23, 1929, was denounced as outrageous by Senator Smith Wildman Brookhart; in correspondence with ACLU John D. Denison (who later became one of the firmest supporters of ICLU) said that it went clearly beyond the law and violated the constitutional right of free speech.[28]

The years 1932 and 1933 were a time of deep depression for most Americans and of desperation for many farmers. In western Iowa farmers tried to raise the low prices of their products by keeping those products off the market: in Cherokee they stopped a milk truck and poured the milk on the ground;[29] they also burned a railroad bridge nearby to prevent the flow of livestock.[30] In promotion of this idea the Farmers Holiday Association was formed. Independent of this—less militant, but with strong sympathy for the same idea—was the Farmers Union. Its leader in Iowa, Milo Reno, originated the idea of a thirty-day "holiday," to end sooner if prices rose; in fact, a rise in the price of milk for bottling from $1.00 to $1.80 a hundredweight was recorded at this time.[31]

With income cut by low prices, many farmers faced foreclosure of mortgages on their farms. When sales were attempted, sympathetic neighbors might interfere or see to it that the farm was sold for a very low price. In 1933 the legislature acted to help those hard pressed. As Governor Clyde Herring stated: "Under the measure passed and signed six weeks ago, there is a two-year moratorium on foreclosures. This does not halt a sale, but the occupants cannot be moved for two years and in that time have the right to straighten themselves out."[32]

The law was unable to satisfy the farmers. At Winterset Judge E. W. Dingwell held it unconstitutional.[33] At Primghar Judge C. C. Bradley refused to promise not to sign foreclosures and was threatened with lynching. This brought a call for the National Guard, and their conduct was the occasion of much concern in the ACLU.[34] They declared martial law in Plymouth, Crawford, and O'Brien counties—indeed, they made arrests in seven counties.[35]

In Crawford County all public business was suspended; military prisoners were held incommunicado.[36] In matters affecting civil liberties, the absence of an Iowa affiliate of ACLU was a handicap. Yet the national office and certain correspondents in the state showed lively interest and, it seems, had some influence.

Thus ACLU reminded Governor Herring that the United States Supreme Court the previous year had "held that the mere fiat of a governor declaring that grounds exist for placing a given district under martial law was not binding on the courts and that an injured party would have standing in the courts to upset such action."[37] The Union insisted that since the acts charged against certain persons were committed before there was martial law, their right to a jury trial must be preserved. For this purpose ACLU offered its services.

In letters and telegrams to various Iowans, the Union also proposed suits against those who had violated farmers' rights. In particular, Lawrence Gasper of Granville, Sioux County, asked a militiaman what warrant he could produce for Gasper's arrest. The soldier pointed to his gun—that, he said, was warrant enough.[38]

Allen Whitfield, a sympathetic attorney in Des Moines, wrote Baldwin (July 19) that he believed a suit might best be entered on behalf of Gasper or of another inmate named North, whom a state agent had beaten in his cell. Two days later, however, a letter to Whitfield advised against action "at this late date and in view of the change in the farm situation."[39]

Support for Milo Reno's Farmers Holiday Association dwindled, partly because of improvement in rural economic conditions. Two excellent accounts of this period are available.[40]

The experiences of George Papcun in 1931 were such that we must regret there was not yet an Iowa Civil Liberties Union. Repeatedly referred to as a Communist, he was, on the contrary, a Socialist. In 1931 and 1932 he was active on behalf of the unemployed. At a town council meeting in Council Bluffs, he criticized the relief administration and was charged with disturbing the peace. Released from the police to a mob, he was beaten and wounded. (Powers Hapgood reported seeing four ugly knife wounds.)[41] He spoke again later in the same city and was arrested.

There should have been investigation and prosecution of the attackers; but Roger Baldwin, receiving an appeal for help, said he did not have the $500 needed.

Powers Hapgood in Council Bluffs was told he could bail Papcun out for $100. But Chief Detective Clarence Ray Brown had Hapgood himself booked for investigation. Asked for his reasons for interest in Papcun, Hapgood said he was interested in free speech. Said a policeman: "Free speech, hell. What they ought to do with these Communist sons of bitches is to take them out and string them up."[42]

In Missouri Valley and Des Moines Papcun met opposition in speaking; in Muscatine he organized button makers.[43] In Davenport he urged the unemployed to make demands on the Board of Supervisors for relief. Accused of vagrancy, he could show that he had employment—from George J. Peck, a Socialist who had been alderman. Asked to leave town, he resisted successfully.

In this period before the founding of ICLU we find the suspension of six students at Simpson College because they would not sign a pledge to obey a rule against dancing. As one consequence, eggs were thrown at A. U. Proudfoot, President of the Board of Trustees.[44]

Intolerance against pacifists was manifested the same year. John K. White, Dean of Men at Abraham Lincoln High School, Council Bluffs, was dropped after half a year for his opposition to war.

The Reverend J. W. Reed, Methodist minister at Tipton, had been active in the cause of peace. Because of the objections of the fathers of two American Legion members Reed was transferred to Toledo, Iowa. Harry Terrell (of the National Council for Prevention of War) went to the Upper Iowa Conference at Dubuque and remonstrated with the superintendent. The latter refused to intervene—a decision to be expected after his conference sermon had denounced war resisters.[45]

This is one of many examples of the perils of the pastorate. In numerous churches the laymen need to learn respect for their ministers' freedom of action and of utterance. "Academic freedom" is a concept so well advertised that teachers have a degree of liberty. It is a question whether the Civil Liberties Union, which has upheld right in schools and colleges well, can do something similar in the churches.

CHAPTER 2

Criminal Syndicalism

THE Industrial Workers of the World (IWW), advocates of industrial unions, refused to join the general support of war in 1917. They were intensely unpopular with most Americans, and there were many governmental measures for their suppression. One of the first works of the National Civil Liberties Bureau (forerunner of the American Civil Liberties Union) was an attempt to secure fair treatment for the IWW. In 1918, when 112 leaders of that organization were indicted, Roger Baldwin, already in charge of the work for civil liberties, issued "The Truth about the I.W.W." and appealed to his correspondents for help. On August 31 he reported that agents of the Department of Justice and of Military Intelligence took charge of his office temporarily, searching all papers.

On September 27 Baldwin wrote an open letter to President Woodrow Wilson, complaining of interference by federal agents with the operations of the General Defense Committee of the IWW: there had been a raid on their headquarters September 5; Justice agents had arrested active members of the defense committee; after the New Republic had printed an advertisement requesting gifts to the defense fund, Justice advised that paper not to reprint the appeal; "The Truth about the I.W.W." of the NCLB, although not declared unmailable, had had its distribution hampered; witnesses for the defense had been intimidated. As for the post office, large quantities of first-class mail had been held up; registered letters were held for months; first-class mail awaited delivery so long that the use of that class had to be abandoned; Senator King had advocated such an amendment to the Espionage Act as would keep the IWW from receiving any funds.[1]

In many states the general fear of and hatred for the IWW were largely responsible for a series of laws penalizing utterances. In sixteen states (including Iowa) such laws, enacted between 1917 and 1921, took the name of criminal syndicalism laws; in about as many others there was legislation to similar purpose but with other titles.

According to the Iowa law (Sec. 12906-9 in Codes up to 1939,

Sec. 689.10-13 in Codes since then) "Criminal Syndicalism is the doctrine which advocates the duty, necessity, or propriety of crime, sabotage, violence, or other unlawful methods of terrorism as a means of accomplishing industrial or political reform. The advocacy of such doctrine, whether by word of mouth or writing, is a felony, punishable as provided" in the following three sections.

There follow details of types of action prescribed under this act, and the penalties.

One may note that the same deeds, if performed to <u>obtain</u> reform, are punishable but can be performed with impunity in order to <u>resist</u> reform. Not all states with criminal syndicalism laws can be accused of such bias. Where Iowa says "as a means of accomplishing industrial or political reform," South Dakota, for instance, says "for the accomplishment of social, economic, industrial, or political ends."[2]

The first prosecution under this law in Iowa occurred in Marion in 1923. Henry Tonn, who was staying in a hotel, presented a check made out to him by the IWW. The police, being notified, searched his room; on the basis of literature of that organization found there he was convicted of criminal syndicalism. Later the Supreme Court of the state reversed the conviction. The judge's instruction to the jury had been prejudicial to the defendant, and no overt act had been proved or even alleged in the indictment. The Court did not pass on the law's constitutionality; but it did find the statute's "provisions from their very obscurity and vague and boundless generalities afford material for endless trouble."[3]

In 1934 relief workers in Sioux City struck for higher pay. Four of them (at least two of whom were Communists) were arrested. It was held that they advocated armed resistance to the government and were therefore guilty of criminal syndicalism. E. O. Bundy and E. C. Newell, with valuable advice from ACLU, defended those accused, with almost complete success.[4]

In October of the same year three were accused in Des Moines of violating the criminal syndicalism law—one was the Communist candidate for governor.

By this time enough citizens of Iowa were alarmed at the use of the law to start a movement for its repeal.

On January 15, 1935, Arthur Garfield Hays of New York, General Counsel and Board member of ACLU, gave a lecture in Des Moines under Jewish auspices. On the same day he spoke at a meeting called to consider means for achieving repeal. He urged that Iowans create an organization, not merely for one piece of legislation but for all the aims of ACLU. Thus the Iowa Civil Liberties Union was founded, as an affiliate of ACLU.[5]

The invitation to this meeting with Hays was issued by the following: Edward S. Allen (Iowa State College, Mathematics), J. C. Lewis (labor leader), Stoddard Lane (Congregational minister), Laetitia M. Conard (Grinnell College, Sociology), John D. Denison (lawyer), and Aron S. Gilmartin (Unitarian minister).

The Iowa Civil Liberties Union was incorporated in April 1935. The articles of incorporation (deposited with the Recorder of Polk

County) name as directors the foregoing six and Joseph I. Brody, a lawyer. Officers were: E. S. Allen, chairman; J. I. Brody, vice-chairman; A. S. Gilmartin, secretary and treasurer.

The law of 1919 on criminal syndicalism had been preceded in 1917 by others (Sec. 12900-5 up to 1939, thereafter Sec. 689.4-9) against inciting insurrection, sedition, treason, anarchy, hostilities, etc. Even before passage of the later law, there had been at least two prosecutions under the earlier ones. In one of them[6] the constitutionality of the statute was attacked on the grounds that the title was bad under Iowa law and that it infringed on the constitutional right of free speech. In the other[7] W. Theo Woodward, vice-president of the Citizen's Bank in Lewis was convicted because of his membership in the People's Council for Democracy and Peace. Not denying membership, he paid his fine of $500; his jail sentence was suspended "during good behavior." He did not appeal the sentence; however, Baldwin wrote: "The law passed by the legislature is so evidently unconstitutional that I am sorry you did not appeal the case rather than pay the fine."

The ICLU, having been organized, found in Gus Alesch, a member of the General Assembly from Marcus, a man who was willing to introduce a bill (HF 398) to repeal Sections 12907-9; it was later amended to include the repeal of Sections 12901-6 also.[8] The Union did not give Alesch the prompt, vigorous, intelligent support he deserved. It did not even have a representative at committee hearings concerning the repeal bill. The bill did not pass.

Hortense Dillon, a Des Moines lawyer who later served ICLU as president, wrote a "Memorandum of Law re Criminal Syndicalism," which ICLU issued that spring. It is addressed less to legislators, urging repeal, than to attorneys defending persons accused of violation.

Along with each argument are given court opinions up to that time—a majority of them upholding laws of this type. The arguments she presented are:

> 1. The criminal syndicalism laws are unnecessary as a means of suppressing violence and disorder; for the reason that acts of violence or incitement thereto are fully covered under the general criminal laws of the various states.
>
> 2. Criminal syndicalism laws, due to their necessarily loose and inclusive language, are easily perverted in their administration so as to reach persons unpopular with the authorities or opposed to the interests of powerful employers; and as such constitute class legislation.
>
> 3. Criminal syndicalism laws in most cases provide punishment not only for mere membership in a radical political party but also for holding meetings of such organizations and for voluntary participation in such meetings.
>
> 4. Criminal syndicalism laws tacitly encourage violence in the <u>prevention</u> of social, economic, or industrial reform.
>
> 5. Criminal syndicalism laws are invoked during periods

of economic crisis, fear, and emotional instability. For this reason they are dangerous and unscientific.

6. Criminal syndicalism laws are opposed in spirit and in their administration to the democratic principles of free speech, free press, and free assembly. In reality, these laws are used solely as a means of suppressing these constitutional rights.

7. Criminal syndicalism laws, even when used infrequently, or not at all, constitute at all times a potential threat to the right of free speech, freedom of the press, and the right to free and peaceful assembly. When not used they are placed in the category of futile, inoperative legislation, and as such induce a popular contempt for all laws.

8. Criminal syndicalism laws create a class of spies and professional informers whose testimony is unreliable and untrustworthy; prosecutions under these laws are almost invariably characterized by unlawful procedure, such as search of premises without issue of warrant, "planted" and "faked" evidence, testimony by ignorant and illiterate witnesses as to the inferences to be placed upon certain discussions of political theory by minority groups.

A leaflet in laymen's language, arguing for repeal, was addressed to teachers and shows why they especially should care for that freedom which the laws in question threaten. Not dated, it seems to have been issued after the legislature's adjournment, for it asks all to write to their representatives that the laws ought to be repealed in the next session.

The American Legion was prompt in damning any attempt to repeal these statutes.[10] Its influence (plus, presumably, the Union's newness and inexpertness) made it impossible to find a single member of the General Assembly willing to introduce a repeal bill in 1937. Neither has there been any one since that time.

The Council Bluffs and Pottawattamie County branch of the Iowa Association for Tax Justice wrote to the Iowa delegation in Congress:

> Arthur Garfield Hays, widely known for his un-American theories, addressed the Jewish Community Forum in Des Moines. In this address he berated our criminal antisyndicalism laws—wanted them repealed. Syndicalism in full flowered in Russia.
>
> Immediately thereafter he started to organize right in our capital city a League of the Civil Liberties Union—the outstanding organization of communism in America.
>
> At least one national magazine is now advocating the death penalty for such activities. Such lecturers giving addresses in Council Bluffs have been given a ride out and told not to come back.
>
> The Jews should know better than to have such a speaker. Americans should know better than to permit it. You and I should know better—or has the United States gone back to

paganism and atheism, or has America gone insane?[11]

The 1938 strike at the Maytag Washing Machine plant in Newton occasioned the use of the Iowa criminal syndicalism law. No other application of it has had such widespread comment as this. No other has involved the Civil Liberties Union to a like extent.

As the date of expiration of the agreement between company and union (United Electrical Radio and Machine Workers Union) approached, the company challenged the union's right to represent the workers. However, an election, under the National Labor Relations Board, gave this union a decisive victory (1189 to 265).

For a new agreement the company then demanded the right (after 60 days) to make such wage adjustments as in its judgment were warranted; however it promised that resulting wage rates would be at least 5% higher than those in the industry as a whole, and at least $.50 an hour. The union, to whom this was unsatisfactory, offered to continue according to the 1937 agreement and submit any change to arbitration.

The company refused, withdrew the original offer, ordered an immediate cut of 10% (May 9), with further reductions in prospect. There was a strike at once.[12]

For nine days strikers held the plant, then left on the insistence of Governor Nelson Kraschel.[13]

On July 9 Carl Bogenrief, the Board member of ICLU by far most active in working on the Maytag strike, reported to Roger Baldwin about the previous two months. The strikers found their cause increasingly opposed by most others. Business was sadly slowed down by the absence of Maytag paychecks. A back-to-work movement grew, counseled by company foremen. The attorney for this movement was Luther Carr, who was also county attorney for Jasper County. In the latter capacity he issued an injunction forbidding all but isolated pickets to oppose return to the Maytag plant. Eventually about half the employees were persuaded to sign back-to-work cards.

There was definitely a connection between the Maytag Company and the city and county governments. On June 18, for instance, with Bogenrief and Hortense Dillon in the courtroom as ICLU observers, a union official asked the mayor to allow a meeting. Before giving the permission the mayor called Umbreit, treasurer of the company. Wilbert Allison, president of the union local at the Maytag plant, charged that the company had stocked the city police and sheriffs with billy clubs and tear gas.

Bogenrief's report spoke of a minimum of violence. In the subsequent trial of William Sentner, a CIO regional official from St. Louis, testimony indicated there was at least some. A timekeeper said that men in his office had prevented his use of the telephone. Pickets, one witness said, had pushed foremen back when they wanted to enter the plant; according to another witness, foremen had tried every day until June 1 to go in, always without success. As for actual physical damage, Bogenrief wrote J. M. Britchey (ACLU) that one shirt had been torn.

About the end of June Sheriff Earl Shields of Jasper County and Mayor George Campbell of Newton issued a call for 1000 peace officers.

On July 8 Governor Kraschel, striving for a settlement, sent two unarmed agents to Newton. He wished to have an arbitration board; the action amounted to an order to the union to cease picketing. Together with this action he asked the company not to try to operate while the board deliberated. The company did not consent to arbitration, and no board was appointed at this time.[14]

July 9 was a day for other action, however. An injunction was issued, limiting the number of pickets at an entrance to three. On this day there were grand jury indictments against a few union officials for criminal syndicalism (William Sentner, Hollis Hall, William Longren, Richard Neibur; also Robert Kirkwood the following day) and a larger number for contempt of court.

The charge of criminal syndicalism roused the Civil Liberties Union to definite action. Arthur Hays, General Counsel for ACLU, wrote:

> Resort to the criminal syndicalism laws has become so rare throughout the country as to occasion widespread surprise that an Iowa grand jury should utilize it. Every criminal syndicalism prosecution in recent years has either failed on trial or in the appellate courts. There is little chance that the Iowa prosecution will be an exception. The ACLU is prepared to furnish counsel and otherwise to aid in the defense. It seems to us incredible that such cases involving only beliefs and opinions should go to trial.[15]

Frank Miles, chief spokesman for the American Legion in Iowa, countered: "Invocation of the criminal syndicalism laws has drawn the usual squawk from the Iowa outfit of the American (?) Civil Liberties Union. . . . The syndicalist laws must be sound, else they would not draw such bitter Communist opposition."[16]

The factory was reopened July 18. At first union men, still on strike, did not interfere with others' return but kept a lookout for "strange faces." Violence began the next day, however; the Des Moines Tribune for July 20 reported that 30 or more persons were knocked down or beaten. The same day the governor ordered National Guard troops to Newton; they arrived at 7:00 PM and closed the plant. Kraschel said it should not open "until the peace of Newton is guaranteed." In his report of July 25, Bogenrief said that Jasper County relief authorities sought to deny relief to strikers, but were told by the governor to grant it to all Maytag employees who needed it. The report ended with the statement that the military regime in Newton was unusually good, and that Bogenrief doubted there would be any gain in protesting encroachment on civil liberty.

With this report, Walter Frank, Baldwin, and Hays, speaking for ACLU, commended the governor for "using troops solely to protect life"; Kraschel thanked them.

National Labor Relations Board hearings on complaints that the Maytag Company had used unfair practices had been begun, interrupted, and reopened until Kraschel stopped them again—fearing that they would increase tension in Newton. They were then transferred to Des Moines. (The Board protested the governor's action as an interference by the state with a federal body.)

On August 4 the New York Times reported that Kraschel allowed the plant to open at noon that day. The company proposed a pay cut of 10%, perhaps 5% more later. If, in the eighteen months ending June 30, 1939, there should have been enough profit to give stockholders specified amounts, pay would rise 5%. The company, which had proposed to bar 109 from reemployment, cut that number to 12.

One member of the arbitration board was R. H. Pollard of Fort Madison. Speaking for the board, which had worked for a settlement, he had recommended a cut of 10% but more generous restoration conditions. To this the union agreed, but the company did not. The strikers rejected the contract the company offered but still voted to go back; they had been defeated.

Scarcely was the factory again operating when the company wrote letters to 275 workers, asking them to explain their part in the original sit-down strike.[17]

How complete was the isolation of the workers from the more prosperous community we see from the fate of the Reverend E. A. Remige, pastor of Newton's First Congregational Church.[18] Early in May he wrote to E. H. Maytag, president of the company, a short letter which contained the appeal: "The Christian way of life leads one to be willing to take a loss rather than cause other human beings to suffer."

A more public act was a letter to the Des Moines Register: "I want to express my appreciation for your editorial, 'Syndicalism, CIO and Arbitration.' We people of Iowa should feel very grateful that we have a paper so unbiased, impartial and free to express itself."

To a group of ministers Mr. Remige proposed that they subscribe to the following:

> In view of the fact that the overwhelming majority of the laboring men of Newton have voted to be a part of the CIO union and in so doing are only within their legitimate rights, the undersigned, members of the Newton Ministerial Association, wish to express our conviction that the non-labor groups of our city should be willing to respect the wishes of the majority of our laboring class and that there ought to be no bitterness of feeling or of action expressed toward them.

His fellow clergymen were not willing even to consider his proposal.

A wealthy member of his church wrote him: "It is almost unbelievable that our church have a minister with communistic tendencies. Since your sympathies are with the poor . . . I am wondering why you accepted a call to a nice church, built by our most substantial people."

By an overwhelming vote the congregation accepted the resignation Mr. Remige had been asked to submit.

The Christian Century, commenting on the social blindness or ineffectiveness of all the Newton churches during the strike, said: "Remige lost his pulpit for actions so mild as to lay any Christian minister alive to the issues involved open to the charge of excessive caution."

Of all those accused of criminal syndicalism, William Sentner was attacked most eagerly. He was an outsider, a district president within the CIO, reputedly a past organizer for the Communist Party. The trial having been transferred to Montezuma, county seat of Poweshiek (an adjacent county), Judge Cooper sentenced the defendant to $2500 fine or 750 days in jail (October 6). The New York Times, October 28, quoted Cooper as saying that "Communism and the CIO are antagonistic to the best interests of agriculture."

The conviction was appealed. A "Bill Sentner Defense Committee" was created in St. Louis, his home city. Both American and Iowa Civil Liberties Unions cooperated in his defense. Finally—as reported in Labor Today, August 1941—the Iowa Supreme Court reversed his conviction.

Apparently no use was made of a valid argument in Sentner's defense. As we have pointed out, it is only the advocates of reform who can be accused of criminal syndicalism in Iowa. In this case it was the employer who wished reform—a lower wage scale; the union was a supporter of the status quo.

In September 1939 five Communists were arrested at Sioux City at a public meeting. The police seized a suitcase containing Communist literature, raided the home of one of the speakers, charged all with criminal syndicalism. Helping in the defense was John Denison, state librarian who had strongly supported ICLU from the start and gave other public service as US referee in bankruptcy; the grand jury indicted no one.[19]

In 1964 Franklin Rosemont of the IWW wrote to Melvin L. Wulf, on the legal staff of ACLU, asking whether the Civil Liberties Union would defend unions if criminal syndicalism laws were used against them. Wulf replied: "These statutes have long been in desuetude. . . . I think the best thing to do is wait until a concrete problem reveals itself. If it does, by all means get in touch with us."[20]

Not convinced that the desuetude of these laws was innocuous, Alan Reitman (long an important member of the ACLU staff) and I, in the summer of 1966, wrote to all affiliates to learn whether there should be a concerted appeal for repeal of criminal syndicalism laws and those closely related to them. There were too few replies showing eagerness to work for repeal, and the project was dropped.

The laws are still on the books in some states and are being used again. Appeals against them were made in Ohio and California courts in 1969. One would hope that civil libertarians would recognize this enemy and act against it with vigor.

After some years of study and debate the Iowa General Assembly in 1976 passed a completely revised criminal code. It omits the criminal syndicalism sections; of the preceding sections of the law on treason and related subjects, only one topic remains—insurrection. The new code is to take effect on January 1, 1978. Then the first objective of ICLU will have been reached—after 43 years.

Norman G. Jesse, who has served ICLU devotedly as Board member and in committee work, was the member of the House of Representatives chiefly responsible for the drafting and passage of the revised code, particularly for the disappearance of penalties for criminal syndicalism. It would be hard to find words to adequately express the gratitude due him.

CHAPTER 3

State Legislation

ATTEMPTS by the Iowa Civil Liberties Union to influence state legislation have been sporadic; in only a few years have they used enough of the organization's energy to justify the denial of tax exemption. (Such denial is general with ACLU and its affiliates; Northern California is an exception.)

The ICLU was founded with the intention of securing the repeal of the laws on criminal syndicalism. It succeeded in getting a bill for repeal introduced in one General Assembly (1935); but being inexperienced, inept in tactics, and faced by "patriotic" opposition, it failed to get the bill passed. Since then no bill expressly for this purpose has been introduced. However, the thorough revision of the criminal code in 1976 will have this effect.

To many it has seemed important that all teachers—more generally, all public employees, all those receiving public funds—be "loyal" and be forced to proclaim that quality. Very soon after its founding ICLU was called on to take a stand on this subject. In February 1935 Bourke B. Hickenlooper (who later became governor and U.S. senator) introduced in the lower House a bill that would require a loyalty oath of teachers. The next issue of the Iowa Legionnaire mentioned it approvingly (but took a friendlier attitude toward members of this profession by not opposing the increase of their monthly minimum pay from $40 to $50).

The bill would have required a teacher's employer to dismiss him if the employer were convinced that the instructor had violated the law. There was no provision for proof of violation, for delay, or for investigation.[1]

The bill was opposed by a "legislature" of students from six colleges,[2] by the Iowa Conference of University Professors,[3] and by the Iowa Academy of Science as well as by ICLU. The first issue of the Bulletin of ICLU summarized its objections: "The real purpose . . . is to gag teachers and prevent them from teaching anything which might change or improve the present state of society."[4] The oath bill was given a quiet death by the sifting committee.[5]

In 1951 the idea was revived in a more drastic form. State

22

State Legislation

Senator Alden L. Douds of Douds (a lawyer) introduced SF 384 dealing with overthrow, destruction, or alteration of the form of government by revolution, force, or violence; it made it a felony to abet or to teach such action or to belong to an organization that does so. Each candidate for office would have to proclaim his innocence. Public employers, such as schools, were required to report how they kept subversives out of their staffs or else forfeit state support. An employee could be discharged if the employer had "reasonable grounds" for believing him a violator of this law—violation was declared a felony.

Opponents of the bill—including ICLU—hoped that the Senate Judiciary Committee would not report it out. This hope was a vain one; five of the eleven members of that committee were sponsors of the bill. The bill, however, was defeated by the Senate.

Douds then sought to save a little. He proposed an amendment to a civil defense bill, which already insisted on oaths by defense personnel; the amendment would have extended the requirement to other public employees. The Senate turned down his amendment two to one.[6]

Iowa was the only state to defeat such a bill by a legislative vote. Among those who helped in this effort were the ICLU and the Iowa Conference of University Professors; the latter urged all chapters to voice their opposition.

Nearly a decade later the federal government decided to refuse federal loans to students unless they filed disclaimers of subversion. Many schools protested, the more so since each school had to serve as a filter for funds coming to its students. The Board of Regents, in control of the state schools of higher learning, expressed its disapproval. But it was Grinnell College which refused absolutely to handle money that would have shrunk the freedom of some of its students. Howard R. Bowen was then president of Grinnell and the man who publicly expressed its reasons.[7]

During the same session of the General Assembly there appeared an antisabotage bill and one that would require, at every school level, one hour a week devoted to teaching "the principles of the Declaration of Independence." The ICLU opposed these two bills, Father Luigi Ligutti and Addison Parker being especially effective. (Father Ligutti was executive director of the National Catholic Rural Life Conference who later became a monsignor and an observer for the Vatican of the Food and Agricultural Organization of the United Nations. Parker was a Des Moines attorney.) The bills did not pass; neither did one to allow wiretapping in the case of a suspected felony—past, present, or future.

The call for insistence on a loyalty oath from employees of state universities came again in 1967 from legislators representing Black Hawk County. In the same season Dubuque Municipal Judge Karl Kenline advocated new laws against dissent, to enforce "100 percent faith in our country and its leaders at all levels, county, state, and national."

Reacting to these and like utterances, ICLU stated, on November 17, 1967:

In times of war, Americans who seek to prove their patriotism by attacking the loyalty of their fellow citizens do their country a great disservice. Citizens who hold views different from the policy of their government have an obligation to express their views and are absolutely protected by the U.S. Constitution from criminal prosecution when fulfilling that obligation. It is critical to American democratic processes that public officials understand the difference between criminal conduct, such as rioting and vandalism, and political dissent and demonstrations, which are among the noblest activities of free men serving a free government.

In 1959 the ICLU took an interest in state legislation in other areas and could note success in a number of ways:

1. The designation of race was removed from absentee ballots.
2. A person arrested acquired the right to telephone an attorney.
3. If one were charged with a felony and could provide no attorney for himself, the judge was directed to appoint one.

Governor Herschel C. Loveless vetoed a bill that would have freed a merchant from liability for libel if he wrongly accused a person of shoplifting.[8]

Until fairly recently the Board of ACLU had not held that capital punishment was a civil liberties issue. Here, as in many other ways, the concept of the Union's proper sphere of influence was broadened. During the spring of 1965 the Board voted: "The ACLU is opposed to capital punishment and will both assert this position in appropriate court cases and attempt to secure legislative repeal of laws authorizing the death penalty."

This position had already been the policy of ICLU—one of the Iowa groups which secured abolition of capital punishment in 1965. In both ICLU and ACLU it was held that it is cruel and unusual punishment, that it denies due process by denying to one convicted the chance of reversing an unjust verdict, and that the poor and the ignorant have least chance to survive a trial.[9]

During the legislative session of 1967 students of Professor George Gordin of Drake University Law School gave ICLU valuable aid. Under his direction they scanned bills coming before the General Assembly, to see which deserved the attention of ICLU. There resulted a number of excellent memoranda concerning pending legislation, over the signatures of Norman Jesse, counsel, and Oval Quist, executive secretary.

One bill proposed that the death penalty be brought back if a peace officer were the one murdered. The ICLU argued: "The reinstatement of the death penalty for even this one crime would create the danger of further 'exceptions' at a time when the national trend is away from the death penalty."

"An act to improve the continuing contract for teachers" was favored by ICLU and passed in 1967. It required that a teacher whose contract was not renewed be given specific reasons. This was a step forward; unfortunately it did not require that the reasons given be adequate; it did not say what sort of reasons would justify dropping a teacher, nor propose that anyone other than the employing school board set standards (see Ch. 6).

A bill to create a professional board to control teaching standards, as originally written, would have made the largest teachers' organization in the state dominate the commission proposed. To this ICLU strongly objected; as the bill finally passed, it gave no power to one organization or to several. In fact, it guarded against excessive power of such groups by stating that a teaching appointment might not depend on either membership or nonmembership in particular societies.

Another bill that was successfully supported provided for release of accused persons before their trial on their own recognizance. Thus the poor, who cannot afford bail, came nearer to equality with the well-to-do in the law's treatment of them. Capital crimes are exempted from the operation of this law. However, since these are defined as crimes subject to the death penalty, the exemption means nothing so long as capital punishment is outlawed in law.

The ICLU opposed a bill to give the Board of Parole the authority to revoke a probation previously granted. It was not passed.

The ICLU also opposed a bill to "establish a merit system . . . for state employees" because of the provision that candidates for state employment might be rejected "where in the judgment of the commission there is reasonable doubt of the loyalty to the nation" of such a person. It was not passed.

A bill on which the legislature did not act as ICLU would have wished was one to restore citizenship rights to convicts on their release. The Union strongly supported this bill, but it was not passed.

With regard to a law "relating to assault of a peace officer" ICLU found the language "too broad, too vague and ambiguous, . . . open to constitutional challenge." Hence the Union opposed it; the bill was not passed.

The legislative session of 1967 passed one bill whose import neither the ICLU officers nor their advisors noted. A "political party" in Iowa is one whose gubernatorial candidate in the last general election received at least 2 percent of the votes. The new law made contributions to such parties deductible from incomes subject to the state income tax. This law gives established parties an advantage over smaller ones (named in Iowa "political organizations"). Since these groups usually show their greatest strength in support of aspirants for posts in Washington, the size of vote for governor is an unfair criterion for any favor granted the large parties, especially that of tax exemption.

In 1970 both houses passed a bill to permit wiretapping under certain circumstances. Opposition caused the introduction of amendments to make it a less serious threat to privacy. The Union voiced strong opposition to all legalization of this practice, even to

the version that had been modified to meet objections. Mark
Schantz, of the University of Iowa College of Law and a member of
the ICLU Board, was the chief spokesman for the Union. In October
1969 he made a presentation at a legislative hearing; a condensed
version of his argument was later sent to all senators. He held
wiretapping not necessary for effective law enforcement in Iowa.
Its invasion of privacy made it a threat to basic American values.
It would put "government in the home and in the office, in private
clubs and public meeting places, on the street corner and in the
automobile." As Schantz contended, the law proposed would authorize
"prolonged and indiscriminate eavesdropping in violation of the
Fourth Amendment prohibition on unreasonable searches and seiz-
ures."[10]

Governor Robert D. Ray vetoed the bill after its passage by
both houses, noting that wiretapping "creates fear of government
and fear of fellow citizens." The ICLU Board then passed a resolution commending him for this action.

Dan Johnston, ICLU staff counsel, was active in organizing
the lawyers' committee opposing the wiretap bill. Among the members of that committee were three ICLU directors: Dean David
Vernon of the University of Iowa College of Law, Robert Mannheimer,
and Val Schoenthal of Des Moines.[11]

During the 1974 session of the General Assembly ICLU was well
assisted by Paul Kilmer, a student at the University of Northern
Iowa serving as legislative interne. He kept track of the status
of bills interesting the Union as they were scheduled for hearings
in committees or in either chamber. He also prepared an index of
the lengthy bill to revise the Criminal Code[12] (no other such index existed). Lobbying was an activity Kilmer was not to undertake.
Beatrice Wall of Grinnell offered her services for this work, and
they were gratefully accepted. Among other students who have contributed willing and valuable assistance to ICLU are Beverly Groos
of Colfax, a graduate student at the University of Iowa, and Craig
Hukill of Cedar Rapids, a psychology student at Iowa State University.

As the session of 1974 ended, ICLU could count nearly all of
its most desired aims achieved.

1. Women had received equal housing rights.
2. The law on rape had been amended.
3. Statewide standards on obscenity had been won (the changes
to affect adults only).
4. The Civil Rights Commission had been strengthened both as
to funds and as to powers.
5. State boards were now required to include public representatives.
6. There was no change in the legal status of abortion (the
Iowa Supreme Court had struck down the old law).
7. Wiretapping had not been legalized.
8. Capital punishment had not been restored.

State Legislation

A couple of desired measures had not had final action; most important was the revised criminal code. The one action ICLU regretted was the increased aid granted to parochial schools, especially transportation of students.

For the legislative session of 1976 the ICLU acquired the services of Robert Hanson as legislative coordinator and lobbyist. A graduate of Drake and Purdue universities, Hanson had taught school, then served the Youth Service Bureau of Story County (under YMCA auspices) for the prevention of juvenile delinquency. Directions of legislative activity to which he proposed to give priority included juvenile justice code revision; penal code; criminal code revision; sexual preference; the adoption bill (as regards termination of parental custody); and prisoners, prison conditions, and prisoners' rights.

CHAPTER 4

The Iowa Civil Liberties Union and

the American Civil Liberties Union

FOR the first twenty years of the American Civil Liberties Union, those with the right to influence policy were the National Board and the National Committee. The Board consisted of members residing in or near New York. Frequency of meetings varied; for many years they were weekly—hence the geographic limitation and also the certainty that the men and women on the Board were devoted to the cause of the Union. The National Committee, chosen by the Board, was composed of persons of distinction throughout the United States; on the whole they sacrificed far less time than the Board to the affairs of the Union. The first Iowan chosen to serve on the National Committee was W. W. Waymack, editor of the <u>Des Moines Register and Tribune</u>; the second was Donald R. Murphy, editor of <u>Wallaces Farmer</u>, who has served ICLU as an outstanding chairman.

The affiliates were recognized by ACLU as bodies devoted to the same principles. However, each had its own membership list and its own financial structure. A person could be a member of ACLU or of the affiliate for his region or of both. Dues paid to one were not shared with the other. Neither were lists of members, national and regional, always exchanged. The region assigned to an affiliate was most often a state, as in the case of Iowa. It could, however, be a part of a state (Northern and Southern California), a county (Erie County, New York), or the vicinity of a city, spreading over state lines (Philadelphia cared also for Camden).

The ICLU expressed little concern about not being consulted on national policy until 1940. In February of that year I was traveling from Ames to Chicago to attend a midwest conference on civil liberties and showed my seat companion mail I had just received from ACLU. I do not remember her identity, but I remember clearly her immediate comment: "That contradicts all that the Civil Liberties Union has stood for."

The resolution of February 5, 1940, which occasioned her judgment read:

While the American Civil Liberties Union does not make any test of opinion on political or economic questions a condition of membership, and makes no distinction in defending the right to hold and utter any opinions, the personnel of its governing committees and staff is properly subject to the test of consistency in the defense of civil liberties in all aspects and all places. That consistency is inevitably compromised by persons who champion civil liberties in the United States and yet who justify or tolerate the denial of civil liberties by dictatorships abroad. Such a dual position in these days, when issues are far sharper and more profound, makes it desirable that the Civil Liberties Union makes its position unmistakably clear.

The Board of Directors and the National Committee of the American Civil Liberties Union therefore hold it inappropriate for any person to serve on the governing committees of the Union or on its staff, who is a member of any political organization which supports totalitarian dictatorship in any country, or who by his public declarations indicates his support of such a principle. Within this category we include organizations in the United States supporting the totalitarian governments of the Soviet Union and of the Fascist and Nazi countries (such as the Communist Party, the German-American Bund and others) as well as native organizations with obvious anti-democratic objectives or practices.

This resolution, approved by a majority of the Board of Directors and of the National Committee, was vigorously opposed by a minority. It resulted in the resignation of Harry F. Ward, chairman of the Board since the foundation of the Union, and a number of others.[1]

A consideration which does not appear on the face of the resolution was the nonaggression agreement between the Soviet Union and Hitler's Germany. As Osmond Fraenkel (a Board member of exceptionally long and distinguished service) explained to me in 1964, war seemed quite possible between the United States, already strongly sympathetic to the cause of Great Britain and her allies, and Russia, a potential ally of Germany. If such a war had come about, the presence of a Communist in a position of influence in the Union could have been embarrassing. Fraenkel himself opposed the resolution. The international agreement did not substantially change the nature of internal policies in the Soviet Union—those policies which ostensibly justified the measure.

About the middle of February 1940, Frank Miles, editor of the Iowa Legionnaire, spoke in Ames. He defended the criminal syndicalism laws (displaying ignorance of their contents) and attacked the ICLU for calling for their repeal; the resolution of February 5, however, pleased him. On February 25 I wrote to Lucille B. Milner, secretary of ACLU: "I felt some shame that the Civil Liberties Union had given Mr. Miles something he was glad to praise—the exclusion of Communists from positions. It enabled him to say of the past: 'But if there had been nothing wrong, why this purging process?'"[2]

It was not she who answered but Roger Baldwin: "I don't think we should be disturbed that anyone in the American Legion should find cause for commending us for anything. The action, while in line with our consistent policy, does merit, I think, commendation for clearing up an awkward situation."[3]

At the March meeting of the ICLU, after a lively discussion, it was voted to write the New York office, pointing out dangers in the resolution of February 5. It was felt that the vague, inclusive language and the creation of "guilt by association" were unfortunate, and hope was expressed that it was not too late to do something to lessen these dangers.[4]

The assertion that the action of February was "in line with our consistent policy" was repeatedly used in its defense. However, there are facts pointing to a contrary conclusion. Elizabeth Gurley Flynn had been a member of the Board of Directors from the foundation of the Union. In February 1937 she joined the Communist Party and so stated at the next meeting of the Board of Directors. No objection was made then, and in 1939 she was unanimously reelected to the Board.[5]

In April 1939 the Board of Directors issued a statement: "Why We Defend Free Speech for Nazis, Fascists, and Communists":

> The Civil Liberties Union has been . . . urged both by friends and critics to take a position denying freedom of speech to the movements those persons characterize as anti-democratic. They have also urged that we declare ourselves in opposition to all anti-democratic theories and forms of government. . . . The attitude of these friends and critics . . . is wholly foreign to the aims and work of the Civil Liberties Union.
>
> The Union does not engage in political controversy. It takes no position on any political or economic issue or system. It defends without favoritism the rights of all comers, whatever their political or economic views. It is wholly unconcerned with movements abroad or with foreign governments.[6]

The resolution had not been referred to the affiliates and, indeed, was deplored by a substantial number of them. It ran counter to principles accepted in the past—in the very recent past at that. It met strong opposition in the Union, its Board, and the National Committee. Thus one might have expected the Board to harbor some doubts about its correctness, but with the majority that was not the case. Some fifteen years after its passage a member of the staff of the New York office told me that the Board was still adamant on the subject.

I have little doubt that this resolution spared the Union and at least a fraction of its affiliates enmity on the part of some in the government, some in the general public. It probably made it easier to get money as well as support from a part of the citizenry.

In addition, the Union could defend the rights of Communists more effectively if it could claim it had no ties with them.

On the other hand, the action of ACLU—one of the earliest of its kind—encouraged many other bodies to act likewise. Declaring that, so far as the staff and boards of the Civil Liberties Union were concerned, Communists were outcasts, it promoted a state of public opinion in which there was much more frequent need to act on behalf of Communists' rights than would otherwise have been the case.

Soon after passage of the resolution, charges were made against Miss Flynn—first, that she belonged to the Communist Party and second, that she wrote publicly in opposition to her adversaries in an inadmissible manner. There resulted her "trial" on May 7, 1940, and her expulsion from its Board of Directors.[7] (In June 1976 the Board adopted a resolution expressing disapproval of its earlier action: "It is the sense of the board that Ms. Flynn [now deceased] should not have been expelled and should have been permitted to complete the term as a member of the board for which she had been elected.")[8]

After these events she spoke in Des Moines on behalf of the Communist Party and expressed her gratitude for courtesies extended her by officers of ICLU—particularly by Forrest Spaulding who, as librarian, had granted the use of the library auditorium for her meeting.

In July 1942 the Board of ICLU was unanimous in requesting the ACLU Board of Directors to submit all controversial questions to local memberships, both for giving the latter information and for securing their opinions. "This should be done before a decision is taken—or, at the latest, before there is publicity on it."[9]

In reply Mr. Luther Stalnaker, then president of ICLU, received "rules on participation of local committees in national policy making." Among these rules is the following:

> Whenever a referendum vote is taken of active membership (Directors and National Committee) local affiliated committees will be given the opportunity to express their views of the issue. Their views, however, are without legal force and will be regarded as solely advisory (dated October 1941).[10]

On October 19, 1942, the Board of Directors of ACLU unanimously adopted a resolution on policy in time of war, of which the essential paragraph was contained in a press release, November 11:

> Recognizing that our military enemies are now using techniques of propaganda which may involve an attempt to pervert the Bill of Rights to serve the enemy rather than the people of the United States, the American Civil Liberties Union will not participate—except where the fundamentals of due process are involved—in cases where, after investigation, there are grounds for a belief that the defendant is cooperating with or acting on behalf of the enemy, even though the particular

charge against the defendant might otherwise be appropriate for intervention by the Union.

Shortly thereafter I wrote to ask whether local branches had been consulted as to this statement.[11] It seemed to me that arguments based on just the war of 1941 were used for conclusions to policy in all wars. Furthermore, "advocacy of such conditions of peace as are now freely discussed by humane men and women could become 'acting on behalf of the enemy.'" In further correspondence I pointed out other situations where the resolution in question might plague us. Baldwin wrote (Jan. 5, 1943) that he had presented my views to the Board; it was evidently their general view that the resolution applied only to the war then in progress. He agreed that the local committees should have been consulted, even though the Board felt that it constituted no change in basic policy.

Intense interest in the resolution of 1940 was expressed in 1948. Successive decisions of the Board of Directors of ACLU determined:

> that this resolution be communicated to all nominees for governing boards, to determine whether it would bar them; that affiliates to be admitted in future be required to adhere to the Resolution; that existing affiliates be requested to adhere to it; that—in view of the fact that the four affiliates declining to adhere to it in principle still did not deviate from it in practice—any departure from such principles by an affiliate or its officers should be grounds for action by the national body.[12]

On March 19, 1949, a conference was held at which affiliates (including Iowa) were represented. A committee recommended an addition to the ACLU constitution, which would replace the 1940 resolution. Presented by Osmond Fraenkel, it read:

> Any member of the American Civil Liberties Union shall be eligible for nomination and election to office in any division of the Union who unequivocally supports the principles of civil liberties as guaranteed by the Constitution of the United States, not only for himself but for all mankind.

This proposal was defeated, 12 to 11; John Haynes Holmes, as chairman, cast the deciding vote.

On May 9 of that year the Board voted that, if an affiliate wished to propose a candidate for the National Committee, it must accept the principles of the 1940 resolution. (I do not know that this disfranchisement of the recalcitrant affiliates was ever put into effect.)

The Board, seeking ways of giving affiliates some influence in decision of policy, proposed that they have a place on the National Committee. This, however, was rejected by those bodies.[13]

A conference of affiliates was held in Des Moines January 14-

15, 1950. The ACLU Board was represented by John Paul Jones, chairman of the New York City Civil Liberties Committee. The purpose of the conference was to improve relations between the affiliates and the national office. Six affiliates had representatives, three expressed interest but could not send delegates, two declined to send any, and four did not answer the invitation.

The conference made a fairly lengthy recommendation which included the following ideas:

> Besides the active members (National Board and National Committee) there should be affiliated active members. Each of these should have two votes. These votes would be counted in determination of policy when there was a referendum, and in the call for a referendum—for which five votes would suffice. It was recommended that the Chicago Division experiment with such integration as later became general. That is, there should no longer be separate lists of members in the Chicago area; funds collected there would be shared on a basis to be negotiated.

The report on the conference spoke of gratification that relations had improved—in particular, that affiliates ought to have an influence greater than an advisory one.[14]

The Committee of the Board on Affiliates, meeting March 13, 1950, made recommendations on all points. In particular they favored the enfranchisement of affiliates by the method proposed; as to determination of what questions should be submitted to the enlarged active membership, we read:

> The extent of policy submission should be covered by the words "any question which seems to the Board to involve new policy or revision of old policy, except where in the judgment of the Board emergency forbids."[15]

The question of the Chicago experiment in integration was to be deferred until a visit by the director (Patrick Murphy Malin had recently succeeded Roger N. Baldwin) to Chicago later in March.

In August of the same year George E. Rundquist of the New York staff wrote me:

> You will have to help us think of Iowa and Des Moines as a part of this office, sitting with us in all of our discussions. . . . This is really a full-scale revolution for us, after too long a time during which we have thought of ourselves as a group which met every two weeks at a Board Meeting. Now we want to think of ourselves as a group united, throughout the entire country.[16]

In 1951 there was another conference of affiliates, May 10-14, in New York. At its conclusion Jerome McNair of Southern California summarized the work of the gathering: It had laid plans for more united and more effective work to meet challenges which were ever more alarming. The conference had produced a welding together of the affiliates themselves and of those groups with the national office, and a feeling of very democratic fraternity.[17]

The staff of the national office drafted, and the conference approved, an amendment to the constitution and bylaws which, it was hoped, would replace the resolution of 1940 as a guide to policy. It stated that "all persons who are members of the National Board . . . shall be unequivocally loyal to democratic government and civil liberties for all peoples." Thus the mention of particular organizations, as in a bill of attainder, was no longer to be part of stated policy.

On June 4, however, the Board (relatively few of whom had attended the conference) voted to add to the statement that this was to be interpreted in accordance with the 1940 resolution. Thus, although those voting for the amendment had generally believed that it would remove the resolution from stated policy, they found it elevated to a place in the basic document of the Union. (For the first time, therefore, condemnation of membership in the German-American Bund went into the ACLU constitution, though that Bund no longer existed.)

As chairman of ICLU, I protested this action in a letter to Ernest Angell, chairman of the Board; justification of the action came in a letter from George E. Rundquist, then assistant director (see Appendix 1).

Not long after this Patrick Malin, director of ACLU, visited Iowa. He asked Donald Murphy, then president of ICLU, whether that body, although it had never adopted the 1940 resolution (as younger affiliates had been required to do) followed it in practice. Murphy answered that there were then no Communists on our Board. In the past, he said, we had had one Communist and one "fellow-traveler." I myself could not identify them. I am sure, however, that their presence on the Board had caused no action which could be a cause for reproach.

A further note on the famous resolution is in order. It has been used not only to exclude Communists from positions where they could influence policy but also to keep specific members of the Ku Klux Klan from boards of southern affiliates.

Early in 1953 three statements were formulated, which, by vote on May 4, were submitted to the whole corporation for a referendum. Their titles are:

1. Nature of Communist Party
   Defense of Civil Liberties Regardless of Associations
   Allowable Consideration of Associations (in General)
2. Allowable Consideration of Associations (in Educational and United Nations Employment)
3. Propriety of Questions and Competency of Authority
   Refusals to Answer Questions about Associations
   Allowable Consideration of Such Refusals (in Government, United Nations, and Educational Employment)

The texts of these statements are given in Appendix 3, as is an alternative to Statement 3 adopted by the ICLU Board, June 1, 1953.

The general tendency of these statements was to restrict the area within which the Civil Liberties Union would defend individual rights.

Affiliates, as well as the National Board and National Committee, were now entitled to vote on referenda. In this case the majority of the latter two approved the statements. Of the sixteen affiliates voting only three favored them. Thus they were defeated.[18] The influential vote of the Chicago affiliate was called in question, and Malin telegraphed a request for the number of Chicago Board members who had voted each way. A telephone inquiry in Chicago then resulted in a majority for approval. When the Chicago Board next met, however, this method of changing their vote after the deadline had been set for the referendum was repudiated, and "no" was the final vote of the corporation as a whole.[19]

The attempt to base policy on the three statements was not at an end, for the bylaws contained a provision that the Board abide by the result of a referendum "except where it believes there are vitally important reasons for not doing so—which it shall explain to the corporation members."

In February 1954 there was another conference of affiliates. From that conference Eason Monroe of Southern California and I brought the recommendation that the three statements be withdrawn and that a tripartite committee be appointed to draft a substitute. Osmond Fraenkel moved that this recommendation be accepted; his motion was adopted.[20]

The tripartite committee proposed a revision of the three statements, and this was adopted with slight changes.[21]

On November 3 of the same year Ernest Besig of Northern California wrote a request that the report in question also be subjected to a corporation referendum. This request was rejected, since it did not come from ten corporation members, as the bylaws required.[22]

For the next few years suggestions for renewed attacks on the resolution were discouraged—just at the moment it would be impolitic even to seem to be partisans (or dupes) of the Communists.

At the 1962 conference of affiliates (they had become biennial) Kenneth Everhart, a leading official of AFL-CIO in Iowa who was serving ICLU as president and representative at the conference, proposed reopening the subject. When asked "Who cares?" he replied, "We do."

Before the 1964 conference ICLU wrote to the New York office and to all other affiliates, urging that this subject be on the agenda of the conference (see Appendix 3). Independently of Iowa, Southern California did the same. However, we were informed that the program as planned was already too full to admit new items. The ICLU Board agreed not to press the issue but instructed the delegates (Val Schoenthal and myself) to vote in accordance with our letter if the occasion arose.

The official sessions did not take up the matter, but all affiliates were invited to an informal conference on the subject. Most active in the discussion were Northern and Southern California and Iowa. It was agreed that the initiative for further action be left with Southern California.

That affiliate did, in fact, propose this substitute: "Support of civil liberties as guaranteed in the Constitution of the United States and particularly in the Bill of Rights is the one and fundamental qualification for membership or office in the American Civil Liberties Union."

This was referred to all affiliates. Only a minority (including Iowa) favored it,[23] and a proposal from Michigan for a committee of the whole Union on the subject was adopted. This committee was to consider not only a new statement on qualifications sought in candidates but also "the total problem of maintaining the integrity, effectiveness and viability of ACLU."

The committee thus authorized proposed the simple requirement that officers, staff members, etc., be "unequivocally committed to the objectives of this Union." However, the final version required commitment also to "the concept of democratic government and civil liberties for all people."

It was then expressly stated that this would "preclude support of those principles which reject or qualify individual liberties and minority rights for all people equally, regardless of race, sex, religion or opinion, or which reject or qualify the freedoms associated with the forms and processes of political democracy." This final version was the result of cooperation of the special committee on the 1940 resolution and the constitution committee.[24]

Thus the Civil Liberties Union no longer creates guilt by association, no longer names specific organizations as anathema. It does, however, forbid an officer or staff member to uphold political systems less democratic than the American, even though they may seem proper in another environment. Corliss Lamont, who had long been a member of the ACLU Board, gives other reasons for deploring the final version.[25] It is to be hoped that, in practice, no harm will come to the Union or its pursuit of freedom in the United States and in lands controlled by it.

For ten years (approximately 1955-65) ACLU membership application blanks contained the caution: "The ACLU needs and welcomes the support of all those—and only those—whose devotion to civil liberties is not qualified by adherence to Communist, Fascist, Ku Klux Klan, or other totalitarian doctrines." This was not inevitably implied by the 1940 resolution, which narrowed the field for officers and staff members only. The Board of ACLU did not ask whether the affiliates approved of it. Accordingly, ICLU avoided the use of the ACLU application blanks and issued its own. Deletion of this sentence from these forms was a natural item in the revision of the constitution and bylaws which did away with the resolution in question.

In 1968 the relationship between ACLU and its affiliates changed again. Instead of a separate chamber of government consisting of the branches, each affiliate now nominates one member to be a member of the National Board. Meetings of that body are held only five or six times a year instead of weekly or fortnightly; the travel expenses of distant members are paid. The biennial conferences, at which the affiliates form a strong contingent, gain in importance; resolutions adopted are given such weight that means for decreasing their quantities and heightening their quality have been devised.

Financial contributions from persons in Iowa to either ACLU or ICLU are shared (except in the first year of a person's membership)—60 percent to ICLU, 40 percent to ACLU. Since some of the aims of the national organization and of each branch involve attempts to influence legislation, gifts to them may not be deducted from one's federally taxable income. Therefore, a national foundation has been created (originally named the Roger Baldwin Foundation) for support of other activities; gifts to this foundation are tax deductible. Affiliates are encouraged to form similar foundations. Accordingly the Iowa Civil Liberties Union Foundation was created in the winter of 1969-70. These foundations are usually of substantial size.

Projects that have enjoyed the support of the ICLU Foundation include the following, some of which are treated more fully elsewhere in this history:

1. The Citizens' Complaint Bureau, which operated in an innercity area of Des Moines during the summer of 1940
2. Legal costs, including those of various trials
3. Support of a conference on women's rights (Des Moines, Dec. 4, 1971), of which ICLU and the National Organization for Women were joint sponsors
4. Research, telephone, taxes
5. Salary of staff attorney

A difference of opinion between the boards of ACLU and ICLU arose when, on September 30, 1973, the former passed a resolution calling for the impeachment of Richard M. Nixon, President of the United States.[26] In the view of the Iowa Board this action was so important and so unprecedented that the affiliates should have been consulted. A resolution to that effect was passed by the ICLU Board, October 26, 1973. The reply of Edward J. Ennis, chairman of the ACLU Board, merits quotation.

> The National Board might very well have utilized the familiar procedure of seeking advice from the affiliates before acting on the impeachment resolution urged by the Southern California, New York and other affiliates. But this was not proposed in the debate, and the Board after long and very careful consideration exercised its authority to adopt the resolution. It did not act carelessly or in haste even though it might have adopted the more deliberate process of consulting the affiliates.
> The grounds of impeachment advanced by the Union care-

fully are restricted to matters not in factual dispute and
matters involving civil liberties. We urge the House to im-
peach on these grounds and to leave to the House its own responsible consideration of any other grounds not involving
civil liberties such as frequent impounding of appropriated
funds or grounds not factually established beyond dispute such
as complicity in the Watergate cover-up. We do believe and
therefore assert that the country cannot withstand the widespread violation of civil liberties involved in President
Nixon's exercise of presidential power. This is our judgment
of what has happened already and not a prejudgment of any
charge which may be brought by the House.

Immediately after the ACLU passed the resolution, the full
resolution was published in The ICLU Defender. With it was a message from President John Chrystal suggesting that ICLU members
could express their views on the issue of impeachment by writing
to members of Congress.

The ICLU Board did nothing further on the question of impeachment until its meeting of April 25, 1974, when the executive committee was asked "to consider taking additional action on behalf
of the ICLU on the issues of impeachment and amnesty."

At the dinner session of the annual meeting of ICLU in Iowa
City (May 11, 1974) the main speaker was Charles Morgan, director
of the Washington office of ACLU. He argued strongly and persua-
sively for impeachment: "The most powerful man in the nation, perhaps the world, would be compelled to submit to the rule of law."

At that time the membership of the executive committee
changed. Since the new committee had not been organized and so
could not act as directed, Russell Pounds, newly elected president, asked me to draft resolutions on amnesty and impeachment
for the meeting of June 6. This I did; the resolution on amnesty
was passed, but that on impeachment was not.

At the Board meeting of July 25, 1974, a new resolution, better reflecting the current situation, was presented. By then, however, a vote favoring impeachment on the part of the House Judiciary Committee seemed imminent. The Board therefore decided to send
a message to the Iowa delegation in the House after that committee's reports. Accordingly the following letter was sent to the
Iowans in both houses of Congress:

> The Iowa Civil Liberties Union, comprised of 1,700 mem-
> bers from across Iowa, is an organization dedicated to pro-
> tecting and preserving the basic freedoms for all Iowans as
> guaranteed by the Constitution and the Bill of Rights. The
> ICLU takes this mandate seriously and has, for nearly 40
> years, opposed, through litigation, legislation, and public
> education, encroachments on the civil liberties of Iowans,
> regardless of how unpopular their cause or their political
> affiliation; whether on the right or on the left.
> With this historical perspective, the ICLU has watched

with grave concern the contempt for civil liberties exemplified in Richard Nixon's conduct in office. His numerous infringements on our constitutional concepts of freedom and democracy led the American people to call for an investigation by the House Judiciary Committee. This committee has in turn recommended to the full House three articles of impeachment. The ICLU feels this was both a fair and wise action.

It is now up to you, Iowa's elected representatives, to help decide this momentous question. We urge you to lay political partisanship aside and vote to confirm the Judiciary Committee's judgment that Richard Nixon be impeached for abuse of power, obstruction of justice, and contempt of Congress, in order that our freedoms be preserved.

Between the time this was mailed and the answers could be written Richard Nixon had resigned from the presidency, and the Congressmen lost their chance to act as ICLU advised.

The reader of this chapter might conclude that there was steady disharmony between the American Civil Liberties Union and its Iowa affiliate. Actually, the resolution of 1940 furnished the only subject for lasting and serious disagreement between ICLU and the majority of the Board of the parent organization, and we in Iowa were heartened by the knowledge that we had the support of some members of the ACLU Board whom we most admired.

Since each affiliate may name a member of the ACLU Board of Directors, ICLU had as its first representative Louise Noun, president of the affiliate. She was succeeded by Dan Johnston in 1971 and Hanna Weston in 1972. In 1970 Gilbert Cranberg of the Des Moines Register and Tribune was elected member-at-large of the ACLU Board.

Two Iowans—Louise Noun and John Chrystal—are members of the National Advisory Council of ACLU. Both are past presidents of ICLU. The council's function is purely advisory; its members are explicitly asked to share in the biennial conferences of ACLU.

In 1975 Civil Liberties Review began publication of Roger Baldwin's "Recollections of a Life in Civil Liberties." The first two installments (Vol. 2, Nos. 2, 4) recount his work and thoughts up to 1940. Although Iowa is not mentioned in these pages, readers of this book will find the account by the chief pioneer in the defense of freedom intensely interesting.

CHAPTER 5

Freedom in the Universities

IN 1943 Theodore W. Schultz was head of the Department of Economics and Sociology at Iowa State College (later renamed Iowa State University). With him in the department was a group of colleagues outstanding not only in individual ability but also in harmony of cooperation. Thus qualified, they initiated a series of pamphlets on Wartime Farm and Food Policy. In September Professor Schultz resigned, accepting a position at the University of Chicago. The reasons for his resignation were so related to academic freedom and to freedom of expression that the episode deserves a place in this history.

Number 5 in the pamphlet series—which eventually ran to ten numbers—was "Putting Dairying on a War Footing" by Oswald Harvey Brownlee. It contained the conclusion that nutritionally oleomargarine compared favorably with butter. This angered the dairy farmers of Iowa and the Iowa Farm Bureau Federation; their clamor brought about the retraction of the pamphlet. However, retraction of the conclusions reached did not follow. About a year later a revision of the booklet appeared—far better supported by evidence and documentation and arriving at substantially the same conclusions, stated perhaps less provocatively. To R. E. Buchanan, then Dean of the Graduate College and director of the Agricultural Experiment Station, goes the greatest credit for his insistence that the initial retraction not be final.

This oleomargarine controversy so dominated discussion of that period that many take it to have been the sole cause of disagreement between Schultz and his department on the one hand and those with authority over him on the other. Actually his letter of resignation named a number of grievances of real importance.

The office of President Charles E. Friley had stopped publication of "Stretching the Feed Grain Supplies" by Brownlee in the April 1943 issue of the Iowa Farm Economist.

Professors William Nicholls and John Vieg had prepared a manuscript for the Wartime Farm and Food Policy series. In its final form it had the approval not only of the regular editorial committee but also of a special committee representing the whole college, appointed by the director of the Agricultural Experiment Station, R. E. Buchanan. Nevertheless, President Friley submitted the manuscript to librarian Charles H. Brown and secured from him a report condemning the work.

Although about a third of the publications of the Iowa State College Press had originated with the social sciences faculty, the president removed the only representative of that faculty from the Press Board—without even notifying that individual.

WOI, the radio station of Iowa State College, had a daily news report directed by a committee of social scientists; the spokesman was Bryce Ryan. The program drew from reliable sources not generally used by papers of wide circulation. Many listeners found it exceptionally valuable. One day at 2:00 PM listeners were surprised to hear that they would not hear Ryan at 4:00 that day—or ever thereafter. No reason or explanation was offered for the sudden termination.

The Rockefeller Foundation had given Iowa State College $10,000 for the study of governmental policies affecting the production and distribution of food. In accepting the grant, the president's office agreed to the project and its direction by Professor Schultz. Nevertheless, that office instructed the business office to pay no further bills drawn against the grant. This was done without the knowledge of Professor Schultz—contrary to the conditions of the grant.

President Friley appointed a committee to reformulate the functions and organization of the Department of Economics and Sociology. Theodore Schultz, although head of the department, was not consulted or advised of the president's plans and purposes in taking this step.

In connection with each of these grievances Schultz's letter of resignation made specific recommendations for remedying what had been done in the past or for preventing recurrences in the future. There were also urgent proposals for improvement of the college as a whole.

While the Farm Bureau had opposed the economists regarding the pamphlet on dairying, its rival, the Iowa Farmers Union, offered them strong support. Its president, D. W. VanVliet, demanded an investigation of the situation by an independent committee to be named by the governor, the American Association of University Professors, and the American Civil Liberties Union.[1] He did not believe that the administration of the college or the Board of Education (the body in control of public higher education) would be unbiased. As a reason for such skepticism VanVliet cited an editorial in the <u>Mason City Globe-Gazette</u>, published by a Board of Education member, Earl Hall. The article, "Responsibility of Academic Freedom," said: "At times when institutional responsibility and academic freedom collide and conflict, it would be our notion that the former should have precedence."[2] Another Board member was quoted as endorsing Hall 100 percent; this was W. B. Rupe, a newspaper publisher in Ames.[3] Henry C. Shull, then chairman of the

Board of Education, rejected the idea of an ACLU inquiry, saying: "Do you think a New York lawyer would be a better judge in this matter than we here?"[4]

VanVliet than approached both ACLU and AAUP directly on behalf of a thorough inquiry. In the end, both the ACLU and the Iowa affiliate preferred to leave to AAUP the task of making an investigation. One reservation is found in the sentence of Clifford Forster (a member of the staff of ACLU): "In view of the request by Mr. VanVliet, the Civil Liberties Union, in one form or another, should participate in any inquiry."[5]

However, ACLU did not go into the case officially; on the advice of ICLU they left it to AAUP.[6]

The references to the AAUP indicate that that organization was in a state of low vitality. As early as November 1943 VanVliet wrote to R. E. Himstead (who then directed the affairs of AAUP) requesting an investigation, since the Board of Education had claimed that the charges were "without foundation in fact."[7] On December 9, 1943, Clifford Forster sent an inquiry to Himstead and, four weeks later, complained of receiving no answer.[8] In April James M. O'Neill, chairman of the ACLU Committee on Academic Freedom, reported to that committee that AAUP had undertaken an investigation. For this reason, and since no legal action was desired, he recommended no further action by the committee, pending a report from AAUP.[9] A letter from Lucille B. Milner of ACLU to Elizabeth E. Hoyt of the Department of Economics (ISC) reported that Himstead said AAUP was investigating; if that association was not actually proceeding, and if its inactivity resulted from a conviction in advance that there was no question of academic freedom, this fact would influence ACLU.[10]

If a violation of academic freedom occurs only when a person loses his job, there was no violation at that time. Professor Schultz had a much broader concept—one that is needed if there is to be true liberty of investigation and of expression. A letter from him expresses this well. Of the period in question he says:

> Members of the faculty were not being fired, but there was great care in who was being hired and there were all manner of social rules and regulations on what was appropriate behavior which added up to a very strong denial of what I consider academic freedom on scores of issues. Even today we are unable to identify most of the underlying conditions and circumstances that impair academic freedom. . . . There is a parallel in all of this in the instances in the last few years with respect to some militant students. Here again, there is a whole family of violations of academic freedom. Most of them are of a type that is difficult to identify to the point where a real and hard judgment can be made. . . . There is very little doubt that there is pressure on reading lists, libraries, the topics that faculty are to avoid or to concentrate on, the refusal to allow a speaker to be heard if his views are contrary to a particular group.

Even today and at many points in our education, academic freedom is impaired and the circumstances that are associated with the impairment are, as a rule, much more subtle and pervasive than a sudden explosion when a president or a board of trustees suddenly decides to dismiss a member of the faculty. The latter is simply not "allowed" to happen, if for no other reason [than]. . . it has become bad publicity and might indeed call for an investigation.[11]

The same letter, using this definition of academic freedom, found that freedom circumscribed and reduced for his department by every one of the acts named in his letter of resignation. He added that credit should be given to Wallaces Farmer and the Des Moines Register for their notable support (editors of both were active in ICLU).[12]

While ACLU did not make a study of the situation at Ames, it became involved. The New Republic for February 14, 1944, contained an article by J. M. O'Neill entitled "Academic Freedom and the Catholics." Having told of violation of academic freedom at the University of Notre Dame, O'Neill set Iowa State on the same level. He did this on the basis of statements in other periodicals—in particular, Reader's Digest for December 1943—without making sure that they were accurate.

> If the press reports are approximately true, he (President Friley) has given up without a fight the fortress for truth and the public interest which he commanded, and he has surrendered to a self-seeking pressure group which is trying to make a profit out of ignorance.

Dean Buchanan, as director of the Agricultural Experiment Station, protested against the article, both in a letter to the New Republic and by letter and by telephone to ACLU.[13] O'Neill had stated that Brownlee was absent on leave. In defense of the president Buchanan wrote to the New Republic:

> President Friley refused to entertain recommendations of pressure groups that there be dismissals in our Department of Economics. Mr. Brownlee is a member of the staff and has been working during the past year on a revision of the manuscript which has now been completed, which has been reviewed by a faculty committee and is in process of publication.

It is unfortunate that O'Neill, like most of the commentators of the time, spoke almost exclusively of the Brownlee pamphlet—the one case in which academic freedom was, in the end, most successfully defended—and neglected the many other items in Professor Schultz's letter. And it is most regrettable that the whole situation was not studied by a competent, impartial committee.

On the departure of Theodore Schultz it fell to his colleague, William G. Murray, to direct the department. Before accepting this appointment, Murray told the president that it would be impossible to attract competent scholars unless they were assured of full freedom of utterance and publication. Such assurance was given and thereafter faithfully observed. It is Professor Murray's considered opinion that the resistance to interference with freedom, both by those who left Iowa State and by those who remained, resulted eventually in bringing the school to a high position as to academic freedom among its sister institutions.

The right of a university to autonomy on research and publication was again challenged at Iowa State University in 1960 and successfully defended.

At issue was a series of reports of studies by the Center for Agricultural and Economic Adjustment; the center operated within the College of Agriculture and the Department of Economics and Sociology. After a first publication in June 1959 there followed "Lower Price Supports—Lower Income" (Oct. 22, 1959) and "Projections for the Feed-Livestock Economy" (Dec. 1, 1959). Authors were Geoffrey Shepherd, Arnold Paulsen, and Donald Kaldor. The studies, originally concerned with hog production and marketing only, were expanded to consider all livestock. These three professors were joined by Francis Kutish, Richard Heifner, and Gene Futrell as authors of the definitive Special Report No. 27 of the Agricultural and Home Economics Experiment Station. It appeared in August 1960 with the title "Production, Price and Income Estimates and Projections for the Feed-Livestock Economy under Specified Control and Market-Clearing Conditions."

It was to the 1959 publications that Charles R. Shuman, president of the American Farm Bureau Federation, objected vigorously. In a letter he sent on January 6, 1960, to James H. Hilton, president of Iowa State University, he said: "It is apparent that the purpose of these studies was to support a certain viewpoint which is that the market price system in agriculture does not work in the interests of farmers. I had heard a number of suggestions in recent months from several people that the real purpose of the Center for Agricultural and Economic Adjustment was, and is, to propagandize against the market system and in favor of political planning, political management and political price fixing. . . . I want to protest in the strongest manner possible the issuance . . . of these fragmentary and biased studies."

On January 14 President Hilton replied with a description of the center and an unqualified defense of its work. Crucial are two paragraphs:

> I wish to assure you categorically that at no time has there been any intention whatsoever on the part of the people carrying on the research or educational program of the Center to propagandize either for or against any proposed solution of the farm problem or for any one marketing arrangement. This will continue to be the policy. Neither will the Center engage in the formulation or promotion of public policy except as dissemination of research findings may contribute to

that end. The matter of formulation of policy and its implementation is the responsibility of the Farm Bureau and other similar organizations.

There is one thing that must be said. And that is, the university must preserve the freedom to do research and to have the opportunity to present the facts in an impartial and objective manner. In this, I am sure you will agree.

Shuman's letter to Hilton also attacked

a statement on farm policy by the inter-state farmers' study group, which is apparently a functional part of the Center for Agricultural Adjustment. . . . I think you will agree that the effect of this statement is to propagandize against the market system. . . . Distribution of this statement by the Iowa State University Information Service certainly implies the assumption of considerable responsibility for its content.

It was Floyd Andre, Dean of Agriculture and director of the Agricultural and Home Economics Experiment Station, who showed how undeserved this reproach was. His letter (dated Jan. 13, 1960) explained that this group, certainly not a "functional part of the Center," had originally consisted of certain Iowans who were members of the dean's advisory committee on agriculture.

After a meeting where these Iowans heard economists working on center research projects, they asked that farmers in five other states be invited to join them. This then was the origin of the "interstate farmers' study group." Meeting at Ames in November 1959, they agreed on a statement relative to farm policy; this action was entirely their own decision.

Ordinarily the news service of Iowa State University finds it proper to report important statements made on the campus—including, for instance, the contents of talks by visiting lecturers; no one thinks of them as spokesmen for the university. In this case it was decided that extra emphasis was needed on the independence of the university and the interstate group. Leon Thompson, editorial assistant for the center, reproduced the group's statement on plain paper and distributed it with a covering letter, explaining that the announcement came from the Interstate Farmers' Study Group, meeting on the ISU campus. Clearly the accusations of Mr. Shuman were not deserved.

Professor Earl O. Heady, executive director of the Center for Agricultural and Economic Adjustment, was also involved in the correspondence; he of course stood firm for the rights of the center as to research and publication.

There followed meetings and exchange of letters between officers of the federation and of the university. In these the mutual respect and desire for harmony were often stated. For this history of freedom in Iowa it is most important that the university authorities successfully upheld the freedom of learning and of utterance on the part of its members.

Chapter 5

Although the Board of Education (now renamed the Board of Regents) had not helped academic freedom when the Department of Economics was harassed in 1943, it has for many years had a liberal influence. From 1965 to 1969 all three universities could rejoice in presidents not only devoted to civil liberties but honored for their devotion. The president of the University of Iowa, Howard R. Bowen, while president of Grinnell College, had accepted the praise of ICLU bestowed on that college for its refusal to accept federal grants to students conditioned on their fulfilling political requirements. W. Robert Parks, now president of Iowa State University, had collaborated with Joseph F. Wall of Grinnell College in writing a series of pamphlets on civil liberties for the Iowa Farm Bureau Federation. This work brought the authors recognition from ICLU. William Maucker, while president of the University of Northern Iowa, received the Meiklejohn Award of the American Association of University Professors for his defense of an instructor's freedom of speech.

The Board of Regents should be commended for their policy on visiting speakers at the universities. Their policy statement, issued October 23, 1964, includes these words:

> It is the policy of the State Board of Regents, expressed through the institutions of higher education under its control, to permit students and staff members to hear diverse points of view from speakers sponsored by recognized student, faculty, and employee organizations. This policy is entirely consistent with the aims of higher education. It is designed to emphasize that in a democratic society all citizens have not only the right but the obligation to inform themselves on the issues of contemporary concern.

In the fall of 1967 Edward Hoffmans, an English instructor at the University of Northern Iowa who had destroyed his own draft card, called for civil disobedience by all who opposed the Vietnam War and the use of the draft in support of it. On the one occasion when I heard Hoffmans speak (at Wartburg College) he insisted that no one should take such a step before he had worked hard at determining the facts and, on that basis, found the war indefensible.

Six members of the Iowa General Assembly asked that Hoffmans be separated from the university. President Maucker stated: "There must be no punitive action taken by the University against anyone because of ideas expressed publicly on political issues." Both Maucker and the Regents refused to act against Hoffmans.[14] It was this action which caused the AAUP to honor Mr. Maucker with the Meiklejohn Award, reserved for an administrator who has given outstanding service to academic freedom.

In 1968 the seven members of the Story County Grand Jury used three months for a study of Iowa State University (which is in that county). The resulting document was largely the work of the foreman, David A. Norris. It called not for indictments because of suspected crimes but for better control of the university by the

Regents, for a fight against the "moral pollution" found there. The jury showed great concern over the influence of "radicals," whether teachers—mainly of the Humanities—or visiting lecturers. "Radicals," never defined but many times mentioned with scorn, seemed to be those persons whose utterances displeased the foreman. The Regents, the document urged, should be selective in the choice of those who might talk to students; then no "censorship" would be needed (of course the authors were against censorship).[15]

In a letter to the Ames Tribune, January 8, 1969, Donald E. Boles (Department of Political Science, Iowa State University) recalled that the Iowa code restricts the grand jury's general duties to investigating indictable offenses and that "moral pollution" is not one of them. A lasting truth about the mission of grand juries was later stated by U.S. District Judge William K. Thomas: "A grand jury is without authority to issue a report that advises, condemns, or commends, or makes recommendations concerning the policies and operations of public boards, public officers, or public authorities."[16]

In the thorough response of President Parks to the jury report we read:

> The main thrust of the grand jury report is a demand for censorship, restrictions on freedom to speak and freedom to listen, and rigid restrictions upon freedom of inquiry in our state university. . . . The Iowa State Board of Regents should be commended, rather than criticized, for permitting the expression and critical examination of a wide range of controversial viewpoints on the campuses of Iowa's three universities.[17]

In the spring of 1969 three state senators—Lucas De Koster of Hull, Joseph Flatt of Winterset, and Francis Messerly of Cedar Falls—introduced an amendment to the appropriations bill for the Regents' institutions:

> No part of the funds appropriated under this act shall be used to provide payments, assistance or education, in any form, with respect to any individual who is, while enrolled as student or while teaching at a university, convicted in any federal, state or local court of competent jurisdiction of inciting, promoting or carrying on a riot, resulting in material damage to public property or injury to persons, unless such person, if a student, shall be re-examined by an admissions officer and be found by him to be of proper character for re-admission as a student.

The amendment was deemed necessary because with it, in effect, "the kooks and degenerates will think twice before they try to incite a riot."

Having been proposed as an amendment rather than as an independent measure, this had little discussion and passed by a narrow

margin. Obvious flaws in the measure were the equal trust in the
judgment of all courts in the United States and the failure to
provide for readmission of teachers, as that of students was en-
visaged. Among those who objected strongly to the "riot amendment"
was the Faculty Council of Iowa State University; that body found
it destructive of "academic due process." Although this measure
was passed, apparently it was never implemented.

In 1969 Francis Messerly had another chance to turn his dis-
pleasure with the state universities into action. He was chairman
of the Senate Appropriations Committee and thus in a position to
call for an investigation of the universities' use of money. However, his study was to cover other matters, in particular teachers'
"social adaptability"—something which, it seemed, the campus
"radicals" would be found to lack. To Mr. Messerly's regret, the
Iowa Legislature's Budget and Financial Control Committee decided
to study finances only.[18]

In the spring of 1970—particularly after students were killed
at Kent State University and Jackson State College and President
Nixon surprised the nation by the invasion of Cambodia—there was
some disorder at the three state universities. For example, paths
to recruiting offices were blocked, and there was a little damage
to university property. Certain newspapers, legislators, and other
persons thought that stern action against those involved was called
for. Accordingly, in July 1970, the Board of Regents set up a code
of personal conduct for the universities, prefacing it with the
statement of six principles which, of themselves, aroused no criticism on the part of ICLU. Indeed, the whole document was milder
in a number of ways than the critics of the universities would
have wished.

The Hawkeye Area Chapter of ICLU, covering the neighborhood
of Iowa City and Cedar Rapids, made a detailed study of the code,
with a number of adverse comments. Thereafter, the Board of ICLU
asked its own Academic Freedom Committee to make a similar study;
on its basis the Board might be able to make a definitive statement. Such a statement was made on October 15. This is briefer
than the Hawkeye pronouncement, but it does not contradict it at
any point.

The Board of ICLU regrets the "failure of the Regents to seek
participation of representatives of the various university constituents" which "may seriously jeopardize relationships between the
Regents and the persons they seek to govern."

Section 5 of the Regents' statement said:

> The foregoing rules shall be construed so as not to abridge
> any person's constitutional right of free expression of
> thought or opinion, including the traditional American right
> to assemble peaceably and to petition authorities.

The ICLU statement discusses sections of the Regents' document that contradict this disclaimer. Section 4, for instance, authorizes the president of a university to bar from the campus—tem-

porarily—any person who, in his judgment, has violated the rules of personal conduct; this provides none of the safeguards usually afforded one accused of violation. Section 4(d) goes further, providing for expulsion or dismissal of a person who disobeys this temporary order. Thus "an innocent person can lose access to his university for violation of what is subsequently found to be an erroneous or invalid order."

Section 1(k) requires a person who has completed his term of suspension to satisfy the president "that he is unlikely to disrupt the university in the future," if he is not to be excluded permanently. This means that he is punished not for what he has done, not even for what he will do or plans to do, but for what the president thinks he may do.

All three universities have accepted the 1940 statement of the American Association of University Professors on academic freedom and tenure (82 professional associations had by 1970 officially adopted the statement); "this must be considered as part of the contractual relationship between the university and the individual professor on tenure"—and indeed, so far as freedom of thought and utterance is concerned, all instructors. Various sections of the rules, the ICLU statement points out, are liable to violate the 1940 principles and the procedures later devised for implementing them; thus a university applying the new rules might lay itself open to censure and possibly loss of accreditation (see Appendix 4).

CHAPTER 6

Rights of Teachers

UNTIL 1967 public school teachers had no assurance that their annual contracts would be renewed or that any reason would be given if they were not. And in the course of the school year "the Board may, by a majority vote, discharge any teacher for incompetency, inattention to duty, partiality, or any good cause, after a full and fair investigation."[1]

In 1967 a new law provided for automatic continuation of a contract unless the teacher resigns or the Board wishes to terminate it. In the latter case the Board must give "a written statement of specific reasons for considering termination." There is, however, no requirement that the "reasons" be reasonable or seem valid to an objective observer.[2] And the "good cause" which might lead to discharge remains dangerously vague. The law clearly needs improvement in both cases.

It should be added that an aggrieved teacher must request the reason for his discharge before he can learn it. Sometimes an experienced teacher is let out to make a place for a cheaper novice. On this subject Ronald E. Thompson, specialist in the Iowa State Education Association for professional rights and responsibilities, has written me (Mar. 1, 1974): "A number of older, or more experienced teachers have been subjected to termination, thus raising the question of age discrimination. The ISEA strongly resists such actions." However, the appeals procedure is so lengthy—and perhaps so fruitless—that some older persons choose to forego it.

The insecurity of teachers has encouraged persons and groups to demand the ouster of one or more teachers. These attackers do not value that freedom of expression which a teacher needs, both as a leader of the young and as a citizen.

A compromise, reached by representatives of the Iowa State Education Association and the School Board Association, facilitated the passage of legislation to improve the rights of public school teachers. SF 205, passed by the Senate in 1975 and (revised) by the whole General Assembly in 1976, is entitled "An Act relating to the issuance, continuation and termination of teachers' contracts."

The first two consecutive years of a teacher's service in a school district are probationary. However, a board of directors may accept a past probationary period in another district in place of such a period in its own; on the other hand, it may extend such a period by an extra year if the teacher consents.

If in a probationary period the board decides against reappointment of a teacher, that decision is final "unless the termination was based upon an alleged violation of a constitutionally guaranteed right of the teacher or an alleged violation of public employee rights of the teacher under (20.10) of the Code." The ICLU will count freedom of utterance as chief among "constitutionally guaranteed rights." The "public employee rights" are those resulting from the certification of an exclusive bargaining representative, a certification that has become possible through other recent legislation (Chapter 20 of the Code).

The board is to establish evaluation criteria to be used in decisions on continuation or termination of contracts. If there is collective bargaining, the board is to negotiate in good faith with the representative; if there is none, it seems that the criteria may ignore the employee's point of view. An adverse decision must be for "just cause." One could well object to the vagueness of "just cause" and the lack of protection against favoritism—for instance, when the size of a staff must be reduced.

For those beyond the probationary stage, continuation of a contract a year at a time is normally automatic. The law gives details on dates of the various communications between board and teacher. There are several stations on the way to termination: a "short and plain statement" of the reasons, which shall be for just cause; availability to the teacher of his complete personnel file, including all past evaluations; a private hearing (should the teacher ask for it) with the board, after advance exchange of expected evidence and witnesses; a shorthand record of the private hearing; optional briefs and arguments of teacher and superintendent after the private hearing; open session of the board, with roll call vote, if through action or inaction of teacher there is no private hearing; within five days after private hearing, board meeting in executive session for final decision (no roll call vote required); open meeting of board with roll call vote; notification to teacher. Should a teacher (not in probationary status) wish to appeal an adverse decision, he or she and the board shall, in a manner fair to both, choose an adjudicator, whose decision will be final unless either party appeals to the district court; from a decision of the district court there may be appeal to the Supreme Court.

Conditions are better in the state's schools of higher learning, but in them also ICLU has had to intervene.

In 1935 Ralph Bergstrom, who had taught manual training in Davenport nearly twenty years, reported that he had not been on the list of teachers to be reappointed. He had written letters to the newspaper predicting (but not, he said, advocating) the downfall of capitalism. He was restored to his position only after signing an undated letter of resignation; the letter would be used if he exercised his right of free speech.[3]

In the spring of 1951 Robert Shorb was ending his first year as teacher in Boone High School. The Board of Education found no fault with his teaching; their complaint was that he—a Roman Catholic—sent his son to a parochial school. They held that failure to send a child to a public school constituted an implied criticism of the public school system, and that criticism—expressed or implied—indicated intolerable disloyalty.

On the last evening for renewal of contracts the Board had a long conference with Shorb. Though they had not then offered his reappointment, they spoke only of school attendance. Assuming that his position depended on his giving in, he telephoned that, under the circumstances, he would not seek to return. This decision, taken after 2:00 AM, was unfortunate. He later refused to sign a statement of resignation and was given no opportunity for reinstatement. The Boone Junior Chamber of Commerce spoke against his dismissal, and there was other publicity in his favor—for which he was unjustly blamed. At the annual convention of the Junior Chamber of Commerce in Sioux City, that body adopted a resolution in support of the Boone Chamber's defense of Shorb. The resolution "strenuously reaffirms the principle of brotherhood of men, and condemns any action of any group or any individual based solely on religious discrimination."[4]

A committee of the Iowa Civil Liberties Union (Warren Gore and Edward S. Allen) investigated the case, speaking with the Board of Education, Robert Shorb, and his lawyer. The ICLU issued a two-page statement on the case, condemning the school board: "The public interest has suffered greatly whenever continued tenure depended on a loss of freedom—especially in a matter of conscientious judgment like the present one. Fear about reappointment may impair the quality of a school system just as certainly as fear of dismissal."

Plans were made for an appeal through the courts (this would have been an appeal, since one court had upheld the Board's right to act as it did), but the plans were dropped when Shorb found a position elsewhere.[5]

In October 1950 Mrs. Mary E. Cassill was a teacher at Lynnville. She was asked to resign and did so.[6] The ICLU studied the case thoroughly before making a statement. George Willoughby, then executive secretary of the Des Moines office of the American Friends Service Committee, gave much time and thought to the investigation. The Union made its conclusions public; they contain the following:[7]

> The action of Superintendent and Board . . . was caused by her advocacy of views—opposition to war, both in general and in the situation of the moment—which were shared by few

others, and by her persistence—greater, it seems, than she herself realized—in explaining these views to others. . . . We need support of freedom by the whole people. We need a recognition that the government which imprisons, the employer who discharges, the community which ostracizes because of advocacy of the unpopular, endangers progress and denies democracy.

In the spring of 1958 Donald E. Laughlin applied for a position as teacher in West Branch. In 1944 he had registered with the Selective Service and had served in Civilian Public Service (the organization that employed conscientious objectors to war). In 1948 he no longer felt it right to register; for his refusal he was sentenced to 18 months in prison, of which he served six.

This was fully known to the Board of Education, but it did not deter them from appointing Laughlin. However, Donald E. Johnson of West Branch, former commander of the Iowa American Legion, pressed for annulment of the appointment. The Board voted 3 to 2 to yield to him. On December 9, 1958, ICLU issued a "West Branch Resolution," reiterating its insistence that a teacher have full freedom of utterance and of association.[8]

The Iowa Civil Liberties Union, anxious to learn how free high school teachers of social studies were, sent a questionnaire to such teachers and received 116 replies. A report was prepared in 1952 by Joe M. Bohlen (Department of Economics and Sociology, Iowa State College) and issued by a committee of which Lauren Soth (Des Moines Register and Tribune) was chairman.[9]

Asked about attitudes related to academic freedom, the teachers were not aware of many encroachments. (Did this mean that they were not sensitive to restrictions or that they were actually free?) They were disturbed, however, by community restrictions—restrictions felt as teachers, not especially as teachers of social subjects. "It is deplorably apparent that these high school teachers have not given much thought to the roles of school board, school administration, teachers in the operation of schools, curriculum development, teaching methods, etc."

As to the teaching of social studies, current events were taught as separate courses in only eight schools. More should be taught, teachers believed, but they felt themselves inadequate to handle such discussions.

Before the school year for the West Lyon Community High School at Inwood began in 1970, there was an orientation for all teachers. Men were then orally informed that they must not wear mustaches. Douglas Flyger, a teacher of social sciences and basketball coach, at that time wore a mustache but obediently shaved it off. After Christmas, however, he returned from vacation with a mustache. This time he was willing to remove it again only if the Board agreed to offer him a contract for the next year and to reconsider its ban in hirsute deviations. This offer was refused, with the remark that Flyger had not used proper channels to assert his hirsute preference. He was, in fact, required to resign in two days. The experience made him so displeased with the teaching profession that he turned to a business career, which he believed would offer him more security.[10]

In view of this fact and the number of "hair cases" ICLU had already handled, the Board of the Union undertook no action on behalf of Flyger.

CHAPTER 7

Censorship

WHEN you hear another say something you disagree with, something that displeases you, you may think:
(1) He ought not to be allowed to say that.
(2) I wish he wouldn't say that.
(3) It is good to hear him say that; perhaps I can learn from him where I was mistaken.

The Civil Liberties Union will almost always disagree with (1), will not criticize those whose reaction is (2), but hopes that its work will definitely increase the number of those with reaction (3).

Censorship of various kinds has been attempted in Iowa from time to time; sometimes the Union has protested, occasionally with effect.

Soon after the inauguration of President Franklin Roosevelt, in a time of severe economic depression, one measure taken to give needed relief and at the same time enrich the cultural life of the people was governmental support of the arts. Thus in 1938 Don Rhodes and Howard Johnson painted a mural, 110 feet in length, in the agricultural building of the Iowa State Fair. The development of Iowa as an agricultural and industrial state was depicted. In 1946 L. B. Cunningham, secretary of the Fair Board, found the mural "an insult to Iowa farmers because it pictured them as clubfooted, coconut-headed, and low-browed." Before the annual fair of that year he ordered the pictures sawed up for use as scrap lumber around the fairgrounds. Destruction, however, was not complete. Paul Backensten, who had helped Rhodes while he painted the work, succeeded in rescuing a ten-foot section; it was shown in a municipal art fair later the same year.

The same sort of censorship of art happened in Cedar Rapids. In 1936-37 murals of historic content were painted on the walls of the federal courtroom. They were the creation of four artists—Robert White (in charge), Don Glassel, Harry Jones, and Everett Jeffries. They showed scenes from the history of this region—not always of a flattering nature.

US District Judge Henry N. Graven, the presiding judge in 1956, disapproved of the murals, feeling that they were not appropriate in a courtroom. In particular he objected to the scene across from the jury box, which showed a lynching. Judge Graven, saying that he had made an effort to have the murals removed and preserved (a process someone thought impractical) ordered them painted over. He asked to have a water-based paint used, to allow for possible restoration later (the originals were probably done in tempera): "It is my recollection that this kind of paint was not used or that it didn't work out, because I think on a later date someone tried to remove a little of it and the mural had been damaged."[1] On May 2, 1956, the <u>Cedar Rapids Gazette</u> reported that the murals were "a thing of the past."

When we recall that the murals were the property of the whole people—who had paid for them—and not of the judge, and that an artist suffers a serious loss when his works are permanently lost to view, we may well ask whether the use of curtains might not have protected both the sensibilities of judge and juries and the rights of the people and the artists.

In 1968 a loan exhibit of paintings at the Des Moines Art Center contained five pictures displeasing to the City Council. They passed a resolution asking removal of these drawings and paintings. The Board of the Art Center accordingly put the five in a room for adults only. The ICLU Board deplored the action of the Council and regretted the yielding of the Board of the Art Center to the wishes of the Council. "The Board of the ICLU views the resolution as an indirect attempt to censor art works by a method which is of doubtful legality and contrary to the public interest."[2] The records also show thanks to Robert Scism (Des Moines attorney, former member of the staff of the state attorney general) for bringing court action against the Des Moines City Council because of censorship without due process of law.[3]

In the same year Sioux City saw a case of censorship of art. The Gagle Art Gallery displayed a poster entitled Pietà. This adaptation of the Michelangelo sculpture had nude figures and was seized by police with a search warrant as being obscene. No charges were filed, and the owner of the shop, backed by the Sioux City Chapter of ICLU, demanded the return of the picture. At the request of the owner's lawyer the ICLU withdrew from further pursuit of the case.[4]

In 1939 the Des Moines Public Library published a "Library's Bill of Rights," from which we quote.

>   1. Books shall be chosen from the standpoint of value and interest to people of Des Moines; and in no case shall selection be based on race or nationality, political or religious views of the writer.
>   2. As far as available material permits, all sides of controversial questions shall be represented equally.
>   3. Official publications and/or propaganda of groups, solicited as gifts, will be available without discrimination.

4. Library meeting rooms are available on equal terms to all organized non-profit groups for open, free meetings.[5]

Following the policy of item 4 the library had given the use of its auditorium for a meeting at which Elizabeth Gurley Flynn spoke for the Communist Party. On September 9, 1939, ACLU sent this message to Forrest Spaulding, the librarian:

> Warmest appreciation of your fine stand at the time misguided veterans broke up a meeting of Communists in the auditorium. Your policy in use of auditorium and schools should be strengthened as more men like you stand by the principles of what is obvious Americanism.

The spirit of Forrest Spaulding is not all-pervasive in Iowa, and the Civil Liberties Union has repeatedly seen deviations from it in the censoring of books and magazines. The social studies textbooks of Harold Rugg have been favorite targets of eager censors, who succeeded in having these books dropped from Cedar Rapids schools in 1940.[6]

In 1948 the judgment of three patrolmen in Sioux City was enough to have the sale of three books stopped: <u>Tobacco Road</u> and <u>God's Little Acre</u> by Erskine Caldwell and <u>Passionate Witch</u> by Theron Smith. The ACLU urged the Chief of Police, Julius Myron, to reconsider the action, pointing out that a jury trial must be the basis of finding that a book is punishably indecent.

The attempt at censorship of broadest scope came in 1959 when Norman Erbe, attorney general of the state, decided that 42 publications (mainly periodicals) were obscene. He requested all county attorneys to "take prompt and vigorous action in requiring magazine dealers to remove these objectionable publications from their racks at once and to bring criminal proceedings" for any subsequent violations.[7]

To the Board of ICLU it seemed indefensible censorship to remove publications from circulation without any attempt to prove a case against them, and even to prejudice future issues of the same journals. Knight Publishing Company and Four Star Publications initiated a suit against Norman Erbe. At the request of ICLU, Sherwin Markman prepared a brief amicus curiae which earned warm praise from Rowland Watts of the New York office of ACLU.[8]

Although the plaintiffs held that it amounted to unconstitutional precensorship, the court upheld the state's right to warn distributors of "obscene magazines."[9] The protests, however, were powerful enough to weaken the force of the attorney general's action.

At Dubuque in 1962 Police Judge Alfred Hughes ordered the destruction of 358 copies of 55 publications, which had been seized in a police raid.[10] He considered them all obscene. The ICLU urged the attorney general of the state to investigate this action. Frank Gillom, Judge of District Court, ruled that books seized in this raid could not be admitted as evidence.

A more recent instance of censorship was noted at Mount Pleasant in 1967. There *The Arrangement* by Elia Kazan was barred from the municipal library as being "too obscene." The publisher then offered to send a copy free to any head of a family in that city who requested it.

The following week John Ciardi, speaking at Drake University, said: "Any attack on one book—even a bad one—is an attack on our greater freedoms."[11]

"Obscenity" is not the only excuse for barriers between utterer and receiver of a message. In 1948 at a Freedom Train in Davenport two students were arrested for distribution of allegedly communistic literature. Judge John J. McSwiggin, however, was aware of Supreme Court judgments and ordered them released; they needed no license and had done no littering.[12]

The *Pterodactyl* was an underground paper issued in 1969 by Grinnell College students. Material for a number—writing and a photograph—was in the hands of the printer (Trico Publishers, Inc.) when agents of the State Bureau of Criminal Investigation asked the president of the company, Eugene Saylor, to give it to him, saying the newspaper was obscene. Saylor complied voluntarily; this fact, and the lack of any warrant, led Assistant Attorney General Douglas Carlson to say that no seizure was involved.

Henry Wilhelm, *Pterodactyl* photographer, held that the printer had no right to surrender what was not his property. This fact and the view that seizure even before the material was printed meant prior censorship led ICLU to intervene in the case, demanding the release of the writing in question. A federal district court held that Attorney General Richard Turner had acted illegally, the writing and photograph were returned, and the issue was printed and distributed. Turner appealed the decision to the United States Supreme Court, which refused to accept the appeal.[13] The ICLU was gratified to see two principles upheld—that censorship must not come before publication, and that a printer is merely the agent of the author and may not act as if he were the owner of the script.

In the autumn of 1971 the State Executive Council, consisting of five selected officials, voted that the State Traveling Library should not renew its subscription to the *Berkeley Barb*. This underground California newspaper had expressed "extremist views." In their action the council overruled a recommendation by the librarian of the State Traveling Library. Melvin Synhorst, secretary of state, voted originally for the prohibition. He later moved for reconsideration but found no support.

Both ICLU and the Library Association urged a reversal of the decision, saying that such a dangerous precedent for censorship by a political body should not be permitted to stand.[14] Although the Executive Council did not reverse its decisions, the attorney general's office ruled that subscriptions were not "supplies" and therefore not under the jurisdiction of the ISTL Board. The library did receive the *Berkeley Barb* through gift subscriptions.

The Executive Council had also ruled that the traveling library should not purchase a recording of *Hair*. That decision, however, they reversed.[15]

Censorship

Barbara Welk of Des Moines, an officer of the Women's International League for Peace and Freedom, spoke to the ICLU Board meeting, May 25, 1972. She and other members of that league showed a collection of posters on environmental problems in Vietnam. The collection had been shown in numerous places including churches. However, the Bellas Hess Shopping Center would not allow it to be shown there; the posters labeled as dangerous certain weed killers sold in that center. When the exhibit was offered to the Des Moines Center of Science and Industry, two items were held to be so "political" they must be omitted. The WILPF refused to show a censored edition of their posters.[16]

Since the United States Supreme Court had ruled that shopping centers are private property, there seemed no recourse in the Bellas Hess Center case. As to the Center of Science and Industry, the ICLU Board asked two members to intercede with its director; regrettably, those named for this mission did not carry it out.

Allied to censorship was the delay after World War II in reestablishing mail service with former enemies—particularly Germany and Japan. Katherine Lucchini, secretary of ICLU in 1946-47, corresponded with Iowans in Congress on the subject, showing interest particularly in the right to send periodicals and other printed matter to those countries.[17]

CHAPTER 8

Police Practices

LIKE most sections of ACLU, the Iowa affiliate is at times called on to see that those who enforce the law also obey the law. As early as 1921, ACLU had appealed to Governor Nathan Kendall on behalf of Ida Crouch-Hazlett (Socialist Party) who had been harassed at numerous places in Iowa. She and three men were arrested at a meeting in Union Park in Des Moines;[1] in Boone she was threatened with arrest if she spoke, even on private property; she had a meeting broken up at Madrid; in Mason City she was kidnapped and driven from town.[2] Such incidents as these were the cause of the appeal to the governor for her protection. Fortunately such appeals had some effect. Within two weeks of her arrest in Des Moines she spoke there again, to an audience of 1000, without interference.

In many cases the American Legion has been prominent in suppression of unapproved gatherings. It is to the credit of V. F. Sieverding of Grundy Center, former state commander, that he stated: "If the law is not violated, such action as is reported is not the proper way to handle the situation."[3]

A police practice of which there is frequent complaint is that of holding an arrested person incommunicado. In 1937 the Des Moines police held a man for 24 hours without any explanation for his arrest and detention.[4] He had caught a ride with two strangers, whom the police apparently wished to interrogate.

In 1939 three men from Garden City were arrested and held for 33 hours without explanation. At the time C. F. Ransom (editorial writer for the Des Moines Register and Tribune) wrote: "[This case] has been a great local scandal, but the Chamber of Commerce and Bar Association have taken such interest that we [ICLU] did no more than pass a resolution."[5]

In 1950 at the suggestion of Hugh Chermley, then the treasurer, ICLU engaged a young man, Kenneth Walker, to be assistant secretary. He lived at the headquarters of the American Friends Service Committee in Des Moines. There he was arrested at 1:30 PM July 25, and given no reason for his arrest. He reported a belief that it might have to do with his registration as a conscientious objector to war. He was questioned at 9:00 AM the next day, and only then was he permitted contact with Lyle Tatum and George Willoughby (connected with both ACLU and AFSC). At 10:30 he was allowed to telephone, and at 11:05 was arraigned. Robert Mannheimer (son of Rabbi Eugene Mannheimer, an early supporter of ICLU) secured reduction of bail and later, defending him, obtained his acquittal.

Kenneth had a brother Max, who was repeatedly (with good reason, it seems) accused of breaking and entering, operating another's car, and the like. Kenneth had formerly helped secure his brother's release after arrest, but this time (Max was then in jail) he had refused to do any more for him. In revenge, Max accused Kenneth of being his accomplice, at least to the point of receiving stolen goods.

As a civil liberties organization, ICLU was chiefly concerned with the police's detention of Kenneth without outer contact. The case gave added impetus to the Union's call for reform in treatment of those arrested.[6]

Nearly ten years later Davenport police held two youths incommunicado for several hours. When ICLU protested, it received an apology; the police had not been aware that the law gave prisoners the right to communicate with their family or lawyer immediately after arrest.[7]

At the biennial conference of ACLU in 1954, Ed Meyerding, of the Illinois affiliate, told of measures used in Chicago to improve police practice. Among them is the wide distribution of a pamphlet, "Your Rights When Arrested." The ICLU is among the bodies that have broadcast such a leaflet; in 1960 the Iowa Peace Officers' Association expressed willingness to use it.

An unusual form of violation of the rights of one arrested came to light in Dubuque in 1961. There a boy of 17, arrested on a traffic charge, was not taken to the nearest magistrate but to a distant justice of the peace—apparently because the arresting officer believed he could secure conviction or a stiff sentence more easily; no counsel was provided for the boy.[8]

Although we have had occasion to criticize the police of Iowa (and sometimes to secure improvement in their practices), we believe that they are among the better police forces in the United States—and generally willing to improve their conduct further.

The Board of ICLU has been disturbed by a provision of law that permits the suspension of one's driver's license on evidence that he has committed an offense which, on conviction, would make revocation mandatory. To the Board this seemed the infliction of a penalty before conviction—that is, the denial of the presumption of innocence.[9] The Iowa Bar Association has also challenged the legality of such suspension.[10]

Responding to an inquiry from me, Captain James R. Smith, assistant director, Drivers License Division, commented on this provision (Section 321.210, Code of Iowa):

> Even though we feel that we do have statutory authority to suspend licenses under these circumstances [the Code actually

names seven different grounds for suspension, all connected with driving a motor vehicle], we do not normally use this particular Section of the Code. We use it only on rare occasions when it is apparent that, for the safety of all concerned, the licensee should be suspended without waiting for final conviction for the offense.[11]

In their relations with the law, poor people usually come off worse than the rich do. This troubles ICLU more and more, and the Union has tried to find ways of making "justice" more just. There is the requirement that a person arrested post bail if he is to be free until his trial. Without money he has the punishment of imprisonment—separation from family, from the chance to earn, from every liberty outside the walls of jail—before any guilt has been proved. The ICLU has urged release without bond if, as is usually the case, he is unlikely to fail to return for trial. Gilbert Cranberg, Norman Jesse, and Dan Johnston, acting for this body, succeeded in getting Des Moines to adopt a new and much more lenient policy as to pretrial release.

To overcome another handicap of those with little money the Union insists on the right of a defendant to counsel at all stages of a case. Too often, according to the ICLU legal committee, the police and county attorney persuade a man to plead guilty and then do not allow him to confer with the lawyer defending him until just before the sentencing.[12] Not only for the original trial but also on appeal, a man is entitled to counsel; and this, if necessary, should be at public expense. Earl Roberts, serving a sentence at the Fort Madison penitentiary, declined to use the court-appointed attorney who had unsuccessfully defended him originally. The Union protested the court's failure to provide a more acceptable defender.[13]

In June 1970 Lewis Stephen Wheeler, a Negro whose home was in Kansas City, had been sentenced to five years imprisonment on a narcotics charge. While being transported to the state penitentiary in Fort Madison he escaped. When Deputy Sheriff William Slycord found and accosted Wheeler in Des Moines on June 18, the two exchanged shots and Slycord was seriously wounded. Slycord fired the full contents of his revolver, but there is no indication that Wheeler was wounded. Two hours later police located Wheeler in a house basement which had an outside entrance. Witnesses have stated that there were two volleys of shots from the police—one while Wheeler was behind a closed door, one after the door was opened. Then an officer fired a rifle shot into the doorway without looking into it. At some time in the procedure Wheeler was killed.

Dr. R. C. Wooters, deputy Polk County medical examiner, made a preliminary report the same evening—a perfunctory report giving conclusions without bases for them; the major conclusion was that Wheeler had been shot by "peace officers acting in the line of duty."

Anxious to have a full and true account of the event—especially whether the killing was justified—ICLU asked for a copy of the autopsy report. This was refused until the ICLU Foundation filed a petition for mandamus under the Iowa Access to Public Documents Act. The autopsy report listed 17 wounds but did not discuss the paths taken by the bullets.

That there had been no thorough investigation by public officials was clear from an inspection of the site on August 19. On that date Oliver Johnson, acting for ICLU, found several spent bullets still lying in the basement entry; he also obtained as much evidence as he could from neighbors who had witnessed the shooting. Johnson was a (black) law student at Drake engaged by ICLU for work in a neighborhood where the Union's presence seemed important.

The investigation did not establish conclusively whether the killing of Wheeler was justified. It did, however, point to the need for a full inquiry, which would require further examination of the autopsy by a forensic pathologist, powers of subpoena, and access to police records—requirements beyond the authority of ICLU.

The county attorney proposed to present the case to the Polk County Grand Jury. This procedure seemed unsatisfactory to ICLU, since the Grand Jury feel themselves a part of the "law enforcement establishment" and are usually biased in favor of the police.

The whole incident confirmed in the Board of ICLU the belief that an entirely independent body, ready to investigate complaints on police conduct, is needed.[14]

In 1968 a school-police liaison system was initiated in the Des Moines high schools. The goals were development of better communication between school, police, and students and development of respect for law enforcement by means of personal contact. Beginning with two officers, by 1969-70 it involved 13 commissioned Des Moines police officers. They had the double function of increasing good will for the police and for law enforcement and of discovering and dealing with cases of delinquency. A committee of ICLU, with Paul F. Dunn (executive director of the Iowa Council of the National Council on Crime and Delinquency) as chairman, was concerned that the pursuit of the latter objective might make the former objective harder to realize.

On March 15, 1971, Dunn presented a five-page discussion paper to the ICLU Board on the subject. He noted that, in the 1969-70 school year, 1,164 juveniles had been reprimanded and released and 494 referred to juvenile court. Attempts to improve "rapport" included 321 speaking engagements (15,563 in attendance). Dunn then recommended "group meetings with police, school administrators, police legal advisers, school administration legal counsel, school board members, Iowa Crime Commission, ICLU, and citizen representation" for more precise guidelines than existed. Other possible steps mentioned were: broad distribution of a handbook or flyer on students' rights; the demand that school staffs know their responsibility to protect students in their charge; an objective evaluation of the system; and clarification of police-student contacts.

The annual report of Dick J. Clemens, coordinator of police liaison, to Richard P. Klahn, director of secondary education (dated Sept. 21, 1972), noted the decrease in juvenile delinquency and claimed some credit for the liaison program. Among the improvements urged in the report is the careful choice of the police to work in schools—selection to be made by a committee of both school administrators and police.

On January 2, 1973, a code on interviewing of pupils by police became effective, on the whole increasing the protection offered the pupil.

Still the Iowa State Education Association, which had been critical of the liaison program from the outset, withheld approval. In February 1973 its delegate assembly, the policy-making body of the association, passed the following resolution:

> The ISEA is opposed to the policy of local school districts which use liaison school personnel such as policemen and private security forces solely to maintain control of students during school hours. The Association encourages school districts to establish an equilibrium between students and teachers within each classroom in order that positive rapport may be developed. The Association believes that additional teachers would meet the educational needs of students as well as maintain necessary control in order to facilitate learning.

CHAPTER 9

Clothing Controversies in Schools

IN the opposition to the war in Vietnam an incident, apparently minor in itself, became quite important in the history of ICLU.
Three pupils in Des Moines schools (two in senior high, one in junior high) wore black armbands in December 1965 "to mourn those who had died in the Vietnam War and to support a proposal that a truce proposed for Christmas Day 1965 be extended indefinitely." The three were John F. Tinker, Mary Beth Tinker, and Christopher Eckhards. Of their parents, Leonard Tinker was regional peace education secretary of the American Friends Service Committee, and Mrs. William Eckhards was chairman of the Des Moines chapter of the Women's International League for Peace and Freedom. The action was taken after joint discussion by the two familes. It was decided that wearing of the armbands should begin on December 16. The principals of the Des Moines high schools, aware of the plan, adopted a policy on December 14 of suspending any student who should persist in wearing the armband. This resulted in the three in question being sent home and suspended until they returned without them. Two younger Tinker children in other schools had similar experiences; however, they had no prominent part in the litigation that followed.
The children had never planned to wear the bands after New Year's Day 1966; thus their suspension lasted only until the beginning of Christmas vacation.
With the support of ICLU the three young people, through their fathers, petitioned the United States District Court to restrain the Des Moines Independent Community School District from disciplining them. They were first represented by Craig Sawyer, of the faculty of Drake Law College. He withdrew, however, partly because he was already involved in another case for ICLU; from then on Dan Johnston, legal counsel of ICLU, handled the petition.
The ICLU Board of Directors acted promptly. On December 17 the following resolution was passed:

   In connection with the present prohibition against the

wearing of black armbands in the Des Moines public schools, the Iowa Civil Liberties Union expresses its regret that the students have been suspended for using what is otherwise a permissible means of expression. While ICLU recognizes the interests of the school in protecting the educational atmosphere of the schools, a complete prohibition of such activity is unfortunate. It is hoped that the school board will review the action of the school administration and in so doing fully recognize and practice the students' rights to freely express themselves, even though the subject matter is controversial or concerns an unpopular point of view.[1]

On March 15, 1966, the petition was filed; after an evidentiary hearing Judge Roy Stephenson refused to direct the school district to change its rules. Although no disturbance resulted from the display of armbands, and there was no threat that any would, he held, on September 1, 1966, that the principals' action was reasonable and constitutional.

The next step was to the Court of Appeals for the Eighth Circuit. In November 1967 that court divided on the question, 4 to 4, thereby leaving the rule still in force. So the final decision was left to the United States Supreme Court. That court, on March 4, 1968, agreed to consider the armband case. Dan Johnston was again the advocate of freedom, acting on behalf of the students as well as ICLU. His able argument was followed by the decision of the Supreme Court, 7 to 2, against the school board. This was delivered on February 24, 1969, by Justice Fortas, with Justices Black and Harlan dissenting.

The following quotations from the opinion are important:

> First Amendment rights, applied in the light of special characteristics of the school environment, are available to teachers and students. It can hardly be agreed that either teachers or students shed their constitutional rights to freedom of speech or expression at the schoolhouse gate.
>
> The school officials banned and sought to punish petitioners for a silent, passive expression of opinion, unaccompanied by any disorder or disturbance on the part of petitioners. There is here no evidence whatever of petitioners' interference, actual or nascent, with the school's work or of collision with the rights of other students to be secure and to be let alone. Accordingly, this case does not concern speech or action that intrudes upon the work of the school or the rights of other students.
>
> The District Court concluded that the action of the school authorities was reasonable because it was based upon their fear of a disturbance from the wearing of the armbands. But, in our system, undifferentiated fear or apprehension of disturbance is not enough to overcome the right to freedom of expression. Any departure from absolute regimentation may

cause trouble. Any variation from the majority's opinion may inspire fear. Any word spoken, in class, in the lunchroom or on the campus, that deviates from the views of another person, may start an argument or cause a disturbance. But our Constitution says we must take this risk; . . . and our history says that it is this sort of hazardous freedom—this kind of openness—that is the basis of our national strength and of the independence and vigor of Americans who grow up and live in this relatively permissive, often disputatious society.

The action of the school authorities appears to have been based upon an urgent wish to avoid the controversy which might result from the expression, even by the silent symbol of armbands, of opposition to this Nation's part in the conflagration in Vietnam. It is revealing, in this respect, that the meeting at which the school principals decided to issue the contested regulation was called in response to a student's statement to the journalism teacher in one of the schools that he wanted to write an article on Vietnam and have it published in the school paper. (The student was dissuaded.)

It is also relevant that the school authorities did not purport to prohibit the wearing of all symbols of political or controversial significance. The record shows that students in some of the schools wore buttons relating to national political campaigns and some even wore the Iron Cross, traditionally a symbol of nazism. [Here the Court was in error; the Iron Cross was a customary German decoration long before Hitler's birth.] The order prohibiting the wearing of armbands did not extend to these. Instead, a particular symbol—black armbands worn to exhibit opposition to this Nation's involvement in Vietnam—was singled out for prohibition. Clearly the prohibition of expression of one particular opinion, at least without evidence that it is necessary to avoid material and substantial interference with school work or discipline, is not constitutionally permissible.

Of the two dissenting justices, Hugo Black spoke with greater vigor and at length. Among his arguments we find the following:

The truth is that a teacher of kindergarten, grammar school, or high school pupils no more carries into a school with him a complete right to freedom of speech and expression than an anti-Catholic or anti-Semitic carries with him a complete freedom of speech and religion into a Catholic church or Jewish synagogue.

In my view, teachers in state-controlled public schools are hired to teach there. . . . A teacher is not paid to go into school and teach subjects the state does not hire him to teach as a part of its selected curriculum. Nor are public school students sent to the schools at public expense to broadcast political or any other views to educate and inform the public. . . . One may, I hope, be permitted to harbor the thought that taxpayers send children to school on the premise that at their age they need to learn, not teach.

It is surprising that Justice Black took such a narrow view of the roles of student and teacher. An instructor who defines his field narrowly serves the education of the whole person poorly. A student learns not only by listening to his teacher but, to a high degree, by arguing with (trying to teach) both teacher and classmates.

Thus a couple of square feet of black cloth occupied the attention of schools and courts for more than three years, resulting in a definite strengthening of freedom for dissenters. The American and Iowa Civil Liberties Unions and Dan Johnston in particular deserve praise and thanks.[2]

When men—chiefly young men—returned to earlier styles of hair, allowing it to grow long on face and crown, there was often resistance from their elders. In schools scattered around Iowa, rules were passed forbidding this new departure. Students objected to such rules as having no support in reason. They challenged the rules, sometimes with support of their parents, occasionally with an appeal to ICLU and to the courts.

When in 1967 Judge Luther Glanton of Des Moines found James Martin guilty of reckless driving, he assessed a fine of $100, which he was willing to reduce to $50 if the defendant would have his hair cut. The ICLU protested.[3]

In September of the same year enough cases of school regulations had been noted to impel the ICLU Board to consider making a statement of policy about grooming.[4] The policy statement which was later adopted contains the following:

> Educational opportunities should not be denied students because their hair is too long to meet the standards of a school administration or school board. A student's appearance, with respect to dress and hair style, should be of no concern to a school unless a student's appearance actually disrupts the educational process or constitutes a threat to safety or health.
>
> It is questionable whether there is any need for a school board to adopt regulations on personal appearance of students. If there are to be any regulations, they should have a reasonable connection with health and safety. They should not be imposed for the purpose of bringing about conformity or expressing the views of adults about how children in public schools should dress or cut their hair.
>
> The Iowa Civil Liberties Union believes that denying education to students because of their haircuts or lack of them violates freedoms assured under the United States Constitution. It has taken this position in appealing to the United States District Court a case in which a Colfax girl was suspended from school last year because her bangs were too long.

> Legal questions the ICLU raises about school hair codes include whether these codes infringe on the rights of privacy, limit freedom of personal expression and constitute unwarranted government interference in a matter which should be left to parents to control.
>
> Regardless of what position is eventually taken by the courts, the ICLU believes it is unwise for school boards to adopt and attempt to enforce personal appearance codes.[5]

The decision in the Colfax case referred to above was rendered by US District Court Judge William C. Hanson:

> School officials of necessity have been given a wide latitude of discretion in formulating rules and regulations to prescribe and control student conduct within the school. However, the discretion is not unlimited. Only those school rules and regulations that are reasonable are permissible. It must, therefore, be recognized that under our democratic system, public school officials may not act autocratically, nor are they vested with absolute authority over their students. . . .
>
> A student's free choice of his appearance is constitutionally protected under the due process clause of the Fourteenth Amendment. Moreover, the court finds that, because every individual should have the right to express his individuality and personality, any rule seeking to infringe such a right will not enjoy a "presumption of constitutionality." In other words, school hair rules are reasonable and constitutional only if the school can objectively show that such a rule does in fact prevent some disruption or interference of the school system.[6]

In spite of this court decision, scattered schools still tried to force arbitrary dress codes on their students. A committee of teachers and students in Dubuque High School had drawn up a very detailed "student appearance guide." One sentence—"Unusual hair styles which attract undue attention are not acceptable"—was the excuse for sending over 100 boys home. Some of them appealed to ICLU, at whose request Professor Gary Goodpaster of the University of Iowa Law College appeared before the School Board. At the conclusion of his appeal he said:

> [The high school] is a place of substantial experience of life and living. . . . To regulate that experience overly, to overdirect, to hide, to mask, is perhaps to deceive, to misrepresent life, to ensure an unpreparedness for living in the very institution which is designed to educate for adult responsibility and roles. The high school should initiate into responsibility, not habituate to conformity.[7]

Maquoketa, Adel, and Decorah were among the numerous sites of ICLU pleas for tolerance. Decorah had had a code which said in part: "All boys will wear their hair in a short, neat and orderly fashion. Unorthodox haircuts or hair styles will not be permitted." On May 3, 1971, United States District Judge Edward J. McManus, issuing a permanent injunction against penalties for violating this code, said:

> Testimony indicates that the principal had the sole, unbridled discretion to dictate the meaning of "short," "neat," "orderly" and "unorthodox." Hence, even if the defendants could show disruption, this court would be forced to invalidate the regulation since it is so vague as to violate due process.[8]

By this time both districts of the federal court system in Iowa had condemned penalties because of grooming. Still complaints kept coming in to ICLU. The Board finally concluded that the Union should no longer enter litigation on its own part. Aggrieved students were advised to bring suit with their own lawyers if they wished; ICLU would furnish them with all the arguments used in earlier cases.[9]

In the winter of 1968-69 a series of speakers had been invited to Grinnell College to talk about "the social, psychological, and sexual aspects of interpersonal relationships." The lecture committee of students and advisers believed that the philosophy of the magazine Playboy was so widely promoted that a thoughtful discussion of that philosophy would be desirable. Accordingly Brice Draper, the college promotion manager of the magazine, visited the school and spoke to a group of students on February 5. During the lecture six women and four men rose and undressed, then resumed their seats and sang "You've Got to Walk That Lonesome Valley." At the same time other students handed out a statement entitled "Playboy Magazine is a Money-Changer in the Temple of the Body":

> PLAYBOY claims to espouse a philosophy that asserts the body is good and the body is beautiful, but PLAYBOY demeans the human body. Pretending to appreciate and respect the beauty of the naked human form, PLAYBOY in actuality stereotypes the body and commercializes it. PLAYBOY substitutes fetishism for honest appreciation of the endless variety of human forms.
> PLAYBOY says the body is good, but posing as liberator it offers us a sexuality of "subjects" and "objects"—of those who desire and act, and those who are desirable and acted upon. Thus sexual activity is dehumanized and depersonalized.
> We believe that the human body is good and beautiful, but a sensual and aesthetic appreciation of the body cannot be divorced from an appreciation of and respect for persons, of both sexes, of all shapes and sizes. We protest PLAYBOY's images of lapdog female playthings with idealized proportions

and their junior-executive-on-the-way-up possessors. The PLAYBOY bunny is an affront to human sexual dignity.

After some fifteen minutes the students dressed once more. The discussion was interrupted by the singing only and lasted about an hour in all. Cameras were active during the demonstration, and reporters very soon knew and told of the incident.

The student deans wrote a letter to the students who had disrobed and to their parents, regretfully pointing out the harm their action was likely to do the school.[10] No penalties were announced. Although there was some thought of discipline on the part of the college, this was abandoned as soon as inquiries from the attorney general foreshadowed prosecution. Students who had planned to circulate petitions denouncing the nudity incident gave up that project after the "intrusion" of the state government.

The demonstrators were, in fact, accused of indecent exposure. They first had L. K. Le Tourneau as attorney and soon thereafter Dan Johnston, partner of Le Tourneau. On February 21 they had a hearing before Edwin Lincoln, justice of the peace. The same evening the Board of ICLU met and passed a resolution: "The legal committee should indicate to Dan Johnston that the ICLU is willing to participate in the Grinnell case if this seems advisable after a conference of the committee with Johnston."[11]

On April 15 eight pled innocent in the District Court at Montezuma. (On the other demonstrators there was insufficient evidence.) The trial began May 27, with County Attorney Michael Enich charging "open and gross lewdness and actions designedly indecent and obscene." The witnesses, who had been at the discussion, said they had seen nothing grossly lewd or obscene.[12]

The eight were found guilty on May 29; Mary Malcolm, spokesman for the defendants, said they would appeal. Sharp Lannon, foreman of the jury, was clearly unhappy: "I think the charge was a foolish one in the first place, and I don't think the jury was given the latitude it might have been given on the question of obscenity and lewdness. As it was, the jury was simply asked if the students had taken their clothes off in public." He then gave his juryman's fee—$21.60—to the appeal fund.[13]

Sentence was to be pronounced on June 30, but an appeal might be made up to June 9. There had been no complaint of lewdness in the disrobing, either in the motives of the students or in the consequences of their act. As Johnston said, no student present on February 5 made any complaint. "It would be hard for me to imagine something more moral and less immoral than what these young people have done." Johnston promptly filed a motion for a new trial; the fines assessed in the first one had amounted to $200. The students had paid the costs of that trial (aided by a collection taken up at the college). For the appeal ICLU agreed to pay the costs (but no lawyer fees).[14]

The Board minutes for August 15, 1969, tell of repayment by three defendants of $40 advanced to each for bail bonds—further indication of the interest and involvement of ICLU.

In the appeal to the Iowa Supreme Court Johnston emphasized that there had been no suggestion of any sexual misconduct. On the other hand, William Garretson, assistant attorney general, said that the court "should preserve public morals."

The majority opinion (5 to 3) held that the law prohibits "intentional public nudity where the exposure occurs in a setting in which firmly accepted norms or rules of public behavior or decency require that people remain covered or clothed." However, Justice Francis Becker stated: "If the acts are shown to be inoffensive to those present, the conviction should not depend on the social or moral norms of those not present."[15] Justice Harvey Uhlenhopp did not take part.

Among the comments in Iowa newspapers, that in the Cherokee Times for June 26, 1970, deserves quoting:

> We must express admiration for the dramatic and imaginative means our younger generation is taking to point out to society at large many of the undesirable norms and practices we put up with because we lack the guts to put our inner feelings into words and actions.

On September 21, 1970, Dan Johnston filed a petition for certiorari with the United States Supreme Court. His brief, submitted on November 12, held that public nudity is not necessarily lewd.[16] On February 22, 1971, the Court declined to review the case. The vote was 8 to 0 with Justice William O. Douglas not participating.[17]

The next month the Playboy Foundation gave the ICLU Foundation $1,000, thus covering the cost of appeals to the Supreme Courts of Iowa and the United States. The gift was made without restrictions and had not been solicited. It was given in recognition of ICLU support for the view that nakedness need not be indecent.

A member of ICLU protested against accepting money from an "organization dedicated to the destruction of human dignity and integrity." But the Board voted not to reject the gift and adopted the following statement of policy:

> We accept the contribution as one of several contributions to civil liberties causes by Playboy Magazine, its publisher and its foundation. In so doing, we note that the Playboy Foundation didn't initiate publicity in connection with the gift and no conditions were attached. We do not feel it appropriate for a civil liberties association to conduct purges of its members or contributors who generally support our goals.
>
> The acceptance does not constitute an endorsement of all of the editorial or commercial policies of the donor, just as our support of a client's right to speak does not constitute an endorsement of the content of his speech.[18]

CHAPTER 10

Child Custody

HAROLD PAINTER of California, a photographer by profession, and his wife Jeanne had a son and a daughter. Jeanne and the daughter were killed in an automobile accident December 8, 1962. For a time Painter kept his five-year-old son Mark. The following summer he began to feel that he alone could not give the boy the care he should have; so he asked his wife's parents, Dwight and Margaret Bannister of Gilbert, Iowa, to care for Mark. There was no agreement that Mark should stay with them in Iowa permanently.

In November 1964 Harold Painter remarried. Both he and his bride Marylyn wished to have Mark return to them in California, but the Bannisters refused to let him leave. Painter accordingly filed suit in June 1965 to regain custody. The trial court held that it was the father's right to have Mark with him.

However, the Bannisters appealed to the Iowa Supreme Court, and that court prevented the return, pending their decision on the appeal. Then on February 8, 1966, the decision of the lower court was reversed and custody was awarded to Mark's maternal grandparents.

The opinion of the supreme court did not hold the father morally unfit but emphasized that Painter's life had been unstable, with frequent changes of jobs and occasional reckless use of money:

> Mr. Painter is either an agnostic or an atheist and has no concern for formal religious training. . . . He is a political liberal, and got into difficulty in a job at the University of Washington for his support of the activities of the American Civil Liberties Union in the University news bulletin.

The court recognized arguments on the other side: the presumption, by statute, of parental preference; Jeanne's will, which named her husband guardian of her children—her mother only if he failed to qualify or ceased to act; the fact that the Bannisters were over 60 years old.

In reaching its decision the court relied heavily on the testimony of Glen R. Hawkes, a colleague of Bannister on the faculty of Iowa State University and head of its department of child development. After extensive interviews and tests with Mark and the Bannisters, Hawkes concluded that it was in Mark's best interests to remain with his grandparents. In reaching this conclusion Hawkes did not investigate either the Painter home or Painter's character.[1]

On February 16, 1966, the Board of Iowa Civil Liberties Union, to whom Painter had appealed, issued the following statement:

> The Iowa Civil Liberties Union Board of Directors voted unanimously to ask its legal committee to prepare within ten days a memorandum and recommendation as to whether the ICLU should enter the Painter case by assisting Mr. Painter and his counsel in petitioning the Iowa Supreme Court for a rehearing.
> The ICLU Board expressed its concern on two points:
> (1) Language in the Court's opinion concerning Mr. Painter's political and religious affiliations, beliefs and activities may raise serious constitutional questions.
> (2) Taking a child from his natural parent without finding the parent unfit may be a deprivation of civil liberties without due process of law.[2]

The next step on the part of the ICLU was the decision to seek permission of the Iowa Supreme Court to file a brief amicus curiae for a rehearing of the case. Val L. Schoenthal was entrusted with this task.[3] It turned out, however, to be necessary to have recourse to the United States Supreme Court. In August ACLU decided to join ICLU in this appeal.[4]

For all proceedings Harold Painter engaged Donald R. Payer of Ames as attorney; J. Henry Covington and Edward Burling, Jr., of Washington, D.C., joined him for later proceedings.[5]

In February and March of 1966 the Des Moines Sunday Register printed a series of articles on the case. Much space was given to the irregularity of Harold Painter's employment and the way in which he handled his finances.

Of the arguments used by the Union and Payer in the futile appeal to the Iowa Supreme Court for a rehearing, two were kept in the petition to the United States Supreme Court for a writ of certiorari:

> 1. The decision infringes on the federal Constitutional rights of Appellee and his son to protection against destruction of their family by state action in the absence of any overriding necessity for such action.
> 2. The decision of the Court violates the federal Constitution because it rests on irrational, arbitrary grounds, without substantial support in the evidence, and infringes the Appellee's rights of freedom of belief and association.

Further, the Iowa Supreme Court was quoted as saying: "We believe security and stability in the home are more important than intellectual stimulation in the proper development of a child." To this the ACLU office commented: "Not this child, note; but any child."

Harold Painter's appeal to the US Supreme Court was supported not only by the Civil Liberties Union but also by the state of California and the Board of Christian Social Concerns of the New York Conference of the Methodist Church.[6] On November 15, however, the Supreme Court refused to review the case. On June 2, 1967, a decree was issued which gave Painter the right to a four-week visit from his son each summer.

While Mark was making this annual summer visit to his father in 1968, a California judge issued an order giving to Harold Painter of Brookdale temporary custody of his son Mark. Custody was made permanent on August 28, 1968.

Reasons advanced by the California attorney, Robert Treuhaft, included the statements that Mark was now more mature than at the time of the original decree and wanted to live with his father and that Dwight Bannister was in failing health (he was hospitalized at the time).

Donald Payer, Painter's attorney in Iowa, objected strongly to this procedure. Mark had gone to California pursuant to the agreement that the visit was to be for one month only; any action for custody change should have been in the District Court at Nevada, Iowa.[7]

To vindicate the superior force of the earlier Iowa decree over that of California, the only practical means would be to challenge Harold Painter if he should at any time return to Iowa.

Mrs. Bannister, in order to make sure what decision Mark really wanted to make, sent a common friend, the Reverend Clay Lumpkins, to San Francisco to visit her grandson. After talking with Mark for two hours, he reported that the boy definitely wanted to stay with his father, even though he felt strong love and affection for his grandmother.[8]

On June 20, 1969, the six children of Charles and Darlene Alsager were taken from their home in Des Moines by a juvenile court officer. Neighbors had complained of the conduct of the six and the disorderly condition of their home. For a time all the children were in the county juvenile home. Two of the six were later returned to their parents. After hearings in September 1969 and March 1970, Judge Don T. Tidrick of Polk County juvenile court found the parents "mentally retarded" and ordered the four other children reared by "persons who could afford them a greater degree of stimulation and discipline." Tidrick's ruling was upheld by the Iowa Supreme Court on October 18, 1972.

To ICLU it seemed clear that the juvenile court had acted on insufficient evidence and without due process of law. It decided, with the cooperation of ACLU, to bring action in the US District

Court on behalf of both the parents and their children. The Civil Liberties Union hoped to get the federal courts to establish principles that will apply to child custody cases throughout the nation. The court was asked to:

1. Rule on what the standards should be in situations where an attempt is made to take children away from their parents.
2. Establish that due process of law requirements should be observed in the juvenile court system.
3. Determine whether there is a conflict of interest in the juvenile court program of Iowa because of the role played by juvenile court officers who are court appointees.

Gordon Allen, staff attorney for ICLU, was asked by the ICLU Foundation to handle the case, with expert assistance from ACLU and testimony from specialists in other states.[9] The first result of this appeal was a hearing, on March 18, 1974, before US Judge William C. Hanson. Rena K. Uviller and Burt Nueborne, attorneys from ACLU in New York, declared:

> The involuntary removal of the children from their natural parents forever, solely because the state believes that some other adult or institution may provide a more adequate or stimulating environment, is the hallmark of a totalitarian society.
> The prospect of the state having absolute authority over the entire minor population, shifting it about at will according to bureaucratic notions of child welfare, is offensive to our way of life.

Appearing as expert witnesses were Dr. Robert Kugel, professor of pediatrics and dean of the University of Nebraska College of Medicine, and Dr. Kenneth Berry, assistant professor of medical psychology in the same college. They agreed that the Alsager parents had no such "mental retardation" as would have justified removal of their children, and that the state made no serious effort to prove either that condition or other grounds for separation from the children. Two of the sons, while living with foster parents, had become so attached to them that, according to the experts from Nebraska, it would be wiser to make the boys' placement in their present homes permanent—if that could be arranged.

These hearings—the first successful steps in the remedy of what seems to the Civil Liberties Union a great wrong—took place nearly five years after the disruption of the Alsager family. This lapse of time speaks to the slowness of the processes of law. Five years in the lives of children mean much more than the same period in adults' lives. Hence it would be desirable to have speedier handling by the courts of juveniles' cases. The state should take great care not to enter casually legal areas where decisions affecting families may take years to correct.[10]

Judge Hanson laid repeated stress on the fact that he was

called on to make a declaratory judgment. That would have been a declaration by the court delineating the legal rights and status of the conflicting parties. However, the court may under certain guidelines refuse to answer the questions asked of it. Judge Hanson made use of this privilege, emphasizing the passage of five years and the great volume of factual material which he assumed he would have to digest. He held that, for these reasons, a judgment would have been ineffectual and dismissed the lawsuit.

Notice of appeal to the 8th Circuit Court of Appeals in St. Louis was filed on December 29, 1974, by the ICLU; at the same time consideration was given to a state filing of a petition of habeas corpus. The appeal to the Circuit Court was successful; as a result Judge Hanson then considered the constitutional objections to the original disruption of the Alsager family. After a study of the case through the autumn of 1975, he found the state law on termination of parental rights too vague and thus open to several interpretations. The parents had no way of knowing what conduct was forbidden, what conduct would bring with it the risk of losing the company and custody of their children.

The decision of December 19, 1975, declared Subsections (b) and (d) of Chapter 232.41.2 of the Code unconstitutional, void, and of no effect—largely because of their vagueness. The wording of this part of the Code reads:

> The court may upon petition terminate the relationship between parent and child:
> 2 If the court finds that one or more of the following conditions exist:
> (b) That the parents have substantially and continuously or repeatedly refused to give the child necessary parental care and protection.
> (d) That the parents are unfit by reason of debauchery, intoxication, habitual use of narcotic drugs, repeated lewd and lascivious behavior, or other conduct found by the court likely to be detrimental to the physical or mental health or morals of the child.

The court also indicated that results of the juvenile court processes were unconstitutional in that they denied the Alsagers substantive and procedural due process. In <u>The Defender</u> for November-December 1975 Gordon Allen commented:

> We can consider this decision a landmark not only for the ICLU and the Alsagers but for constitutional law in particular. Family unity and integrity were declared to be a fundamental right, therefore necessitating the showing of a compelling interest by the state before termination could occur. A high threshold of harm must be shown before the state can so drastically intervene in family situations.

During the time of Judge Hanson's study of the case, most of the Alsager children visited their parents, coming from the foster or group homes where they had been placed. This was most difficult in the case of George, the oldest, since he was in the Iowa Security Medical Facility at Oakdale.

The Alsager parents had sought $50,000 damages, but this was denied them by the decision of Judge Hanson.

The state filed notice of appeal from the decision favorable to the Alsager family, for it was not satisfied to have these sections of the Code held unconstitutional. This appeal was tried in St. Louis in November 1976 and the sections were held to be unconstitutional.

The Alsager family was reunited June 3, 1976. During the months from June to October the state again sought to have the Alsager children placed in foster homes and succeeded in this attempt. After six months the situation is to be reviewed again.

The original case, in which the ICLU was involved, rested on constitutional grounds. The state's second attempt to separate the children from the custody of the parents seems to involve no violation of constitutional rights or of due process; hence the Union has not contested it.

The Alsager parents challenge both disruptions of their family on substantive grounds. Gordon Allen serves as their attorney, but in a private capacity with no implication of ICLU involvement.

CHAPTER 11

Miscellaneous Litigation

MANY sections of this history have dealt with litigation, generally under outstanding categories. The large and growing list of cases and types of cases ICLU handles calls for a section on miscellaneous litigation. It will of course contain only a small sample of the work the Union has done and keeps on doing in this area.

Suspicion of Sodomy

In 1938 Archie Carter was editor of the Dubuque Leader, a labor paper. He had the reputation of being an effective advocate of labor interests. He had led truckers through a strike to successful negotiations; he helped bring about the election of labor candidates to city council and school board;[1] he was also vigorous in a fight against corruption. He claimed, for instance, that the sheriff or county attorney in most Iowa counties either took money for the protection of slot machines or was in that business himself. He was about to publish accounts of corruption in Dubuque when he was arrested for sodomy.

Carter lived in a room at the city YMCA. Those who expected to charge that he was homosexual had bored a hole through the wall of his room and installed a dictaphone to record the words and sounds inside.

He was in the room with Donald Emerson; observers were on the other side of the wall. The state charged that sodomy took place. The defense said that Emerson had asked Carter to massage him—so as to get him into a position that could be misinterpreted—and that Emerson had been coached to simulate sounds of sodomy. It was also noted that the observers, who took turns as knothole spies, disagreed as to which of two beds was being used. Emerson's father was held to be in white-slave, marijuana, alcohol, and heroin concerns. Carter associated with the son in the hope of learning facts to help his efforts—in particular to discover the source of marijuana.[2]

Emerson, the partner in the alleged crime was not arrested. His mother, Cecilia Emerson, said later that she was convinced there had been no sodomy. On the day of Archie Carter's arrest, she said, her son had called on her where she was employed, exhibited a roll of bills, and stated that he was flush with money and was going to be taken care of financially.[3] Emerson left the state immediately for Milwaukee. It was reported that he received $50 while still in Dubuque and participating in the case, then $10 a week in Milwaukee.[4]

Concerning the trial which resulted in Carter's conviction, J. F. Wirds, the lawyer who appealed for a new trial, stated that the first jury vote in the original trial was 7 to 5 for conviction; of the five, two said they changed their vote for fear of being "framed."[5] John Connolly, a labor attorney, later characterized the original trial as "a mess." He offered to do all he could to secure a parole for Carter, the victim of a frame-up, whether or not he was guilty.[6]

After the trial and conviction, Archie Carter sought to interest the American Civil Liberties Union in his defense and engaged J. F. Wirds as counsel. Wirds was successful in locating Donald Emerson in Milwaukee. Emerson then made and signed a confession. In this he said the district attorney and police officials had planned the frame-up. When Emerson refused to sign a statement that would accuse Carter of a moral offense, he was threatened by police officials with prosecution for the same charge. The police also forced him to leave town by threat of arrest.[7]

A few days after this confession by Emerson, the attorney general of Iowa called the police in Milwaukee and was told that Donald Emerson had repudiated the statement he had voluntarily signed.

The support of labor unions and of the Civil Liberties Union was needed. Yet both, perhaps out of fear of association with one who might be guilty of a sin so generally condemned, were hesitant and reluctant to furnish the money needed for an effective appeal. For instance, the ACLU offered $100 for a bail bond when $250 was needed.[8]

Both in New York and Des Moines there was indecision as to whether this was a "civil liberties case" at all. At any rate, failure of the ACLU to give prompt and adequate support led Wirds to write to J. M. Britchey (ACLU):

> When we needed you very much when it would have saved Archie Carter, you were all scratching your head and thinking things over for fear you might get your fingers smeared up. . . . There is nothing that you people can do at this stage of the game excepting to aggrandize your own organization through interference in the Carter case.[9]

Out of admiration for Wirds the ICLU had appointed him to its advisory committee. He, however, became so disappointed with the organization that he asked to have his name removed from the letterhead.[10]

Miscellaneous Litigation 81

It should be noted that Wirds was wrong in saying that the Civil Liberties Union could have "saved" Carter; there was no appeal to either ACLU or ICLU until Carter had been convicted and help was asked for an appeal.

Carter, having been sentenced to ten years' imprisonment, was released after five. He then wrote: "I wish to thank you for the efforts of the C.L.U. which at least resulted in my receiving enough good time back to bring about my release, which occurred yesterday."[11] Although he did not specify any particular individual, he might well have given special thanks to Carl Bogenrief; as secretary of ICLU in 1938, he worked hard and without hesitation for Archie Carter.

Protesting Pacifist

Walter Gormly of Mount Vernon is so devoted a pacifist that he uses unusual means to express his disapproval of war and of all support of it. Thus in 1962 he made a protest sit-in at the Federal Building in Des Moines. He was then indicted for unwarranted loitering, sleeping, and assembly. The next step on the part of the government was to send him to Springfield, Missouri, for psychiatric examination; there he was found mentally competent.

In the jury trial that ensued Gormly was defended by Sidney Levine at the request of ICLU (whose president he became that year). Levine argued that the indictment be dismissed since the action violated due process and the guarantee of freedom of petition and was not based on regulations too vague to be valid. He did not secure acquittal, but the sentence imposed was that of only one day of imprisonment.[12]

Swift and Careless "Justice"

The case of Dennis Ashby occupied the attention of ICLU for some two years. On October 7, 1965, this 17-year-old boy, with three older companions, held up a filling station in Ringgold County. Later the same night they were captured in nearby Missouri and returned to Iowa. Dennis then gave his age as 19 and did not correct this misstatement until two weeks later, when he was already in the reformatory at Anamosa.

The case was prosecuted by Justice of the Peace Edna Thompson and Judge H. J. Kittleman in succession, so speedily that Ashby entered the reformatory two days after the holdup. The attorney assigned for defense did a perfunctory job; in fact, the defendants neither requested counsel nor objected to the rapidity of the trial without a jury. Ashby pleaded guilty and received a 25-year sentence.

On March 16, 1966, Norman Jesse, Robert E. Mannheimer, and Thomas George attacked the conviction and sentence in a petition for a writ of certiorari in the Iowa Supreme Court. They held that Thompson and Kittleman had acted illegally in that they had failed to ascertain the true age of Dennis Ashby and to proceed accordingly; that he had been denied the effective assistance of counsel and a trial by jury.[13]

At the September meeting of the ICLU Board Thomas George was able to report that already, as a result of this case, new rules of procedure were being adopted by southern Iowa District Courts.

The Iowa Supreme Court decided against Ashby's appeal on July 11, 1967, with Justice Becker dissenting.[14] But ICLU and the cooperating attorneys were unwilling to take this answer as final and appealed to the United States Supreme Court. That Court, however, denied a rehearing.[15]

Dennis Ashby, who had been released from the reformatory during the appeal, was then sent back to Anamosa. After a couple of years he was paroled; since then he has been employed and has been active in the Model Cities program in Des Moines. He is married, has a child, and has given no cause for complaint as to his way of life. At this writing he conducts an amusement center for young people—one at which no alcoholic drinks are sold. Gilbert Cranberg has given him continuing, sympathetic support and deserves gratitude for it.

Clerk's Transcript

In February 1966 ICLU announced a challenge to the constitutionality of the Iowa system of "clerk's transcript" appeals. The clerk's transcript contains copies of pleadings, instructions, etc. but no transcript of the evidence. Criminal appeals, under the system challenged, were decided by the Iowa Supreme Court on the basis of the clerk's transcript when no action was taken to file briefs and arguments after notice of appeal was given.

Louise Noun, president of ICLU, stated, "We are concerned about appeals being decided without the benefit of arguments by attorneys before the Supreme Court, especially when this results because of ignorance of how to obtain full-dress review or inability to pay a lawyer to prosecute a full-dress appeal."

At that time Craig T. Sawyer, cooperating ICLU attorney and assistant professor of law in Drake University, represented Orrington Spencer Gardner and Price Clay in habeas corpus actions. They were then serving sentences respectively for robbery with aggravation and for second-degree murder.[16]

Soon after this ICLU became interested in the case of Harvey Entsminger, then serving a ten-year sentence on a forged check charge. The attorney appointed to perfect his appeal did no more than submit a clerk's transcript. Entsminger's own petition for certiorari was denied by the Iowa Supreme Court in October 1965. He then appealed to the United States Supreme Court; Craig Sawyer and Val Schoenthal, on behalf of ICLU, filed a brief as friends of the court.[17]

On June 20, 1966, the petition for writ of certiorari was

granted. On October 10 the petition for the appointment of counsel was granted, and David W. Belin was named.[18] (Belin was an attorney who served on the staff of the Warren Commission to investigate President Kennedy's assassination and became executive director of the commission headed by Nelson Rockefeller which studied CIA and FBI activities.) On May 8, 1967, the Supreme Court of the United States decided that Entsminger's counsel must perfect a plenary appeal—the clerk's transcript was insufficient. However, after the appeal was presented to the Iowa Supreme Court, it affirmed the original conviction. For the prisoner the appeal process, which he had begun on November 27, 1964, gave no relief. But the principle had been firmly established that a lawyer assigned as counsel for one appealing a conviction must work conscientiously on his behalf.

In 1968 the Iowa Supreme Court limited the number of appeals to result from this ruling; it held that the requirement of more than a clerk's transcript need not apply to an appeal made in 1965, before the pronouncement of the United States Supreme Court.[19]

Lèse Majesté

In the spring of 1966 some boys were behaving roughly on the lawn of Judge George M. Paradise in Sioux City. When he ordered them to disperse, telling them that he was a judge, they refused and attacked him. Thereupon he found them guilty of contempt of court, sentencing them to six months' imprisonment, exacting a fine of $500 from each. The ICLU protested; the protest contained the following:

> Although we feel that the legal basis for the use of contempt of court under such circumstances is questionable at best, the summary procedure used by the Court raises more basic questions of fundamental fairness in the use of the contempt power of courts instead of the usual criminal law. If the historical procedures of due process of law, such as formal charge and trial by jury before an impartial and disinterested court, can be denied those whose criminal conduct happens to be directed toward a judge but does not impair the integrity of the court, statutes can be enacted denying the same procedures in cases involving other groups as victims.

Dan Johnston, acting as attorney for the boys without fee, first applied for a writ of habeas corpus; Judge Donald Pendleton in Woodbury District Court refused to issue it. Johnston then appealed to the Iowa Supreme Court. That court provided for release of the boys while it reviewed the case.

When the Supreme Court made its decision, it did not reverse the judgment of Judge Paradise but did reduce the sentences of the boys from six months to sixty days. The ICLU paid the costs of the case.[20]

Segregation of Migrants

In the autumn of 1969 a nursery in Hampton, which provided housing for its migrant workers, denied access to these workers' camps. The employers' claim was that the houses were their private property and that they could control the people coming on it. They seem especially to have objected to visits from social workers, who could observe conditions and hear complaints. On behalf of ICLU Melvin H. Wolf of Waterloo filed suit in the Federal Court in and for the Northern District of Iowa. The suit alleged that the property took on the nature of public property when it became people's homes and the proprietor of the farm who employed the migrant workers could not exercise absolute dominion over it. Wolf wrote:

> The case never came to trial as the new director of the Migrant Action Program in the Mason City area made arrangements with the nurseries that his personnel and other personnel in the community could have access to the camp and asked that we drop the lawsuit. I think the lawsuit had the effect of opening this particular camp, but there is no court decree or any decision in Iowa covering this rather important problem.[21]

Priority Projects

Occasionally the ICLU Board has approved a list of types of litigation that should have priority without, of course, barring the possibility of other litigation. Thus in September 1973 six "priority projects" were voted:

> (1) Challenging Iowa's statutory requirements on naming members of examining and licensing. (In many cases the Governor was required to appoint those nominated by certain professional organizations, thus excluding public representation.)
> (2) Testing constitutional requirements that banned registration and voting by persons committed to public (but not private) institutions for the mentally ill.
> (3) Challenging the Iowa law which required corroboration for the crime of rape committed against a woman (but not that against a man).
> (4) Establishing the right of persons confined for mental treatment in either a public or private institution to call a lawyer and communicate with other persons.
> (5) Establishing the rights of individuals in cases involving dissolution of marriage to have a court-appointed attorney if they are indigent.
> (6) Seeking monetary damages in at least one case a year for violation of Iowa's civil rights laws.

By March 1975 new legislation had rendered (1) and (3) moot;

(6) called for no new legislation—only enforcement of existing law and a better supported and more active Civil Rights Commission. Type (4) was being tested in the courts. It, as well as (2) and (5), were the subjects of bills already in the General Assembly.

So it is clear that basic aims of the Civil Liberties Union had become accepted by a substantial part of the people of Iowa.

Management of War Memorials

The ICLU is concerned with the delegation to named private organizations of preferred rights in public business. Iowa law decrees that the management of war memorials, aided in construction or maintenance by public funds, must lie with representatives of eight particular societies—from the Grand Army of the Republic to the American Veterans of World War II. For instance, the Des Moines Veterans Memorial Auditorium is a public building, and tax money is used to pay operating losses as well as principal and interest on bonds. The bias of the governing commission has been demonstrated twice: in 1959 when Jehovah's Witnesses were not allowed to rent the hall, and again a decade later when the promoter of a telecast of a fight between Mohammed Ali and Jimmy Ellis could not secure its use. In both cases enmity to those who refuse military service was the reason for rejection. (The decision against the showing of the fight was reversed, but too late for the reversal to be effective.)

In 1972, supporting the challenge to this monopolistic management by a spokesman for the Vietnam Veterans against the War, Polk County District Judge Leo Oxberger upheld the ICLU contention that the law was unconstitutional. The Iowa Supreme Court reversed the Oxberger decision for the technical reason that the veteran who sued was not a resident of Des Moines, hence not liable to taxation in support of the auditorium (he lived in West Des Moines).[22]

In 1974 ICLU again challenged the method for naming the board. This time four persons, all living in Des Moines, claimed they were denied equal treatment under the law which the Constitution guarantees. One plaintiff, Mark Bennett, was not a veteran and so can raise the question of whether the public at large can and should have a voice. Another was a woman, Ione Shadduck, who had served with the US Army in Korea. Her grievances came from the exclusion of women veterans from all organizations privileged by the law. The other two, Jay Schweitzer and Alfred Semple, had been in the armed forces in Vietnam but had not joined any of the named groups.[23]

CHAPTER 12

Religion and the State

JEHOVAH'S WITNESSES appear often in civil liberties news. They are a sect noteworthy for their devotion and courage but also marked by the hostility they arouse in others. For them there must be no obeisance before the civil government if that conflicts with their tenets. Thus they will not salute the flag. Neither will they join the armed forces. They could have been classified as conscientious objectors to all wars, thus winning exemption from forced service, but for one thing: they do look forward to the Battle of Armageddon, in which they are to fight and to emerge victorious.

The Witnesses claim freedom from conscription on the basis of their religious ministry, for each of them is held to be a minister. It is not surprising, then, that they are sometimes denigrated by those for whom reverence for the flag and willingness to fight for that flag and its nation are essential parts of patriotism.

A frequent method of Witnesses' propaganda has been the use of phonograph records, which they beg to be allowed to play for whoever answers the doorbell. The message is likely to speak harshly of Roman Catholics.

The Civil Liberties Union has been called upon to defend the rights of Jehovah's Witnesses fairly often, but less often than would be the case if their own office did not have excellent legal counsel.

In Germany during the Hitler era, Jehovah's Witnesses were among Hitler's most courageous opponents. The Brockhaus Encyclopedia gives 2000 as the approximate number of his victims among this sect.

In Iowa we have records of many cases of ill treatment of the Witnesses, at least as early as 1940. In June of that year Reginald Bourne got permission to use the school grounds in Carson for a meeting. A crowd gathered, trying to have the permission revoked. The Pottawattamie County sheriff, then 38 miles away, was appealed to by telephone; he merely advised that Bourne's party (including a baby 20 days old) leave. The ICLU protested the negligence of the two deputy sheriffs who had been on the spot, pointing out that mob action should be punished, not condoned.[1]

Jehovah's Witnesses had planned a convention in Columbus, Ohio, in July 1940, but the governor and the Ohio State Fair Association canceled the contract for use of the grounds. Members of the sect in Iowa circulated petitions for the cancellation to be reversed. Cynthia Lucas, one of the members, reported to ACLU that the sheriff of O'Brien County had jerked such a petition out of her hands and torn it up, saying: "You are petitioning against war."[2]

Other Iowa towns where Witnesses were harassed that summer include Toledo, Belle Plaine (where a man was threatened with loss of relief if he attended Jehovah's Witnesses meetings),[3] Grundy Center, Clear Lake, Coon Rapids, Mount Pleasant, and Grand Mound. By December, however, Willard Johnson was able to report to the ICLU Board of Directors that sheriffs were then protecting Jehovah's Witnesses, perhaps partly through ICLU's influence.

But strong optimism was not yet justified. During a 1941 meeting at Laurens the demand was made that the American flag be saluted. About the same time a member of the American Legion bought a copy of the Watch Tower, which Jehovah's Witnesses publish, for three cents; he then had the seller arrested because of a local ordinance on peddling, and fined $25.00.[4]

At Bellevue George Sullivan was distributing booklets of the sect. When distributors told of their rights according to the Supreme Court, the mayor said: "To Hell with you and Jehovah. The Supreme Court decision has nothing to do with Bellevue—we are running Bellevue, not Jehovah. Who the Hell is Jehovah? He doesn't mean anything to us, anyway. I am the one who says what can be done or can be given away here." The Witnesses, refusing to pay a fine, were imprisoned for four hours and then warned not to return to the town.[5] (Bellevue had an ordinance forbidding anyone to ring a doorbell or knock at a door without a previous invitation or request.)

In that same year, 1941, the Iowa Supreme Court reversed the conviction in Clinton of four Witnesses for selling pamphlets on Sunday.[6]

In 1943 members of the sect complained of discharge from employment because of their religion and of inability to secure union cards.

Up to this time ICLU as a body had taken just one step for the protection of the Witnesses—a memorandum to county sheriffs reminding them of First Amendment rights. In a number of cases, however, members of the Union served as legal counsel to aggrieved individuals.

The Union became directly involved in a Jehovah's Witness case in 1946. Charles E. Sellers, a member of that group, had asked for the right to use the park of Lacona for meetings on September 1, 8, 15, and 22 (all Sundays). Two members of the town council consented; the mayor also upheld their right to hold meetings. The first gathering was marked by some harassment, and on the following day the council restricted the use of the park to meetings approved in advance by that body. However, Jehovah's Witnesses were not informed of this action. The next Sunday when they came back, they found the bandstand occupied and benches overturned. They were attacked and suffered bloody faces, black eyes, and broken teeth and eyeglasses. They had no protection during the fight, but the sheriff did protect them as they left—without a meeting.

On September 14 Sellers wrote to the mayor and the sheriff, complaining of violation of civil rights and lack of protection. That same day, however, the town council authorized special marshals to maintain "peace and order"; the sheriff, having conferred with two deputies of the attorney general, advised that no meeting of any kind should be permitted on the 15th and that a blockade be set up around Lacona. Roadblocks were then established on Sunday by the sheriff, 100 deputies, and some highway patrolmen; only residents and physicians were allowed to pass.

Shortly before the 29th Sellers asked the mayor and council to allow a meeting on that day, and also brought action against them, the town marshal, and the town to secure the civil rights of the Witnesses. Federal District Judge Charles A. Dewey of Des Moines, although admitting that the town had violated constitutional rights, still held, among other findings, that the sheriff had acted properly on September 15 to prevent riot and bloodshed. The plaintiffs' petition was dismissed.

The Iowa Civil Liberties Union insisted, and the Federal Circuit Court at St. Louis later agreed, that the plaintiffs were in the right. Briefly, that court found: (1) that Jehovah's Witnesses have the right to hold religious meetings in the public park of Lacona; (2) that the resolutions of the town council requiring a permit are unconstitutional; (3) that Jehovah's Witnesses are entitled to protection in the exercise of their constitutional rights. The United States Supreme Court, by refusing to review this decision, brought the case to a satisfying conclusion.[7]

In 1959 there was some denial of this group's rights of assembly but better defense of those rights. In Marshalltown the Memorial Coliseum Commission let them use the coliseum, in spite of protests from the American Legion and others.[8] Although the Veterans' Memorial Auditorium in Des Moines was barred to those who refused to bear arms, the fairgrounds did welcome the Witnesses. In this case the mayor and the state legislature succeeded in reversing the first decision of inhospitality.[9]

Jehovah's Witnesses are not the only sect to suffer from intolerance in Iowa. As early as 1922 ACLU took note of an attack on Holy Rollers in Cedar Rapids. In January of that year a crowd stoned a gathering of this group, seized their leader (Rev. H. A. Ferguson), and threatened to throw him in the Cedar River. The police rescued him.

Another sect to which ICLU has given close attention is that of the Amish—particularly the most insistently conservative segment, the Old Order Amish. Their religion calls on them to avoid such changes in their way of life as telephones, automobiles, and clothing deviating from their traditional garb. They are industrious farmers, with crime almost unknown in their community. The chief settlements in Iowa are near Hazleton (Buchanan County), near Kalona (Washington County), and more recently in the neighborhoods of Milton (Van Buren County), Bloomfield (Davis County), Leon (Decatur County), and Riceville (Mitchell County). The rate of increase in the number of settlements (recently about one every four years) has as causes the large size of families and the desire to restrict the number of families in one group. Some of the young leave, either to join other Mennonite settlements or to enter the outside world; but this attrition is too small to stop the total growth of the Old Order Amish in Iowa.

Two small schools near Hazleton have been sites of an acute dispute with the public educational system. The Amish hold that schooling beyond the eighth grade is not only superfluous for their manner of living but likely to be harmful. They have their own one-room schools, taught by their own members or others in sympathy with them; thus the boys and girls are kept free of the unsettling ways of town life.

The language of Amish home and religious life is German; children have two hours of instruction in that language each week.

When the law required that all schools (including private ones) have "certified" teachers rather than "competent" ones, a consequence was the demand that schools with no certified teacher close. Such an order, issued in November 1962, had serious effects for the two schools near Hazleton. Because their children did not learn from a certified teacher, eight Amish men were convicted; they preferred to go to jail rather than to pay fines.[10]

In later prosecutions, however, the option of time in prison was not offered. Further, since each day that a child was not in an approved school constituted a separate offense, the fines accumulated fast, threatening the farmers with loss of their property. At least twice anonymous donors put off such a result.[11] Pressures of this sort induced a number of families to migrate to Canada or Wisconsin. Nevertheless, the number of pupils in the two schools grew from 37 in 1962 to 55 in 1967.[12]

In 1965 Attorney General Lawrence Scalise, who sympathized with the Amish, offered three methods by which their wishes could be fulfilled within the law: Amish teachers might be certified by passing tests; private money could be sought to enable a certified teacher to be engaged; a separate, private room could be provided in a public school. The school committee of the Old Order Amish rejected all three.[13] A fourth proposal made by Scalise was that these private schools be made part of the public school system, which would provide teachers and transportation. The school board of Oelwein, whose district included the two Amish schools, turned down this proposal.[14]

During that year ICLU studied the Amish situation carefully. In October it declared:

> The Supreme Court has consistently held that the right

to practice one's religion can be restricted by a reasonable exercise of a government's police power. . . . The representatives of the government of Iowa are acting in accordance with guidelines spelled out by the Supreme Court. . . . The ICLU while strongly supporting the rights of the Amish and all others to their religious beliefs also strongly supports the Supreme Court in its difficult task of preserving a system of balanced rights in a complex, pluralistic society.

The Church-State Committee of ACLU subsequently considered the case but could not agree on a position. By a 7 to 6 vote the National Board of ACLU disagreed with the premise of the ICLU position and on May 23, 1966, urged support for abolition of the certified-teacher requirement in favor of a program of testing to determine academic achievement. The ICLU Board did not agree, believing this should not be done until the General Assembly (not then in session) could act and that this would be only a temporary solution if, under uncertified teachers, the Amish youngsters did not pass the tests.[15]

Influential in reaching an agreement, at least for a time, were the sympathetic concern of Governor Harold Hughes and the offer of $15,000 by the Danforth Foundation to hire certified teachers. The agreement provided:

1. The schools would be rented to the public school system.
2. There would be two certified teachers.
3. No public funds would be required.
4. The state standards on attendance would be met.
5. The curriculum would be adjusted to the views of the Amish parents, within the law.
6. The Board of the school district would select the teachers, attempting to satisfy the Amish.
7. The schools would meet housing standards.
8. This was to be dependent on legislative action.
9. The governor would propose suitable legislation.
10. Both sides—Amish parents and public school authorities—would try to make the system work.[16]

In the conference which constituted the annual meeting of ICLU for 1966, schools for the Amish furnished one of the main topics. W. W. Sendlinger, lawyer for the Amish, criticized ICLU for failing to see the issue of freedom of religion. In reply Val Schoenthal of the ICLU Board again distinguished between freedom of belief and freedom of practice.

Even under this agreement there was a minor difference. The Amish parents wanted the school year to end on May 11—when the children would have had the 180 days required by the state law. The Oelwein School Board objected because during some of that time there had been no certified teacher; the schools continued until May 27.[17]

Looking toward a more permanent arrangement, Governor Hughes recommended a grant of $50,000 a year. Rather than name these particular schools, the plan would insist that schools to benefit from it should be rural, with a previous record of operation without certified instructors. Soon after proposing this, the governor named a group of men to study the problem. Among them were Methodist Bishop James Thomas, Episcopal Bishop Gordon Smith, Howard Bowen, president of the State University of Iowa, and I. J. Lubbers, president of the Iowa Association of Private Colleges.[18]

The advice of this group, which followed the recommendations of ACLU and had the approval of Governor Hughes, resulted in a law that would exempt such schools as those of the Amish from certification laws. It was to apply to any group that had been established for ten years and "professes principles or tenets that differ substantially in objectives, goals and philosophy of education in Iowa." However, the State Board of Public Instruction was given the right to order the testing of students in such exempt schools and promptly stated the intention to do so. The first permit ran for two years; after that, each ran for one year at a time.

The renewal was made regularly until 1971. Then it was noted that the record of the pupils in the Amish schools was definitely lower than the average in the state. One other fact was disclosed: only two or three schools had originally asked to have uncertified teachers; however, when they had been granted exemption, other Amish schools asked for and received the same privilege—even though they had, without complaint, used certified teachers until then. As a result, some 250 children were involved, compared with the original 37.

In July 1971 the Board of Public Instruction voted (5 to 4) to require that all pupils be taught by certified teachers.

Through all this time there was general sympathy with the Amish and a respect for freedom of religion. Yet for many (and for a majority of the Board of ICLU in 1965) the right of the boys and girls to have such education as would fit them for life outside their home communities was also important. For not all the young people were destined to remain farmers in Amish communities; the size of their families made that quite improbable.

The decision of the Board of Public Instruction to put an end to exemption was at once challenged, and not only by the Amish community. At the time there was before the United States Supreme Court a very similar case in Wisconsin, and its decision would affect what would be permissible and desirable in Iowa. Furthermore, the vote was taken so near to the reopening of schools at the end of summer that both the small Amish schools and the public schools in the same districts would have found it hard to plan for the changed situation.

Accordingly, Governor Robert Ray expressed the hope that the Board would reverse its decision and allow the schools to go on for a year longer. Likewise, the Board of ICLU urged the Board of Public Instruction to extend the exemptions and sent a resolution of similar import to ACLU.[19] Since then the exemption of Amish schools has been renewed a year at a time. At the end of 1975 there were 17 such schools, and they have joined in a concerted effort to improve the education offered their young people.

An interesting and informative account of Iowa's Old Order Amish has recently been published.[20]

Throughout its history ICLU has been concerned about keeping church and state independent. Before this affiliate of ACLU was founded the parent organization gave support to a bill in the 1933 General Assembly which furthered that independence: it forbade any inquiry into the religion of an applicant for public employment. It became law that year but was put into effect very slowly. In 1959 Richard Stephenson, a staunch member of ICLU, reported to the Board that state government employment forms still contained questions on church membership.[21] Now, however, there is no such question on these forms.

As in many states, churches in Iowa hoped that the public school system would help their pupils get that religious teaching which the school personnel did not, could not, or should not give them. A method often favored is to free boys and girls from the regular school program for a specified period, that they may be taught by a religious leader. Donald Boles distinguishes between "released time" (for instruction in the public school building) and "dismissed time" (for instruction given elsewhere).[22] Many others say "released time" in both cases.

The United States Supreme Court in the McCollum case (1948) held released time unconstitutional, thus reversing the Supreme Court of Illinois, which had sanctioned it. The ACLU filed a brief against released time. In the Zorach case (1952), however, the Supreme Court refused to condemn dismissed time.

In 1953 Attorney General Leo Hoegh was asked whether Iowa might permit dismissed time. There seemed to be no state law covering the question—except that the truancy law (Iowa Code 299.2) stated that absence from public school should not be named truancy if it were for the sake of attendance at a religious service or for receipt of religious instruction.

Here and there in the state, religious periods in public schools continued, causing occasional objections. For instance, in 1957 there came a complaint that a chapel service was regularly held in the schools of Milton, with a Methodist minister taking part.[23]

When ICLU drew the attention of Iowa members of Congress to the use of prayers in schools, Senators Hickenlooper and Miller expressed approval of the practice; Representative Neal Smith was noncommittal.[24]

The files of ACLU have three letters from George F. Serson, a Baptist minister at Confidence, to Charles Frizzell, superintendent of the Cambria-Corydon School District, complaining of Roman Catholic bias in the schools. Grievances named were: the song "Dominique" was sung, his daughter was required to wear green on St. Patrick's Day, and no meat was served on Fridays.[25]

The question of religious education in the public schools recurred so often that the Board of ICLU favored sending a questionnaire over the state to discover what the actual practice was. Donald Boles and William Robinson were asked to formulate such a document. They were aided in this by the example of Ohio, which had already taken similar action.

The questions were sent to all school superintendents in Iowa. The covering letter said nothing of such laws as might be applicable. It asked that the respondents not sign the responses but indicate only the size of the school on which they reported.

There were 33 questions. The main groups referred to prayers in school, Bible reading, hymn singing, invocations on various occasions, religious festivals, religious instruction during school hours. Answers came from 72 percent of the 453 superintendents. A greater fraction of the larger schools replied than of the smaller ones.

To the question whether organized prayers of any kind were said during school hours 15 percent replied affirmatively. This, however, gives a rather false picture, inasmuch as most of the 15 percent said their prayers were uttered in "a few classes." Ten percent reported Bible reading during school hours. In a majority of cases this reading was part of the general study of literature.

In nearly 30 percent of the schools hymns were sung during school hours; in a large fraction of these cases this was a part of vocal training. Where it did not have this purpose, pupils were generally not required to participate.

As to invocations, ranging from grace at lunchtime to commencements and building dedications, about 17 percent reported them during the ordinary school program, but a majority reported they were said on special occasions.

Seventy-nine percent of the schools observed religious festivals. This is probably an underestimate, since some superintendents did not regard Christmas as such.

Approximately 12.5 percent had "released-time" religious programs: 4.9 percent reported programs in the building, 12.2 outside. It seems that some schools had both types (released and dismissed), perhaps in different grades. Of those with a program outside, the most common arrangement was for the pupils involved to go together to a church building for the last hour of a school day; other pupils stayed in the school. "Sectarian" instruction occurred in 1.8 percent of the schools.

A welcome comment came from one superintendent:

> We believe in freedom of religion. We feel no obligation to quote or read prescribed prayers. We feel we are privileged to pray if we wish, read the Bible if we wish, discuss religion if we wish, the same as any other subject. We don't offer it as a course. I'm proud we can have religious freedom and that we are not told and required to accept documented worship of any kind.

Although it was clear that a minority of schools further religion (or a certain kind of religion) in ways declared unconstitutional, ICLU has not followed up this questionnaire with a sustained effort at universal separation of church and state in the public schools.

Aside from the pressure of many other problems, some justification for a low level of action may be found in the address given by Professor Robert J. Levy of the University of Minnesota Law School at the 1960 biennial conference of ACLU. The title was "Views from the Wall—Reflections on Church-State Relationships." We quote a few sentences.

> Clear thinkers who take any position along the Church-State spectrum must recognize the need for cooperative effort to find a middle ground. The American Civil Liberties Union must be a buffer between extremists on both sides of the "Wall." . . . The Union, and its individual members, should be careful not to foment or support disputes about trivia. . . . But often dispute is inevitable. Then, if the plaintiff's injury and the issues are worth the struggle, the case should command all available resources. An individual willing to battle his community needs aid and sympathy. . . . In conclusion I can only hope that I have not added to making love and praying another activity which should be indulged only in private—making speeches on Church and State.

Since 1964 a new arrangement has become more common. This is "shared time"; pupils subject to it spend some hours in public school, other hours in parochial school—the latter not only for religious teaching, as would be the case in "dismissed time." The public schools involved are subsidized by the state on the basis of the number of pupil-hours in these schools. This arrangement of shared time has come to be widely used, chiefly with schools directed by the Roman Catholic and Dutch Reformed churches; it has not been challenged by either the courts or ICLU.

Until 1974 pupils attending these schools might travel in public school buses between their homes and the public schools but not between the private school and either homes or public schools. In 1974 the General Assembly passed a law "to provide auxiliary services, including transportation, for nonpublic school children and to provide appropriations." This law (predictably opposed by ICLU) requires that each school district provide transportation on the same basis for pupils in public and nonpublic schools, with the state paying a substantial part of the costs. This provision went into effect in the summer of 1975. It allowed a bus for private students to cross the boundaries of public school districts at state expense, but a bus for public school students had to stay in one district. (The justification may well have been that the parochial schools, being fewer, were farther apart.) The practice was challenged by ICLU and Americans United for Separation of Church and State and in December 1975 was found to be unconstitutional by Circuit Judge Roy L. Stephenson and District Judges William C. Hanson and William C. Stuart. Their finding of violation of the Constitution rested on the fact that "non-public school children are being afforded benefits that are not available to public school students." In 1976 the General Assembly remedied this inequity by giving the public school buses the same privilege. The ICLU continues to oppose all use of public funds for transportation of parochial school children.

Provision of the other "auxiliary services" to pupils in private schools is, in contrast to transportation, optional with the school district (or system). Such services "may include health services, special education services, services and materials for remedial education programs and library and resource centers, audio-visual services and materials, guidance services, scientific instruments, school testing services, and other services and materials."

Two books by Donald E. Boles, professor of political science at Iowa State University, give further information on relations between state and church.[26]

CHAPTER 13

The Disadvantaged

THROUGHOUT its history a major concern of the Iowa Civil Liberties Union has been the rights of the disadvantaged—whether that disadvantage be physical, racial, political, economic, or discrimination because of sex.

The Mentally Ill

In 1938 a state committee was formed to study the treatment of the mentally ill in Iowa, and ICLU was invited to cooperate. The Union offered to do so, but only in the protection of sane persons from treatment as if they were not sane.[1] The ACLU at that time was willing to act only if the commitment of a sane person was clearly caused by his political or economic views or activities.[2]

In Chapter 11 we reported on an incident involving Walter S. Gormly. Because of his sit-in on behalf of peace in 1962, he was sent to Springfield, Missouri, for psychiatric examination. Since this was a case in which an unorthodox view, expressed in an unusual manner, was taken to imply a mental disorder, ICLU intervened on Gormly's behalf.

Beginning with that year ICLU has often considered the treatment of the mentally ill, the institutions in which they are placed, and the attitude of society toward them when they are released. Richard Stephenson has been an important advocate of this interest, a source of information, a willing investigator. Having been a patient in a state hospital, he first drew attention to the difficulty those in his position have in securing employment.

The Union, looking into many aspects of the treatment of those who are (or are held to be) mentally ill, found a number of improvements urgent. County homes received many such patients when the hospitals were full but had no means of treating them. If a man in one of the state hospitals for the mentally disturbed became unruly, he could be transferred to the state reformatory at Anamosa. There all in the ward for "criminally insane" were treated alike—no better than those convicted of crimes: those who had been convicted and had later become ill, those who had been charged with crimes but because of their mental condition had had no trial, and those who had been accused of no crime but had become a burden in the hospitals. For those thus confined at Anamosa (125 in 1962) the available staff consisted of one full-time psychiatric nurse, one physician present a half-day a week, and one social worker in the summer only.[3]

The ICLU saw as its first task the release from the reformatory of some who had not even been charged with a crime—had not even had a judicial hearing. Without resources to intercede for all in this category, the Union took up the case of Ronald Long. Norman Jesse argued that his treatment violated the Constitution and secured from Judge Maxwell of Anamosa his return to a mental hospital.

The success of the Civil Liberties Union in this case contributed markedly to the willingness of the legislature to vote $2.6 million for a maximum security hospital for the mentally ill; this they did in 1965.[4] A more immediate effect of the Union's activity on behalf of Long and of the principle that only convicted criminals should be treated as criminals was the early improvement of treatment for all those confined at Anamosa merely because of mental disease.

The ICLU shared with the Iowa Mental Health Authority the cost of a comprehensive study of civil commitment, both for mental disease and for alcoholism. The excellent and thorough report was written by James Polson and Randall Bezanson, two senior students of law at the University of Iowa.[5] The conclusion of this study begins:

> The participants in the Iowa involuntary hospitalization process are ordinarily conscientious, fair and sympathetic. They are generally confident that the performance of their duties results in just and beneficial treatment of the patient. Any trepidation which they express focuses around their intense concern that patients not be railroaded into mental institutions.

The article points out shortcomings in the existing law as well as the frequency of deviation from the statutory standard for involuntary hospitalization—sometimes in the interest of the patient, but very often to his disadvantage.

Following the publication of this study, Louise Noun, president of ICLU, appointed a committee of nine to recommend whether the Union should take action—action which might mean challenging the civil commitment law and practices in court and work for legislative revision of the law. The committee was also requested to make recommendations as to problems of commitment and treatment of alcoholics and drug addicts. Mary Dresser of Mason City was named chairman of the committee; the authors of the report, Polson and Bezanson, were also included in its membership.[6]

In 1972 the ICLU Board, while considering various questions

of suffrage rights, noted the constitutional ban on voting by an "insane" person. This provision, in the view of the Union, is so vague and broad (there being many definitions of "insane") that it is unreasonable and in violation of the Fourteenth Amendment of the United States Constitution.[7]

The drafting of a thoroughly revised civil commitment statute was ultimately taken up by professors of the College of Law in the University of Iowa—at first Robert Bartels and later Randall Bezanson—with the aid of students.

In the State Senate, John S. Murray of Ames was especially active. Bartels met with the Joint Committee on Mental Health and Juvenile Institutions, within which Murray was chairman of a subcommittee; they worked with representatives of the Iowa Bar Association and the Iowa Medical Society. In March 1974 the Senate Human Resources Committee held a public hearing on the proposed draft and received testimony from ten speakers—including persons from the Clerks of District Courts Association, a mental health institute, and the Polk County Legal Aid Society. Spokesman for the last society was its director, Robert C. Oberbillig; he also represented ICLU, on whose Board of Directors he had worked for years on legislative concerns.

In 1976 the General Assembly passed a comprehensive law on the hospitalization of the mentally ill. Senator Murray was chairman of the Senate committee and influential in drafting the bill. Major new features include the following:

1. A person, to be committed, must receive notice in advance of the hearing.
2. There is a new definition of mental illness justifying involuntary commitment (one must be mentally ill _and_ dangerous to himself or to others, either physically or emotionally).
3. Emergency treatment of one who is physically dangerous is specified. A magistrate meets the respondent (prospective patient) at the hospital, holds a hearing, and issues a warrant if probable cause is found. There must then be a formal hearing within 5 days.
4. Periodic medical reports are to be filed with the appropriate court after the first 15 days (an extension of no more than 7 days is possible). Later the interval between such reports may be 60 or 90 days. The initial medical finding may be one of the following: (a) no mental illness, (b) illness requiring outpatient care only, (c) illness requiring inpatient care, (d) illness with no likelihood that treatment will bring about improvement.
5. The county hospitalization commission is replaced by one person—a judge or referee.
6. Initially a respondent has a lawyer. After the hearing the lawyer is replaced by a mental health advocate (analogous to a public defender) who is to represent the interests of the patient. He must review the periodic medical reports and may visit the patient and his institution.

To the ICLU it is particularly gratifying that arbitrary involuntary hospitalization and unjustifiable retention of the patient are both prevented.

Minority Races

On Iowa's road toward equal treatment of races are some bright spots worth recall. In the United States Congress James F. Wilson of Iowa was chairman of the Judiciary Committee during the Civil War. A law he introduced in 1862 forbade the army to return fugitive slaves. In 1864 he introduced a resolution for the abolition of slavery. In 1865 he proposed the enfranchisement of Negroes in the District of Columbia; the law was passed the following year.

Another Iowan, James W. Grimes, was a member of the committee that framed the Fourteenth Amendment to the Constitution; he was particularly influential in securing the second section of that amendment, which applied pressure for giving Negroes the vote in all states. Iowa was the first state to forbid racial discrimination in the franchise; this was in 1868. In the same year Susan Clark, a black girl, was admitted to a "white" school in Muscatine. In 1873 a Negro woman was awarded damages for her forcible removal from the dining room of a Mississippi River steamer at Burlington.

Since it was founded the Iowa Civil Liberties Union has been much concerned with the rights and interests of those whose race puts them at a disadvantage. In most cases these are Negroes. At one time, however, the Union tried to help those of Japanese descent. During the war with Japan the US government, inexcusably but with the pretext of wartime need, had moved Japanese and descendants of Japanese living near the West Coast to concentration camps in the interior. Among the first to be allowed to leave these camps were the young men and women whom colleges and universities would admit as students. In 1942 ICLU wrote to 23 colleges, urging them to give such relief as they could. The resulting situation was surveyed early in 1943: 34 Nisei had come to Iowa colleges; of these 25 were at Drake University, 4 each at the State Teachers College (now the University of Northern Iowa) and Cornell College. Sympathetic replies came from Central, Simpson, and William Penn colleges. The presence of a bomber base at Sioux City was said to prevent Morningside College from being hospitable. The state institutions at Ames and Iowa City were slower in opening their doors than their sister school in Cedar Falls.

There had been a Quaker boarding school—Scattergood Academy—near West Branch. The school had been given up (to be revived later, with distinct success), and the American Friends Service Committee had for some years used the buildings as a welcoming center for refugees from Europe. There the Committee helped fit them for American life and sought employment for them in this region. In 1943 the AFSC wished to reopen the "hostel," in order to help Japanese-Americans in similar ways. The opposition of two American Legion posts caused the abandonment of the project. And the Iowa

Senate, with no protest, passed a resolution that called for the return of all Japanese-American students in Iowa colleges to their camps, on the grounds that their racial extraction made their patriotism doubtful (see Appendix 5). The Young Men's Christian Association, on the other hand, earned the praise of ICLU for the work of its committee to place Nisei in jobs.[8]

The work of ICLU on behalf of Negroes was mainly concerned with access to public accommodations, employment, and housing. Iowa had long had a law (Civil Rights Law of 1884 amended in 1892) forbidding discrimination because of race, creed, color, national origin, or religion in "inns, restaurants, chophouses, eating houses, lunch counters and all other places where refreshments are served, public conveyances, barber shops, bathhouses, theaters and all other places of amusement." This law was quite generally ignored at the time of the founding of ICLU. Perhaps its existence was in the minds of those cafe owners who claimed the right to select their own customers or to seat them as the manager directed.

In 1943 Des Moines became a center for the training of WACs (members of the Women's Army Corps). After some complaints the Restaurant Owners' Association promised there would be no racial discrimination. It was noted that, when marching, the black women were grouped together with white officers.[9]

Progress in some places could be recorded by 1947. The Des Moines YMCA abolished segregation and discrimination; Negroes found housing in a trailer camp of Iowa State College; some were admitted to dormitories at the State University. The Civil Rights Law was increasingly cited—successfully at both Davenport and Des Moines.[10]

In 1948 Negroes were consistently refused service at the lunch counter of the Katz Drug Store in Des Moines—although they could buy in all other sections of the store.[11] The Civil Liberties Union pursued the case by legal means. In the end the suits were settled out of court, with the store promising to serve all persons with equal courtesy.[12]

The Surf Ballroom at Clear Lake, after its purchase by a Chicago firm, excluded Negroes. In 1952 two men were denied entrance; one of them, Isadore Patterson, sued the manager and the doorman. The ICLU, allied with the labor union to which the Negroes belonged, supported the suit. The first jury to which the case came acquitted the manager; they found the ballroom was not a "place of amusement," thus subject to the Civil Rights Law, but a "place of recreation."[13] On appeal, this decision was reversed. The ICLU would have contested a further appeal by the defendant, but he preferred to pay the $500 required of him and to promise to discriminate no longer.[14]

In November 1944 there was the complaint that barber shops in Iowa City would not serve Negroes.[15] Negroes were excluded from the Marshalltown municipal swimming pool in 1948.[16]

Both race relations and the rights of speech were involved in a case calling ICLU to act in 1947-48. On October 13, 1947, Alfred Twitty, a Negro from Washington, D.C., was in Pacific Junction (Mills County) seeking odd jobs. Mayor John Lutter accused him of being a vagrant and ordered him to leave town in an hour or be arrested. When Lutter tried to arrest Twitty, Russell Coppock (a school teacher) and five others objected. The mayor did not proceed with the arrest (out of fear of the six, he said), and Twitty stayed in Pacific Junction overnight to finish a job he had started. However, Lutter did arrest the six men and charged them with "violent and tumultuous assembly" and interference with the administration of justice. The jury of six businessmen in a justice-of-peace court found the six guilty and fined each of them $25. They were defended by I. T. Genung of Glenwood. Coppock later heard that one juror had said he did not believe the charges valid but "they wanted to pin Coppock's ears back"—a teacher ought not to do such a thing.[17]

Russell Coppock alone decided to appeal the conviction. The ICLU saw the importance of the case; on its behalf Paul James of Des Moines associated himself with Genung and filed an appeal.[18] Since there had been hostile articles in a newspaper of Mills County, a change of venue to Pottawattamie County was sought and obtained. Meetings to interest the public in the case were held: in Des Moines by ICLU, in Omaha by the Committee for Interracial Understanding and the Packing House Workers' Union, in Omaha and Council Bluffs by the National Association for Advancement of Colored People. Many people in Iowa and Nebraska contributed to the costs of defense.

The trial was held in Council Bluffs in March 1948, with Vernon Johnson as judge. Paul James asked prospective jurors whether they were prejudiced against Negroes; Drake, county attorney for Mills County, asked them whether they belonged to ICLU. In the trial James said that the six had wished to protect the civil rights of the Negro. Quoting the state's motto, "Our liberties we prize, our rights we will maintain," he said it was hardly conceivable that it should be made a crime to live up to this motto. After four hours of deliberation the jury acquitted Coppock.[19] Unfortunately, Twitty had disappeared and could not testify in the trial.

In editorial comment on the outcome, the Des Moines Register expressed gratitude to ICLU and to those who had contributed for Coppock's defense. It noted three gains: rights of minorities had become a bit more secure; petty law-enforcing officials would be more conscious of the extent of their duties and the limit of their powers; it had been shown how, through cooperation, the cause of justice can be advanced.[20]

In 1953 Attorney General Hoegh earned the praise of ICLU by pointing out to the associations of owners of hotels and restaurants their duties under the law. James Morris (Negro attorney and publisher of The Defender, which gave news of the black community in Des Moines) and others called his attention to many violations of the Civil Rights Act in southern Iowa and to discrimination against Negro delegates to an American Legion convention in Des Moines and against members of a conference of the African Methodist Episcopal Church at Council Bluffs.[21]

The right to equal chances for jobs—and equal treatment in

these jobs—is demanded by minority races. Typically a factory manager might say: "I would employ you, but you lack the needed skill and training." A trade school official might tell the candidate: "We will be glad to train you—if you have a prospective employer." In 1941 it could be reported that Des Moines had made progress in ending this dilemma—thanks mainly to the efforts of John S. Coleman.[22]

The ICLU has shown a steady interest in equal employment opportunities and has been active in urging laws to further it. In 1942 Charles F. Ranson, then president of ICLU, told of discrimination against Negroes in defense employment and training.[23] He recommended that the Union set up a standing committee on the subject. A year later the Union discovered that four of the sixteen war plants in Des Moines allowed Negroes to work.[24]

A later experience of discrimination came to Lawrence Howard, a Negro student at Drake University. He applied for employment with the highway patrol and was told that applications were accepted from whites only.[25]

It became clear that a law compelling fair employment practices was needed. Such a law was proposed in the General Assembly of 1947 but not passed. It called for a commission to oversee its enforcement. Employers and labor unions would be forbidden to discriminate. Neither an employer nor an employment agency might advertise any limitations that would involve discrimination. The bill provided for complaints, investigations, and hearings.[26]

Again and again ICLU pressed for such a law, pointing out the successful use of others like it in various states; Iowa finally adopted it in 1965. The Civil Rights Act of that year incorporates the older prohibition of unfairness in public accommodations along with the new provisions as to employment.

The Union itself has practiced equality in employment and has had five black members of the Board, of whom two were women. Serving as (unpaid) secretaries were W. Lawrence Oliver and Willie Glanton, lawyers; John M. Estes, Jr., who has held offices in NAACP and the Des Moines Chamber of Commerce; Edna Griffin; and Russell G. Pounds, who became president of ICLU in 1974.

The third area of discrimination—that of housing—was the hardest to fight. Restrictive covenants claiming a piece of land for Caucasians in perpetuity were not unknown in Iowa, although the Supreme Court has declared such agreements unenforceable. More widespread, and very effective, have been informal pressures—fears that a dark neighbor might shrink the value of one's own house. The proprietor of a small business had rented a room to a Negro. Accused of "harboring" such a person, he found his clientele dwindling to such an extent that he felt he must ask his guest to go elsewhere.

Urban renewal and new highways are all too likely to displace those who find it hard to get other homes—especially if they are Negroes. Donald Boles pointed this out in a Board meeting as early as 1958.[27] The next year Malcolm Higgins (an early director of the Iowa Civil Rights Commission and, from 1957 to 1959, executive secretary of the Des Moines Commission on Human Rights) reported to the Board that in some areas real estate brokers would show an available house to Negroes only;[28] in other areas the reverse was true.

In 1959 the concern of residents of Des Moines over forced separation of races led to a "Statement of Conscience," which was printed as a prominent advertisement in the Des Moines Register:

> We welcome into our neighborhood any residents of good character, regardless of race, color, religion or national origin.
> We have signed this statement to indicate that we believe in brotherhood and welcome the opportunity to practice it at our own neighborhood level.

Among the sponsors of this statement, which had 2000 signers, were ICLU and the Des Moines Commission on Human Rights.

In 1961 the Des Moines Commission on Human Rights and Job Discrimination made a significant study of about 50 Negro families who had moved into predominantly white neighborhoods; 30 answered the questionnaire. They had bought their new homes, half of them with mortgages, largely through building and loan associations; only three had difficulty in financing. (It may well be that such difficulty had kept others from entrance into the group interviewed.) Over a third had met bitterness and hostility. Displacement from former homes for the building of a new freeway was the most important single cause for the families concerned to move at this time.[29]

That year the ICLU Board urged the passage of a fair housing ordinance in Des Moines.[30] Such an ordinance now exists in a number of Iowa cities: a report of the Iowa Civil Rights Commission (Feb. 1970) lists 20 cities with human rights ordinances; all but two include housing among their provisions.

In 1967 the Civil Rights Act of Iowa was amended by the inclusion of provision for fair housing. Exempted from its demand of equality for all were: housing for particular religious groups, houses for two families, houses occupied by the owner and renting out not more than six rooms. A provision that was contested by ICLU and many others calls for one complaining of unfair treatment to post a bond of $500. This requirement was soon found unconstitutional and was repealed. In 1970 discrimination because of sex was added to the practices condemned by the act.

The Iowa Civil Rights Commission was established in 1965 to enforce the Iowa Civil Rights Act as amended in that year; it continues to work for enforcement of the act after further amendments. Lacking coercive power, its function is rather that of education and persuasion. As one of its activities the Commission held human rights conferences at Ames and Iowa City in June 1970. Out of these conferences came 21 recommendations urging more power, more funds, better organization, and educational work.[31]

In 1970 ICLU recognized that neighborhoods whose people are

largely poor or largely black need extra help when there are complaints against government or other so-called establishment agencies. Therefore, Oliver Johnson, a law student at Drake University, was engaged for a summer project, with an office in Des Moines entitled "Citizen's Complaint Bureau." His most notable work was the investigation of the killing of Lewis Wheeler by police (see Ch. 8). Other matters on which his action or advice was sought included unfairness in employment, estrangement of a married couple, complaints that officials made unsupported accusations against the Black Panther Party, inadequacy of work of a defense attorney, reduction of bond, Social Security benefits, custody of a man's daughter, and repossession of furniture.

The annual meeting of ICLU in 1972 took place in Cedar Falls, close to Waterloo—a city with considerable racial tension. Appropriately, racial issues were the subject of an important part of the meeting.

Jesse High, in charge of urban school planning for the State Department of Public Instruction, said that the state had no position on school segregation. He advocated as such a position that it is wrong to deprive children, because of color or economic status, of exposure to different kinds of educational programs. He spoke for the employment of more black teachers and warned that local control policy decisions often aid and abet discrimination.

Mark Schantz, associate professor in the University of Iowa Law College and member of ICLU Board, called President Nixon's antibusing proposals vague and subject to serious constitutional question. He held that the real national issue was not busing but the depth of our commitment to equal educational opportunity.

Ruth Anderson of Black Hawk County (which contains both Cedar Falls and Waterloo), educational chairman of that county's National Association for the Advancement of Colored People, spoke for total integration, vigorously opposing de facto segregation.

Mary Burdell, social worker at Waterloo, noted a confrontation between the schools and the community; the former were more willing to have changes that would equalize educational opportunity.[32]

The Iowa Civil Liberties Union has worked for many years for racial equality and has had growing cooperation in this from public officials and others. Much improvement is still needed, and the Union promises to persevere in its active concern.

Conscientious Objectors

As we have seen, the ancestors of the American Civil Liberties Union were the American Union against Militarism and the National Civil Liberties Bureau, which AUAM established. Both of these bodies were actively opposed to conscription or—when that institution seemed inevitable in the United States—concerned with the rights of those conscientiously opposed to war.

On April 12, 1917, AUAM issued a memorandum which urged recognition of these principles: (1) Individuals should have exemption on the ground of their own beliefs. (2) Authority to grant exemption should be in the hands of a civil tribunal. Three groups of objectors were to be expected, and AUAM proposed appropriate provisions for each: for those who would not bear arms personally, noncombatant service; for those rejecting such noncombatant service as would aid military operations, types of alternate service which most would gladly perform; for absolutists who refused all compulsory service, full exemption, especially if their normal or voluntary employment were socially valuable.

To this memorandum was added the note: "In offering this memorandum we do not imply support of the principle of selective draft, which we are obliged to oppose as in itself dangerous to democracy." Authors of this document were Lillian D. Wald, Jane Addams, and Norman Thomas.[33] We should here add that throughout his long life Thomas remained persistent as an opponent of conscription in ACLU.

There was hope of disputing the constitutionality of the law. In this connection Charles T. Hallinan quoted Daniel Webster: "A free government with an uncontrolled power of military conscription is a solecism, at once the most ridiculous and abominable that ever entered the head of man." A court decision that the draft was not forbidden by the Constitution soon ended hope of opposing it on this ground.

In the winter of 1917-18 eleven conscientious objectors were held at Camp Dodge.[34] In the spring seven other men were sentenced to 25 years' imprisonment and one to 20 years' at that camp; they were condemned for resisting orders, conscientious objection "seeming the motive."[35]

In the early years of ACLU the ever-broadening field of its activity left opposition to conscription as such largely neglected.

The ICLU was not very active on behalf of objectors during the Second World War. Its Bulletin of March 1943 notes that in three months there had been 19 convictions for violations of draft laws from religious motivation. The objectors were mainly Jehovah's Witnesses, basing their claims for exemption on the status of each member as a minister. Some had refused to go to civilian public service camps, since these, though under civilian direction, were nonetheless a part of the conscription system. Bail bonds in a southern district of Iowa were increased from $2,000 to $6,000-$7,000;[36] ICLU protested.

Two Iowans who were denied exemption were Lyle Tatum and J. Lloyd Spaulding. The hearing officer denied that they acted from religious grounds, although Tatum was a lifelong Quaker and Spaulding an active Methodist. Both were given four-year sentences; both had had legal support from ICLU,[37] which regretted that its meager resources prevented its entering other cases.

An active concern of ICLU was the practice of renewed prosecution of those who had served one sentence for refusing military service and then still refused it. To the Union it seemed that the persistent rejection of induction should be regarded as just one act, justifying no more than one sentence.[38]

Universal military training was proposed soon after the end

of the war in 1945. This time ACLU opposed such a law, and it was not passed by Congress.

In 1947, shortly before Christmas, President Truman granted amnesty to many violators of the Selective Service Law. Lyle Tatum was one of the fifteen whose convictions had taken place in Iowa.[39] Spaulding had been paroled in 1944.

The issue of required military service was emphasized in 1948 when Kenneth Boulding applied for naturalization. He had been born in England and was a professor of economics at Iowa State College. A Quaker, Boulding stated that he would not defend the Constitution by arms. Fearing an adverse ruling from the judge in the case, he was ably assisted by Robert Mannheimer and Addison Parker of ICLU; they in turn had valuable counsel from Julien Cornell of ACLU.[40] Boulding was granted citizenship. Members of the American Legion were indignant, demanding his dismissal from the college. In this they did not succeed; however, when the University of Michigan invited Boulding to a professorship there he accepted, and Iowa State lost an outstanding scholar.

The concern of the ICLU Board of Directors for those resisting the Selective Service System was voiced on January 15, 1949, in the following resolution:

> The Iowa Civil Liberties Union and its parent organization, the American Civil Liberties Union, have repeatedly expressed the belief that conscription in peacetime is a grave infringement on the liberties of citizens, to be justified only by such extreme need as does not now exist. However, the Selective Service Act of 1948 was passed. [Just before that there had been a period of 16 months when America was free from forced military service.]
>
> A number of young men have, on the grounds of conscience, failed to register—in spite of the recognition that many would be deferred, even under the Act's narrow definition of conscience.
>
> We must recognize the vast difference in motivation between those who violate most criminal laws and those who, for reasons of conscience, will not obey the demand to register under the Selective Service Act. The latter are showing deep concern for their fellowmen; and many reasons for punishing those who violate laws for their own profit or to others' harm do not apply at all to such conscientious objectors. We therefore approve the far-sighted action of those judges, who, while compelled to sentence these violators of the Selective Service Act, parole them at once for work of distinct benefit to society.

Early in 1950 ICLU reaffirmed its stand against peacetime conscription.[41] Conscription in general was opposed on grounds of history—its rejection in most of the nation's past and American pride in those immigrants who came to escape forced service in Europe. There was, the Union held, no pressing need that could justify the draft. Particularly repugnant features of the law then proposed were the narrow grounds of belief as a basis for conscientious objection and the fantastic harshness of penalties for counseling against compliance with the law.[42]

Again toward the end of the same year ICLU returned to the subject. The resolution this time said:

> If any law for compulsory military trainer service be enacted, it should be only for a definite, brief term or for a clearly defined, temporary, abnormal situation. Any such law should broaden the existing definition of conscientious objection, not defining conscience in terms of any particular religious belief. Whatever provisions be made for conscientious objectors, they should be completely free from military direction.[43]

The Board of ACLU had at that time voted not to oppose conscription, unfortunately without consulting affiliates on this decision. Furthermore, if conscription—an institution most destructive of freedom—is an inevitable consequence of the war system, it would seem to be our business to do away with that system.[44]

Generally, however, the Board of ACLU has held that it must not make a pronouncement on the foreign policy of the United States; that it should leave to other bodies (to which many supporters of ACLU belong) activity on behalf of peace or any specific policy in relations with other nations. In 1955 ACLU urged the Department of Justice to refrain from second prosecutions of conscientious objectors (similar to the action of ICLU in 1943), arguing that they would not increase society's security but would harm it through an appearance of vindictiveness.[45]

In 1917 a law had been enacted declaring various classes of persons ineligible for employment by Iowa municipalities; among them are those who have claimed exemption from military service as conscientious objectors. The ICLU had noted and deplored such a policy in Des Moines. In 1959 the state Senate voted to repeal the provision, and Norman Erbe (then attorney general) held it unconstitutional.[46] It is still in the Iowa Code (365.17), but a bill for its repeal was filed in 1971 and ICLU urged its adoption.

The distinction between just and unjust wars, for many centuries a part of church doctrine, naturally leads to conscientious objection to particular wars. This has become much more prevalent during the conflict in Indochina, and the Civil Liberties Union has sharpened its concern for the selective conscience.

There are those whose protest against conscription takes the form of forbidden acts. In 1965 a young man, Stephen Smith, burned his draft card and then had trouble finding a lawyer to defend him. It was through the efforts of ICLU that Craig Sawyer of Drake University undertook this defense. Since then ICLU has taken similar action in numerous other cases.

Until 1970 both ACLU and ICLU avoided the extreme positions of approving conscription under all circumstances or under none;

when the two bodies differed, ACLU was farther from the latter position than ICLU.

In 1969 the Board of ACLU stated its belief that the Selective Service Act then in operation was unconstitutional. Louise Noun, the member of the Board nominated by ICLU, voted with the majority. In the same year John de J. Pemberton, Jr., executive director of the ACLU, became one of the sponsors of the National Council to Repeal the Draft. This he did with the sanction of the Board of Directors of ACLU, even though that Board itself had not decided to call for this repeal. However, when the expiration of the existing law (June 30, 1970) approached, ACLU took a decidedly active part in working against its renewal. Lauren Selden was the man who worked energetically and resourcefully to this end. In the end, the Congress did give this institution two more years of existence.

On January 27, 1973, by direction of Secretary of Defense Melvin Laird draft calls ended. This did not mean an end to the system of conscription. Young men were still expected to register and, if they wished, to ask for classification as conscientious objectors. It was a step that weakened the strength of appeals for a definitive end to the whole system.

A topic related to conscription was that of amnesty for a great variety of persons who had suffered penalties related to the Vietnam War and the military system. The subject took up an increasing amount of attention on the part of ACLU, and a growing number of others showed a strong interest in it.

Many were the types of persons for whom an obliteration of penalties and threats of penalties were sought. Some had gone abroad (mostly to Canada or Sweden) rather than enter military service; others "went underground" within the country. They may have been conscientiously opposed to all war or selectively to the conflict in Indochina. In the latter case, their objection could be that the war was unconstitutional (the main consideration for ACLU) or that it was a national sin because of its history, its methods, its probable effects.

For some, the revulsion against the American part in the Vietnam struggle arose only when they were in the midst of the destruction, seeing some of its effects. Harshness and unfairness on the part of the military "machine" account for many who deserted or suffered greatly through undeserved punishment.

Outside the armed services were many who opposed the war or conscription through determined action (for instance, taking part in demonstrations or destroying draft records) and were then subject to arrest, conviction, imprisonment, or other penalty. The ACLU called for wiping out all harmful effects of a legal frown or condemnation, to benefit everyone whose word or act was contrary to war in general or this war in particular.

Many proposals for partial amnesty have been made—for instance, that the one forgiven must still perform such service of value to society as was required of conscientious objectors during the war. The ACLU opposed any such stretching out of punishment time, calling for unconditional and universal amnesty.

The Disadvantaged

As early as December 1970 the Board of ACLU published Policy 108 calling for amnesty for war resisters, and the Project on Amnesty became a major source of concern in the Union. As its director, Henry Schwarzschild, said, "The burden of proof of conscience should not be on those who refused to fight the war, but on the society that pursued the unconscionable endeavor."[47]

In June 1974 the Board of Directors of ICLU passed the following resolution.

> For all persons still under any sort of disability because of opposition to, or abstention from, the war waged by the United States in Southeast Asia, we bespeak amnesty. From the general amnesty we would exempt only those who had been convicted of violence against persons.
>
> Amnesty would not be a statement that all of those granted amnesty were guiltless. Amnesty is rather, to quote from a publication of the American Civil Liberties Union: "the discretionary act of a sovereign state of deciding to abstain from prosecuting groups of citizens who may be in conflict with the law for political reasons. Amnesty is the forgetting of certain acts in the interest of social justice and reconciliation."
>
> Amnesty would benefit those who took the position that the war was unconstitutional or unjustifiable. Disapproval of the war (as well as disapproval of war in general and of conscription) led many, as a matter of personal conscience, to avoid military service. They did this by leaving the country, by going underground in the United States and by other methods.
>
> Amnesty, of course, also would benefit some whose motives were less admirable than those who acted as a matter of conscience. However, any case-by-case examination of war resisters would require an intolerable amount of time because of administrative or judicial problems and would call for making extremely difficult judgments about motives of individuals. A case-by-case approach also would discriminate against the uneducated and underprivileged individuals who were not able to express their philosophical position about the war as well as could educated and articulate individuals.

Welfare Recipients

The ICLU is concerned for the rights of the poor—especially those so poor that they depend on public relief.

In 1937 the Supervisors of Dickinson County ruled that "relief shall be discontinued for any person or persons expressing dissatisfaction with the care or relief being furnished them by the county." In response to an inquiry from ICLU Mrs. Ethel F. McMichael, director of relief, wrote: "Dickinson County has a definite plan whereby relief for the needy is budgeted according to

the number of individuals in their family and their income. In
most cases this is acceptable, and relief claimants are willing to
reimburse the county with labor for relief received. We can see no
reason why dissatisfaction should be expressed."[48] However, the
ruling was rescinded, and ICLU was given credit for this action.[49]

In 1945 a man and his wife, both injured, were in Sioux City;
a social worker told them to go to California, where they had been
previously. They were unwilling to go, and the social worker had
them committed as feeble-minded.[50]

In 1961 Polk County ordered a family to leave, on the grounds
that they were likely to become public charges. Sherman Markman,
for ICLU, filed a brief which challenged the order as unconstitutional; Judge Dring Needham agreed with him.[51]

The original provisions on Medicare in Public Law 89-97 (enacted July 30, 1965) assured hospital insurance benefits to all
persons age 65 and over, if they were entitled to cash monthly Social Security or railroad retirement benefits. No exceptions were
named. However, there were about 2 million aged residents of the
United States who were not entitled to these retirement benefits.
Section 103 of the law provided hospital insurance for most of
these, if they met certain conditions. What interested ICLU was
the exclusion from this insurance of "those persons who were members of any organization registered, or required under a final order of the Subversive Activities Control Board to register, as a
Communist-action, Communist-front or Communist-infiltrated organization."

Applicants in this "uninsured" group for Medicare benefits
were expected to check the no blank after a question about membership in organizations of the types described. This check mark was
all that was required—no affidavit, no notarization, no witness.

Naturally ICLU was opposed to such a penalty for affiliation.
At the request of Louise Noun (president), Executive Secretary
Oval Quist wrote to the Iowa delegation in Congress as follows:

> It is the feeling of the Iowa Civil Liberties Union that
> provisions of the Medicare legislation which exclude from
> hospital benefits members of certain organizations and require
> that they are not (and for twelve months have not been) such
> members be repealed.
>
> The Iowa Civil Liberties Union hopes you will be able to
> assist Congressmen Ryan and Farbstein (and Senator Javits) on
> humanitarian grounds as well as on Constitutional grounds.
>
> The Des Moines Tribune stated opposition to the restric-
> tions in a commendable way when it said editorially:
>
> "The sensible thing to do would be to eliminate polit-
> ical views and affiliations as a qualification for benefits.
> If the Government is willing to collect taxes from individu-
> als without regard to their politics, it ought to be willing
> to provide the benefits their taxes buy."

However, it was not congressional repeal but court action which
put an end to the objectionable inquiry and requirement. Shortly

The Disadvantaged   111

after the Medicare law went into effect on July 1, 1966, a Federal
District Court held the Communist exclusion provision to be unconstitutional. Since November 1966 no political affiliation of any
kind has been inquired into or considered in decisions regarding
entitlement to Medicare or any other benefits.[52]

The Cardinal Area Chapter has received the complaint that certain classes of Story County residents granted public funds have
their names published in the daily press.

Similarly, the Hawkeye Area Chapter told of protests by county
welfare workers about the new reporting system of the Iowa Department of Social Services. Some workers were opposed to including
the names, addresses, and Social Security numbers of their clients
in forms filed with the State Department. They contended that this
is a violation of confidential relationships with clients and
that there is danger of information getting to people not entitled
to receive it when this is filed in a data bank. The Department
replied that such identification information was essential for its
use and that safeguards had been established to protect confidentiality.[53]

Women

Within the Iowa Civil Liberties Union the two sexes have always been treated as equal, although most Board members have been
male. One of the founders of ICLU was Laetitia M. Conard. Soon
after the founding in 1935 Hortense Dillon produced the study on
criminal syndicalism laws—one of the most thorough and important
works produced by this Union. Louise R. Noun has had the longest
tenure as president; it is to her credit that this was a period of
great growth in membership, financial support, influence, and
breadth of concern. In 1975 Elizabeth S. Turner became president
of ICLU. A social worker, she has been director of casework and
consultant in community development with the Iowa Children's and
Family Services Agency since 1948.

However, explicit interest in the rights of women as such
came quite late. An important session of the biennial conference
of ACLU, held in New York in 1970, was devoted to inequalities in
the treatment of the sexes. Among speakers especially noteworthy
were Dorothy Kenyon, whose wisdom and wit had enriched ACLU for
most of its years; and Pauli Murray, lawyer, poet, professor at
Brandeis University. Professor Murray's account of the many ways
in which women are treated worse than men was revealing and probably cause for new activity in ICLU as well as other affiliates.

At the conference six resolutions on policy were presented
and later adopted by the ACLU Board. A number of them were reflected in the program of the next annual meeting of ICLU, held at
Des Moines in 1971. Robert Webber, director of Planned Parenthood
of Iowa, spoke for a more liberal abortion law and better distribution of birth control information. Marita Jones, assistant dean
of students at Iowa State University, named employers, employment

agencies, and unions as discriminators. In colleges and universities women are especially poorly represented among the higher ranks of the hierarchy—trustees, administrators, full professors. Women, she reported, have lower pay and slower promotion in the faculties.

Alvin Hayes, Jr., executive director of the Iowa Civil Rights Commission, reported that a third of the commission's cases refer to sex discrimination. Such discrimination, he said, is socially acceptable and fashionable. Women should speak with a strong voice and should encourage others to report their grievances to the Civil Rights Commission.

Leona Durham, editor of the Daily Iowan (student paper of the University of Iowa), spoke of the medical and legal professions as critical to rights of women. She advocated insistence that the professional schools of these disciplines be forced, by specified dates, to have women form 51 percent of the student body and 51 percent of the faculty. She spoke of subtle discrimination such as the discouragement of girls' study of mathematics, thereby excluding them from a large variety of careers.[54]

Senator Jack Miller of Iowa proposed an amendment to the United States Constitution (S.J.R. 138) which would guarantee women equality under the law with respect to education and employment, while at the same time guaranteeing "the validity of any law . . . which is essential to enable women to perform their responsibilities as homemakers or mothers." Louise Noun wrote Senator Miller, commenting on the proposal:

> The two aspects of this amendment are patently contradictory. If women are compelled by law to perform their responsibilities as homemakers or mothers, then their rights to education and employment are limited by how these responsibilities of homemaking and motherhood are defined by our lawmakers. Instead of securing equal rights for women, this amendment represents a giant step backward in women's fight for legal equality by incorporating into the United States Constitution a provision which, in effect, says that women's place is in the home.[55]

In the summer of 1972 the ICLU Board was confronted with two issues where women asked for equality of rights. In Davenport women, on registering to vote, are required to list names of their spouses or parents. No such demand is made of men. The ICLU called for reform. A woman in Dallas County needed an attorney in a divorce action. She could not afford one, and that small county has no legal aid organization. The ICLU sought to establish her right to counsel.[56]

Iowa has two training schools for juvenile delinquents—one for boys at Eldora, one for girls at Mitchellville. A comparison of the two reveals inequalities of various kinds. Girls are sent to Mitchellville on more trivial grounds—e.g., "waywardness." They are subject to senselessly restrictive rules while there and have far poorer facilities for education toward future employment. The small and dwindling number of girls sent to this school would make the cost of service equivalent to that at Eldora very high. These are among the reasons the ICLU Board voted to recommend that the Mitchellville school be phased out, to be replaced by services offered nearer the girls' respective homes. In many cases, it was believed, family counseling would be a superior substitute. A special investigating committee, with Sally Hacker (Department of Sociology, Drake University) as chairman, prepared a resolution to this effect; a mail ballot of the Board approved it.[57] The school has not been closed, but substantial reforms in its operation have been made.

In 1972 Northwestern Bell petitioned the Iowa Commerce Commission for a substantial increase in telephone rates. At the same time the company's treatment of women was under scrutiny as to pay and chances for employment and advancement, especially to administrative positions. An increase without assurance of a policy of full equality would amount to state sanction of bias. Concern over the position of women was brought to the company's attention by ICLU through personal conferences of the Union's women's rights committee with company officials.[58]

The Board was informed of sex discrimination in the commercial field. Kathryn Kirschbaum of Davenport had applied for a credit card to BankAmericard. That firm said that her husband must also sign the application. She reported that he would not do so. Her husband, Ray Kirschbaum, is a member of ICLU Board and was present at the meeting where this was related. Kathryn Kirschbaum is mayor of Davenport, and as such may sign a million-dollar contract with the federal government even without her husband's cooperation.

The ICLU has been concerned about sex discrimination in public schools. The change in treatment of students in the case of marriage or pregnancy has repeatedly interested the Board. Specifically referring to Des Moines, the Board suggested a policy statement:

> Marriage, pregnancy, or parenthood do not exclude a student from the ordinary expectations and privileges of all students. However, school officials may, at the request of a student or his or her parents, make special and individualized arrangements for students who are married, pregnant, or parents, as long as the arrangements are consistent with the primary educational function of the school system.[59]

Unequal support of physical education for boys and for girls at many levels of schooling troubled ICLU several times in 1972. Early in the year the Hawkeye Area Chapter succeeded in cutting down the difference in the Iowa City school system. The Quad Cities Chapter also sought to get more nearly equal treatment in its area.

A specific complaint was brought to the ICLU Board at its December meeting. Three girls from Franklin Junior High School of

Des Moines told of trying in vain to have interscholastic competition for girls, as is provided for boys. Sally Hacker, a Board member, strengthened the girls' case by stating that up to nine times as much money is assigned to athletics for boys as to the corresponding program for girls. The Board then decided on a letter to the Des Moines superintendent of schools, asking for an affirmative action program in preparing the school budget which would move toward providing equal funding for boys' and girls' athletic programs. The position of the ICLU was also to be reported to the State Department of Public Instruction, in view of the extent of this type of discrimination.[60]

This discrimination in the funding of athletics was a subject of a federal complaint filed by ICLU with the Civil Rights Division of the Department of Health, Education and Welfare. The same complaint included a protest against the failure of the Des Moines school system to appoint more women to administrative positions.

The increase in the influence of women within ICLU, from a time when they numbered one or two in the Board to the end of 1975 with ten of the eighteen at-large members female, is noteworthy. One step was deliberately taken—the increase in the size of the Board—in the hope that the members would use the extra election to choose women for some of the vacant posts. Some of the candidates were men, but enough voters respected the purpose of the enlargement (and found those for whom they voted well qualified) to achieve the present ratio.

In the spring of 1974 Nanette Coak, age 12, wrote to Attorney General Richard C. Turner, asking his help in getting her admitted to Little League baseball. Replying sympathetically, Turner wrote: "There are some things even an attorney general can't do, and I'm afraid this is one of them. But I will pass your letter along to the Governor, the State Ombudsman and the Iowa Civil Liberties Union." The Union was glad to have its influence implied by Turner.[61]

The issue of sex discrimination in sports is neither local nor confined to secondary education. Title IX of the Higher Education Act of 1972 bans sex discrimination in education programs of universities and colleges if those programs receive any federal aid. There was pressure on Caspar Weinberger, Secretary of Health, Education and Welfare, to "soften" the guidelines telling schools what they must do in the field of athletic programs and activities. An ICLU letter was sent to Weinberger, Iowans in Congress, and President Nixon, opposing any weakening of women's rights. Specifically ICLU holds that there should be equality in facilities and their use; equipment and its use; opportunity to learn athletic skills; participation in interscholastic competition; funding of athletic, intramural, and physical education programs. It calls also for the representation of females on athletic governing boards.[62]

In the annual meeting of ICLU held at Iowa City May 11, 1974, there was a panel discussion of "Equality of Women in Athletics," dealing especially with high schools. Wayne Cooley, secretary of the Iowa Girls High School Athletic Union, said that Iowa had 17 different competitive sports for girls, far more than any other state. In the years 1969-74 the number of schools offering gymnastics for girls grew from 13 to 54. Ione Shadduck, physical education professor at Drake University, said that, while Iowa was ahead of other states, sexism continues in the number and salaries of women coaches and in media coverage.

Among the rights of women interesting the ICLU is that of abortion, particularly in the case of a pregnant woman who does not wish a child. The Iowa law forbade an abortion not needed to save the life of the woman, but the situation was changed by the decision of the United States Supreme Court (Jan. 22, 1973) that no state might forbid abortion in the first six months of pregnancy. States could, the Court said, regulate and even prohibit abortions in the last three months of pregnancy, unless the health or life of the mother depended on the operation.

After this decision the ICLU Foundation and Iowans for Medical Control of Abortion challenged the Iowa law; the plaintiffs were two Des Moines doctors and two pregnant women who had been unable to obtain abortions. Gordon Allen, staff counsel of ICLU, named clarification of the situation as the purpose of the suit. The state, conceding that the Supreme Court opinion removed illegality from early abortions, sought to retain the old Iowa prohibition for the last three months. However, the panel of three federal judges to whom the case was referred ruled that the Iowa law was not enforceable in any respect.[63]

The Iowa law on rape was so unfair to women that it roused strong (even though belated) opposition from the Board of ICLU. A man could not be convicted without corroboration of the statement by the accusing woman. This was a requirement not usual to other crimes of violence and quite out of place when the crime is most unlikely to have any witnesses. The law also admitted as evidence (which might make conviction more difficult) the record of former sexual behavior on the woman's part. In these regards the law was amended in the spring of 1974, as ICLU had urged.

CHAPTER 14

German Visitors

IN 1950 the State Department invited a number of Germans to the United States, that they might get acquainted with our way of life. As a part of this program ICLU was asked to be host to ten of these visitors for a week. I was placed in charge of arrangements. However, Miriam Zahradnik, who acted as secretary, did most of the work of arrangements; the office of the American Friends Service Committee in Des Moines gave her a room with telephone.

The guests were of various callings—teachers, social workers, journalists—from different sections of West Germany, but all eager to build democracy and freedom in their country. They came in two groups of five each in November and December and were guests in private homes in Ames.

The first group met with a Community Chest Board and remarked that such private welfare agencies as were there represented were rare in Germany—aside from church organizations. In a conference with members of the staff of the <u>Des Moines Register</u> one German expressed amazement at the defense and protection given to a man accused of murder. She saw the League of Women Voters and similar groups as the greatest asset to American life and democracy.

They were then taken to Paullina (O'Brien County) where they were in time for a quarterly meeting of the Religious Society of Friends. After a session with the sheriff of the county, they were guests at a community gathering in their honor. It was there that the local residents were asked what the general attitude would be in case a Negro should wish to settle near Paullina. The answer, spoken with regret, was that it probably would not be cordial—all the people thereabouts were white.

The second group of five did not go so far from Ames. They attended a Board meeting of ICLU and were guests at a community gathering in Slater (Story County); thus they too came together with men and women from farms and a small town. A happy memory of this visit is that of the group waiting at the station for the train to take them away, singing one German song after another.[1]

116

We have personally maintained contact with some of these guests from Germany—most lastingly with Dr. Kurt Apfel, a journalist from Stuttgart. In 1953 he wrote of his regret that Germany had too little support for civil liberties, and that what there was was too scattered. He was consoled at least that his country had no such phenomenon as was associated with the name of Joseph McCarthy.[2]

My wife and I were in Europe for several months in 1955 and, planning in advance with valued help from Roger Baldwin, could visit men and women working zealously for human freedom in Germany, Italy, England, and other lands. In Germany we confirmed what Kurt Apfel had written. In Bonn we had a good conference with lawyers from the government's civil service; they told us that no lawyers in the city, outside the government service, supported the Liga für Menschenrechte (the organization affiliated, as is ACLU, with the International League for the Rights of Man).

CHAPTER 15

Chapter Activities

THE Iowa Civil Liberties Union was 15 years old when the first recorded suggestion of a local chapter was made. In January 1950 Max D. Gaebler of Davenport wrote to Jeffrey Fuller of the ACLU office about the possibility of an organization in his city. George E. Rundquist wrote to me about the inquiry, and I had some correspondence with Gaebler within the month. Nothing further seems to have developed at that time.[1]

Quad Cities

In late 1969 a chapter was formed to cover Scott County, in which Davenport lies, and Rock Island County, Illinois. It has equally close bonds with the ACLU affiliates in Illinois and Iowa. The official name is "Quad Cities Chapter."

Recorded are interest in a speakers' bureau and participation in a television panel. The chapter took up the cause of a woman who was denied a license by the realtors of Davenport because it was assumed that, with children under age 12, she could not give enough time to the real estate business.[2]

The Palmer College of Chiropractic at Davenport had the practice of denying admission to those who had been convicted of a felony and those whose hair style violated the code of the school. The Quad Cities Chapter protested both types of discrimination in 1972.[3]

Mrs. Genevieve Bailey of Davenport, who received Aid to Dependent Children funds, was charged with violating the law on welfare fraud. Bail was set at $500, and an acquaintance paid the $50 necessary as bail bond. Judge Philip Steffen had the policy of not naming a defense attorney if bail has been posted. He told Mrs. Bailey to secure an attorney, for which she clearly had no money. When she appeared in court several times without an attorney, Municipal Judge Jack Broderick, on recommendation of Judge Steffen, sentenced her to 30 days for contempt of court.

Chapter Activities

Both the Quad Cities Chapter and ICLU asked: Is the Davenport court ignoring the state law that calls for release without bail of an individual with ties to the community? Is the court ignoring Supreme Court decisions upholding the right of indigents to be defended by a court-appointed attorney? The case was appealed to the Iowa Supreme Court.[4] In November 1973 that court ruled that Judges Steffen and Broderick had acted illegally in finding Mrs. Bailey in contempt of court.

On October 30, 1973, the Quad Cities Chapter Board sent a telegram to Illinois Congressman Tom Railsback urging him, in his capacity on the House Judiciary Committee, "to proceed with dispatch in the investigative phase of impeachment proceedings as resolved by the House members against President Richard M. Nixon."

Hawkeye Area

In 1961 a chapter in Iowa City was recognized.[5] Irving L. Allen was named chairman. The Daily Iowan reported that the chapter was not participating in the petition for the hiring of qualified Negro teachers but had no wish to hinder the project.[6] The branch (soon naming itself the Johnson County Chapter, since Iowa City is in that county) was, nevertheless, concerned about racial questions. Its secretary, H. William Fischer, wrote ACLU to learn what the Oregon affiliate had done concerning discrimination at the University of Oregon. The answer came from Charles Davis, chairman of the ACLU of Oregon. The state board of higher education of that state had directed that the charters of fraternities and sororities not complying with board racial policies by January 1, 1963, would be withdrawn.

The chapter formed at that time apparently made no deep impression, for in 1967 Dean David Vernon of the Law School spoke for the formation of a chapter in Iowa City.[7] Reasons given were the number of ICLU members in the city and the fact that the rapidly increasing number of men wishing to claim the status of conscientious objectors had no place to turn for advice or help.

The formal organization of this chapter was completed in 1968 and was renamed the Hawkeye Area Chapter. It extended its territory to the following nine counties: Benton, Cedar, Iowa, Johnson, Jones, Keokuk, Linn, Muscatine, Washington.[8]

The bylaws naturally stated that the chapter should be guided by the rules and regulations of ICLU. In 1970 the Hawkeye Area Chapter requested, in a reciprocal territorial claim, "that ICLU take no action, conduct no investigations, issue no press releases, sponsor no events in this area without prior knowledge and consultation with the Board or Executive Committee."[9]

As related in Chapter 5, a committee of this chapter made a thorough study of the rules of conduct enacted by the Board of Regents for the three state universities and wrote the first report on them.

Some 80 Iowa City citizens objected to sex education in the

public schools. The chapter board, reacting to this discussion, passed the following resolution:

> The Board of the Hawkeye Area Chapter of the ICLU declares it is a fundamental right of students, under Iowa's compulsory school attendance laws, to learn the facts of human sexuality. Simply because these students are below the age of majority is no reason for those setting public school educational policy to deny students this right. Courses of study and components of courses which relate to human sexuality may be appropriately included in every public school. The level of professional educational ethics prevailing among our teachers is adequate to protect against the abuses feared by many parents.[10]

The chapter has concerned itself actively with rights of university students (particularly in connection with protest gatherings), student teachers (said to have no rights), and secondary school students. In Cedar Rapids high schools, principals were urged to accept the concept that students should not be penalized academically for disciplinary infractions.

The treatment of persons held in Johnson County jail was protested. For instance, only the closest relatives were allowed as visitors—not even common-law wives or female friends; one inmate was kept on a ration of coffee and bread for six days for not shaving his beard.

The Hawkeye Area Chapter in 1971 decided on a nine-county study of the policies of sheriffs in the handling of prisoners in such areas as visiting privileges and censorship of mail. Policies in the detention of prisoners were also to be investigated.[11]

The chapter took steps to contest the Cedar Rapids ordinance that prohibited the showing of films in places with Class B liquor licenses.[12]

On July 6, 1966, Donald E. Thomas was convicted in Cedar Rapids of first-degree murder in the death of his wife by shooting. Judge William R. Eads presided in the case, which resulted in a life sentence for Thomas. Just after the trial, however, Judge Eads said he thought there were issues in the case that ought to go to the Iowa Supreme Court. With compassion he told Thomas, "You have drawn one of the short straws in the lottery of life because of your background."

In 1967, in *Entsminger* v. *Iowa*, the US Supreme Court ruled that anyone convicted of a felony is entitled to at least one appeal as a matter of due process—with the aid of counsel whose duty it is to see that the appeal is pursued effectively. Three weeks after Thomas's trial his attorneys, Robert Matias and Robert Wilson, did indeed file notice of appeal. But they did nothing to perfect the appeal, so in March 1969 the Iowa Supreme Court dismissed it. Neither the defendant nor any of his relatives was informed of the dismissal.

Months thereafter John M. Ely, Jr. (a former state senator

Chapter Activities 121

and a leader in ICLU and its Hawkeye Area Chapter) talked with a relative of Thomas about other matters and happened to learn of the case reported here. He wrote to the Supreme Court and learned from them that the appeal had been dismissed. Ely then wrote to Thomas reporting that the appeal had been dropped and offering assistance to secure new legal counsel to reenter the appeal if Thomas would give his permission. At first the prisoner replied his case was hopeless and advised dropping the matter. It took a second letter to persuade the inmate of Fort Madison to exercise his right of appeal. On behalf of his chapter of ICLU Ely convinced a young Cedar Rapids attorney, Michael Fay, to see what could still be done. Action was further delayed because records of the case could not be found at the Supreme Court; they were finally discovered in the office of the attorney general.

In the attempt to get an effective appeal Ely was helped by Judge Eads, who had presided over the original trial but had been troubled by some features of it. In September 1972 Eads formally appointed John Platt, another Cedar Rapids lawyer, to handle a new appeal. Fay and Jon Kinnamon, a third young lawyer, aided Platt in preparing the appeal. This was successful, and a new trial was ordered.

It is to the credit of Judge Eads that he took a personal interest in the case from the time he presided over the trial. He not only allied himself with Ely in urging Fay to action but offered to write Governor Robert Ray, asking him to consider commutation of Thomas's sentence.

In its 5 to 4 decision on the appeal, the Supreme Court introduced a new rule of law into murder trials in which defendants plead insanity. Instead of a defendant being compelled to prove his insanity, the burden of proof is shifted to the prosecution who must prove the defendant's sanity.

Subsequently Thomas entered a guilty plea to murder; after two hearings to determine degree of guilt, he was found guilty of murder in the second degree by Judge Robert Osmundson. After having served nine years in prison, Thomas finally had his day in court for his legally available appeal, resulting in a reduction of sentence from a term of life to a term of 50 years—and a new rule in Iowa law from that day forth.

Previous to May 10, 1970, Leona Durham had been engaged to be editor of the **Daily Iowan**, beginning on the 11th. On the 10th, however, the Board of Student Publications, Inc. (SPI) voted to retain her predecessor, Lane Davis, for an indefinite period of time; the effect was to prevent Durham from taking office. In fact they did dismiss her on May 14. This occurred a few days after the invasion of Cambodia and the fatal action against students at Kent State, both of which she had protested with vigor. Ascription of motives without the most convincing evidence must be avoided. Hence it is impossible to assert (as Miss Durham did) that her firing was an act of political censorship. There were other alleged grounds for the action of the board—"an erosion of mutual trust" (which would not exclude censorship) and lack of experience (she had worked for three publications at the University of Wichita).

At the hearing on May 14 she was represented by William Buss of the Law School faculty and thereafter, on the advice of Buss, by Dan Johnston.

The Hawkeye Area Chapter expressed an interest in the matter and invited both sides to present their views. After hearing them, the chapter passed a motion urging the Publications Board to reconsider the dismissal action.

The Board did, in fact, create a panel for this purpose: Louise Noun, selected by Miss Durham; John McCormally, editor of the <u>Burlington Hawkeye</u>, selected by the Board; and Ronald Carlson of the Law School faculty, chosen by the other two. This panel found in favor of Durham; accordingly the Board, though not legally bound, did restore her to the position from which she had been suspended.

It should be stated that neither Dan Johnston nor Louise Noun, though both were officers of ICLU, acted on behalf of the Union.

Miss Durham wrote me (Jan. 16, 1976):

> My own assessment of the Hawkeye Chapter's involvement is that, while it was not extensive, the impact of their request that the board reconsider was considerable in result. I have no question that the dispute was more speedily resolved as a consequence of the interest the membership took in the problem. . . . I consider that I owe a debt of gratitude to the Hawkeye Chapter.

Grinnell

The Grinnell Chapter was founded in 1962.[13]

Harry J. Kilmer, a farmer in Poweshiek County (in which Grinnell lies), was suspected of vandalism. The sheriff, William Welch, called Kilmer's son Carl (age 6) from school and asked the boy about his father's activities. According to testimony of Welch and of the principal, Herbert Haas, the latter was present during the questioning.

Kilmer sued the sheriff for this violation of the rights of his son and himself. The Grinnell Chapter supported the suit, and the ICLU Board voted $200 toward the costs. Usually the Union has taken the side of a defendant; here the rights of both child and parent had been so clearly violated that a deviation was deemed fully justified.[14]

Kilmer belonged to the National Farm Organization, and the vandalism with which he was charged was supposedly connected with that group's activity. Since feeling against the NFO was running rather high at the time, the chapter preferred a decision by a judge rather than by a jury. The judge decided against Kilmer, even though there was clear violation of the civil liberties of a minor child. Since neither Kilmer nor the chapter had funds for an appeal to a higher court, the suit died there.

The chapter protested racial discrimination when a Negro was refused permission to buy a lot at the Holiday Lake resort.

The Grinnell Chapter itself dissolved during the year 1964-65.[15]

Northeast Iowa

Waterloo and Cedar Falls (seat of the University of Northern Iowa) lie in Black Hawk County. A chapter for that county and a separate one for the college were reported to ACLU in 1962,[16] with a list of members and officers. Duane Campbell, president of the college chapter, requested recognition of ICLU.[17]

His successor as president, John Neith, drew attention to the Dixon case, in which a federal court held that no student might be expelled from a college for nonacademic causes without a hearing. The chapter successfully requested the administration of the college to allow two students to apply for readmission; they had been arbitrarily suspended without a hearing.[18]

In 1970 Black Hawk County was central in the creation of a new, greatly enlarged chapter—the Northeast Iowa Chapter. It covers the following fifteen counties: Allamakee, Black Hawk, Bremer, Buchanan, Butler, Chickasaw, Clayton, Delaware, Dubuque, Fayette, Floyd, Grundy, Howard, Mitchell, and Winneshiek.

Like many other sections of ACLU, this chapter has worked actively for the right of students to vote in the cities where they study. On behalf of the chapter Melvin H. Wolf (a Waterloo attorney who has been state senator, president of the Northeast Iowa Chapter, member of the ICLU Board) wrote to the city clerk of Dubuque:

> In our opinion residency for voting purposes is not the same as domicile and any student declaring his residence in your community should be entitled to vote there if, in fact, he resides there during the academic year and meets the length of residence requirements as to precinct, county, and state.[19]

The Northeast Iowa Chapter was among the many agencies called on to defend the right of boys to decide the length of their own hair; as usual, it was successful.

There is a tendency to put an end to a program established for a purpose generally approved when any of its members takes action that challenges the established order—even when he makes his protest as an individual and not as part of his work for the program. Thus the Board of Supervisors for Black Hawk County decided to eliminate the VISTA program after members of it had picketed a store. The ICLU authorized the chapter to bring action to challenge this decision.[20]

Northwest Iowa

The Northwest Iowa Chapter was organized in 1970. Its territory covers these counties: Buena Vista, Clay, Dickinson, Emmet, Kossuth, Lyon, O'Brien, Osceola, Palo Alto, Pocahontas, and Sioux. Most active in its organization was John Denison of Spencer, son of one of the founders of ICLU.

Two students at Buena Vista College, Storm Lake, solicited signatures to an antiwar petition outside St. Mark's Lutheran Church. Dennis Freeman, a state legislator, seized the papers. The students enlisted the aid of ICLU and an attorney, David J. Stein. The latter wrote a sharp letter to Freeman, reminding him of his oath to support the Constitution. After three days Freeman returned the papers and said this act of restitution did not result from expectation of legal action.[21]

The Northwest Iowa Chapter was discontinued about two years after its foundation. John Denison, zealous and effective in gaining members for ICLU, found none who would give it effective life. One probable cause is the large area covered, with no substantial number of adherents in any community.

Sioux City

In 1962 Kenneth Everhart, traveling around Iowa on behalf of ICLU, reported that a chapter could be expected at Sioux City.[22] Actual organization took place in 1967.[23]

The defense of the Gagle Art Gallery was discussed in Chapter 7. The Sioux City Chapter protested the expulsion of a student from Morningside College, holding that he had not received a fair hearing. The ICLU Board stood back of this protest. The student, being a foreigner, might have been in danger of deportation. Louise Noun, president of ICLU, helped to have him admitted to another college, so he was allowed to remain in America.

In 1970 the Chapter protested the revocation of permission for a sanctioned school club to hear a controversial speaker. The superintendent of schools replied that there had been no revocation of permission but rather a request that an expression of an opposing view also be scheduled.[24]

With his letter Superintendent Anderson proposed guidelines on teaching controversial issues, among these guidelines we find: rights of pupils, including "to form and express his own opinions without jeopardizing his relations with the teacher or the school community." Criteria for determining the appropriateness of an issue are part of the curriculum. They include the following: "The issue should be current, significant, real and important to student and teacher." (This seems too restrictive.) "The classroom is a forum, not a committee for producing resolutions." "If a teacher expresses his opinion, he should not claim it to be authoritative." "Teachers of subjects involving controversial issues are assured of the Board's support, if it is found that they have been subjected to unfair criticism or partisan pressures."

On the whole, the code seems fully acceptable on civil liberties principles.

Cardinal Area

In October 1967 a chapter was organized in Ames; it was recognized by the ICLU Board in November.[25] The limits of its jurisdiction were vague at first. In 1970 the territory was defined as comprising the following counties: Boone, Hamilton, Hardin, Marshall, and Story. The chapter then adopted the name of Cardinal Area Chapter.

In the summer of 1969 the Ames City Council passed an ordinance which, among other things, made it a misdemeanor to be in a place where there were illicit drugs. The chapter, not meeting at that season, did not protest. The following year, however, it tried to have the ordinance repealed or, if that were impossible, so amended that the chance of conviction of perfectly innocent persons might be avoided. Amendments to this effect were introduced by two Council members, but the other three members—in spite of reasoned appeals by students and ICLU members—voted against reform. About a year later (after two members of the Chapter Board had been elected to the City Council) the ordinance was repealed, without opposition and with the approval of the police.

The City Council wanted to prohibit policemen from earning at other work during their free hours. The chapter protested this as an invasion of the police officers' privacy; the protest, together with that of the police, was successful.

Following the invasion of Cambodia and the killing of students at Jackson and Kent State universities in the spring of 1970 there was widespread indignation at Iowa State University. The armory was occupied for one night, and some damage was done to it. Officials of the university were at all times in harmonious contact with the student leaders and found it wise to impose no penalties.

Not long afterwards a protest mass meeting had an aroused audience of about 3000 persons. From this demonstration some went to the field where ROTC drill was in progress and disrupted it. Another large group started a spontaneous movement downtown—a quite orderly two-mile march, with marshals helping direct it. The march ended at the draft office, for the crowd opposed not only the Vietnam War and the brutal suppression of dissenters but the institution of conscription which fed the war.

Soon thereafter a small group blockaded the office of Selective Service and for a time prevented a busload of prospective recruits from leaving Ames. With the aid of tear gas the police evicted the dissenters from the building; a considerable number were arrested and held for a time. When they appeared in court, sympathizers were in the audience and expressed resentment, particularly because of the high bail exacted. One girl was charged with contempt of court; an obscene epithet had been hurled at the municipal judge, and he believed it came from her. Very soon afterwards another girl told the judge it was she, not the one arrested, who had shouted; he insisted on making an example of the first girl, who then spent seven days in the county jail at Nevada.

The chapter as a body was not active in defense of the dissenters. However, some individual members took care to be accurate observers, helped gather needed bail funds, spoke at the mass meeting, and in other ways expressed their solidarity with the opponents of the war. Stanley M. Yates, head of the special collections department of Iowa State University, recorded interviews with many who participated in these events in the spring of 1970. They will be invaluable as a source of knowledge about that excited period.

The rapid growth of data banks in Iowa and at Iowa State University aroused fear of their misuse—through inclusion of data that are false, merely matters of opinion, or invasions of privacy. At the chapter's invitation, Clair Maple, director of the ISU computation center, spoke of the dangers and the possible ways of cutting down the chances of misuse. His special emphasis was on the need for building such safeguards into a system at the outset. It was the general opinion in the meeting (Feb. 1971) that everyone should have a right to know what dossiers about him exist and what is in them.

The issue called for immediate attention when in 1972 a "crime computer system" was set up to cover Iowa. Named the Traffic Records and Criminal Justice Information System (TRACIS), it was the subject of four articles in the Des Moines Register, beginning June 30, 1972. On July 9 the same paper told of an interview with Governor Robert Ray; he was concerned about possible abuses of the system and looked forward to legislation to prevent them.

George F. Covert, systems analyst in the Ames laboratory of the Atomic Energy Commission, proved invaluable because of his thorough knowledge of computers and his deep concern for civil liberties. Having testified before the Confidential Records Study Committee of the legislature November 21, 1972, he was a chief speaker in an open meeting of the Cardinal Area Chapter on December 16. This meeting drew up a resolution for the ICLU Board to consider; that body revised and passed it on December 22, hoping that it would result in laws protecting the rights of privacy (see Appendix 6 for the text of the resolution). The cooperation of Hanna Weston of Iowa City, chairman of a committee of ICLU on the same subject, should be acknowledged.

One example to show the complex nature of the question is the following. Suppose that Iowa has effective ways of keeping information in a data bank such as TRACIS from those who have no right to it. This bank, however, will be linked to banks in other states with no such safeguards. The ICLU proposes that data from Iowa not be sent to other states unless they in turn give equivalent protection.

Students of Ames High School were well represented at the chapter meeting in September 1970. They expressed dissatisfaction with the school's arbitrary and authoritarian direction. Soon thereafter an underground paper, Dog Breath, was issued and distributed in the school. The distribution took place on a Wednesday. There was no central organization for the publication, but 17 persons were named on one page as having had a share in its production. The following Monday all of these were suspended from school. Charges against the paper were that it had a scurrilous reference to a member of the school staff, that payment was accepted for a few copies, that it contained a list of the prices and qualities of illicit drugs then obtainable in Ames (but no hint on how to use these facts).

The suspended students were told to return with their parents, in order to be readmitted to the school. Most suspensions were for three days or less, although a few were much more severe. Usually a "change of attitude" was demanded—even when no incorrect attitude had been proved. The high school principal, Dr. Ralph Farrar, was among the invited speakers at a chapter meeting for consideration of these events but was unable to stay for discussion.

The chapter recommended that all regulations in the schools conform to four principles: (1) there should be no penalty imposed before investigation, (2) it should be clearly known what acts would be punishable, (3) such acts should be only those that interfere with the educational purposes of the school, and (4) so far as possible, the penalties themselves should not interfere with those purposes. It seemed that all of the principles had been violated in the case of Dog Breath.

Since this incident the Ames school board has issued a statement of discipline policy, which substantially agrees with the principles advocated by the Cardinal Area Chapter.

Students at Ames high school in 1971-72 received a 34-page handbook prepared by an elected committee of four teachers and four students, with the principal and vice-principal as ex officio members. Besides the welcome joint authorship, it should help prevent some practices the chapter condemned. It does not provide for appeals for redress of grievances in general; if there is suspension, appeal is made only within the administrative system—the superintendent and school board. The handbook does not mention any grievance committee of students. Such a committee had been discussed with Civil Liberties Union members, and the chapter had offered to hear appeals that could not be satisfactorily settled in the school system.

Occasionally the Cardinal Area Chapter arranges—usually in cooperation with other groups—for a general meeting of larger scope than a normal monthly chapter meeting can be. Such a "town meeting," of which another sponsor was the Ames Peace Center, discussed conscription. Spokesmen for three positions were heard—abolition of the draft, renewal of the existing system, and replacement by a system with more civilian alternatives. A petition for each position was provided, urging legislators to support that position. Only the petition for complete abolition had any signatures, and it carried 45 names to Washington.

For more than a year the Cardinal Area Chapter as well as other bodies had realized that there should be unofficial observers of court proceedings—both at Ames and at the county seat, Nevada. Such a system of court watchers was brought to effective reality after the chapter had heard Walter Chidester, director of the American Friends Service Committee Justice Program (Des Moines), speak in Ames on September 14, 1972. He had been observing court sessions in Story County, found court watchers needed, and offered to help in starting the system. It was set up by the chapter, in cooperation with the Committee on Criminal Justice. It worked well in Ames but, because of lack of volunteers, lasted less than a year. The chapter hopes to revive the system both in Ames and in Nevada.

In 1974 the Cardinal Area Chapter decided to have public observance of Bill of Rights Day (Dec. 15). Two radio stations broadcast interviews on the Bill of Rights and ICLU. The library of Iowa State University offered display space for an exhibit, which attracted visitors from December 9 to January 7. Most prominent was a large copy of the Bill of Rights, together with the words of Thomas Jefferson: ETERNAL VIGILANCE IS THE PRICE OF LIBERTY. Books from the library collection and sample copies of a number of periodicals completed the exhibit. Observers were offered copies of The Defender as well as information on ICLU and forms for seeking membership or information. The office of ICLU later reported an increase in the number of Ames members but could only guess that these resulted from the library display.

Residents of many neighborhoods in the United States have in the past taken part in attempts to restrict their areas to Caucasians only. To that end, there went into every deed the promise that the buyer would bind himself and every successor to exclusiveness. Even after the Supreme Court had declared such "restrictive covenants" legally unenforceable, they remained in the documents. Two classes of persons were likely to obey the covenant—those who did not know that they were no longer bound by law to do so and those who, aware of the legal situation, would still feel morally bound by every clause in the chain of title bearing their signature.

This situation was discussed at a 1974 Board meeting of the Cardinal Area, attended by John S. Murray, state senator as well as Board member. From the discussion came the idea of requiring each new transfer of real estate to outlaw the snobbish practice explicitly. So it came about that Murray, on March 7, 1975, introduced a bill (SF 284) to amend the law which already required filing of each instrument of transfer with the county recorder. Added to the old law would be this provision:

> The recorder shall not file an instrument conveying an interest in real estate unless the instrument contains a provision stating that any restrictive covenants on the basis of race, color, national origin, sex, creed or religion which occur in the chain of title to the real estate are invalid and unenforceable by law.

Des Moines Area Committee

The members of ICLU in Des Moines never succeeded in establishing a chapter to care for local problems, as other chapters do. In order to free the central organization of some of Des Moines' worries John Chrystal of Coon Rapids, president of ICLU, named a committee of ten residents of the city (all of them present or past members of the Board) to form a Des Moines Area Committee. Its purpose is to study and investigate civil liberties in the Des Moines area, to express its views before local governmental bodies, and to make recommendations to ICLU. David Goldman became the first chairman of the committee.[26]

An early activity was the investigation of a drug raid which had taken place at 11:00 PM, October 13, 1972, in a predominantly black area of the city. Two hundred persons, who were in two taverns, were searched and ordered to leave the area. The committee found that rights of individuals were violated when they were searched without probable cause. The committee urged the office of US District Attorney Allen L. Danielson, which worked with a special federal agent to coordinate the raid, to give assurance that no future mass raids would be made in which civil liberties of individuals were violated.[27]

As we have seen, the three active chapters covering several counties account for 29 of the state's 99 counties. The Sioux City Chapter will go beyond its county when its neighbors have cases that justify such action. The Quad City Chapter is split between two states. In Iowa it has official jurisdiction in Scott County only but will not ignore civil liberties problems in other nearby counties. Thus nearly half of the state can claim the attention of some chapter. The energy and effectiveness of chapter work will naturally vary from chapter to chapter and from year to year. Civil liberties interests in the rest of the state rely on the central ICLU.

The activity of chapters helps make ICLU a truly statewide organization. Also helpful for this purpose is the invitation to each chapter to name a member of the ICLU Board. Board members who live at a distance from the Board meeting (whether they were elected on the nomination of a chapter or by the members at large) may be reimbursed for the miles they travel in going to a meeting.

CHAPTER 16

Organization

Awards

FOR some twenty years the Iowa Civil Liberties Union has usually honored one or more persons during the annual meetings. The praise was given either because of service in and for ICLU itself or because of action promoting the ideals of the Union.

Among the former group we should name:

    Charles F. Ransom (1953)
    Donald R. Murphy (1958)
    Gilbert Cranberg (1959)
    Edward S. Allen (1961)
        also Founder's Award (1973)
    Kenneth Everhart (1963)
    Louise R. Noun (1971)

With the exception of Cranberg all these persons have occupied the presidency of ICLU. Cranberg, editorial page editor of the Des Moines Register and Tribune, has given long and valuable service as a member of ICLU, and in 1970 was elected to the Board.

George Dunn of Waterloo, who had led in the prosecution of the Surf Ballroom for exclusion of Negroes, was honored in 1954 "in recognition of his work in helping to establish new legal precedents in the field of civil liberties and in leading with vigor and self-sacrifice in the continuing struggle to maintain the Bill of Rights."[1]

In 1955 it was journalist Clark Mollenhoff who was praised "for turning the relentless spotlight of truth and simple justice in the Wolf Ladejinsky case."[2]

"FREEDOM—Study It; Understand It; Maintain It" was the title of a pamphlet published by the Iowa Farm Bureau Federation in 1955. For this contribution to the cause of liberty ICLU gave the 1956 award to its authors, W. Robert Parks (then professor, later president of Iowa State University) and Joseph F. Wall (then professor, later dean of Grinnell College).

In 1959 a program of federal loans to college and university students was begun, which required each one benefiting from it to sign a political disclaimer. The Board of Regents, who direct the state universities, were among those making a vigorous protest. Grinnell College rejected all money that would thus cut down on freedom. In praise of this action ICLU honored that college in 1960. Howard R. Bowen, its president, in accepting the award, made it clear that it was not he alone but the entire college which merited praise. Norman Thomas of New York, long a leader of the Socialist Party and six times its presidential candidate, was one of the founders of ACLU and a devoted member of its Board ever after that. He was the speaker at that annual meeting of ICLU and received a similar award.

St. Paul's Methodist Church in Cedar Rapids aroused resentment by selling a house it owned—a house in a "white" neighborhood—to a Negro. For this action against racial segregation in housing the church received praise from ICLU in 1962. At the same meeting Bishop F. Gerald Ensley of the Methodist Church was commended for his work for democratic education and for his stand against groups whose activities threaten the Bill of Rights.[3]

In 1965 two awards were given. Donald E. Boles, who had worked diligently on the relations between church and state, was cited "for his distinguished service to the cause of civil rights in Iowa for many years and particularly for his work as chairman of the Governor's Commission on Human Rights." The second award went to Joseph R. Knock, who had served in a Freedom School at McComb, Mississippi, the previous summer. His citation reads: "In recognition of his own services to the cause of racial justice and also because he represents the many Iowa young people who went to Mississippi and other states to work in Freedom Schools and in the campaign for full voter registration."[4]

Dan Johnston was honored in 1969 for his presentation of the armband case to the Supreme Court, his help in obtaining volunteer attorneys to represent the ACLU, and for other services in supporting civil liberties.[5]

In 1970 Governor Robert D. Ray received the award for his veto of a bill that would have legalized wiretapping in Iowa. In receiving the award Governor Ray said: "The rights, liberties and freedoms of this country do not belong to any one group, sex, color or creed, but are the property of all our citizens. These priceless virtues are for the benefit of our people and likewise to be respected by our people."[6]

Francis H. Becker, a member of the Iowa Supreme Court from 1965 to 1972, received the 1972 award of ICLU from its president, Louise Noun. She pointed out that Justice Becker, while on the court, was often at his best when speaking and writing for himself in dissent. His dissent in the Grinnell *Playboy* case (in which some students disrobed to protest *Playboy*'s exploitation of sex) said: "Despite the majority assertion to the contrary, defendants were protesting what to them is an important issue. Here the free expression of ideas is in fact being inhibited by a vague reference to violation of the 'accepted norms of social behavior.' Our democracy has enough strength and vitality to withstand such shocking conduct without resort to criminal sanction."[7]

At the annual meeting in 1974 two persons were honored for outstanding contributions to civil liberties. Roxanne Conlin, assistant attorney general of Iowa, had been active in pressing legal actions involving civil rights cases as well as in efforts on behalf of equality of women. Arthur Bonfield, professor of law in the University of Iowa, had had an important role in drafting the Iowa Civil Rights Act in 1965 and had worked on the Administrative Procedures Act passed by the General Assembly in 1974—an act to protect individual rights before state agencies and boards.[8]

The Iowa area office of the American Friends Service Committee received an award from ICLU in 1975. That office's efforts in the areas of criminal justice reform and peace education were recognized as having served to strengthen the constitutionally derived rights of all Iowans. At the same time William Faches, former Linn County attorney, received a similar award for his exposure of violation of civil rights by Cedar Rapids police.

In 1976 those receiving awards were Claudia Morrissey, who was ending her service as executive director, and Gordon Allen, continuing as legal director.

The variety of grounds for presenting these awards gives some idea of the breadth of ICLU's involvement in the work for freedom and equality.

Publications

As early as 1936—the second year of existence for ICLU—a publication called the _Bulletin_ was sent to its members. In 1960 the title was changed to _The Defender_. There was rarely a regular schedule of publication; usually four numbers appeared annually. Lately, the number of issues in a year has been at least six.

Editorial headquarters have been located in Des Moines except for a period in the 1950s when preparation and publication of the paper took place in Ames. At that time the printing service of Iowa State College was willing to care for both printing (by mimeograph) and distribution, paid for by ICLU. A group of members in Ames served as authors and editors. The activity of ICLU in the state then reached a level that allowed the _Bulletin_ to go beyond the borders of Iowa for its news and comments. The contents of one number (Nov. 1953), chosen at random, will serve as a sample. It begins with a quotation from President Truman: "If we deny freedom to the least among us, we cannot protect the rights of the rest of us." Then the following items:

Our treasury—with an appeal for more members
Corliss Lamont and Joseph McCarthy (defense of Lamont's refusal to answer questions)
Insomnia—quotation from _The Reporter_
Praise for the Board of Education (now Board of Regents) for its handling of anonymous attacks on professors

Praise for Attorney General Hoegh. He had reminded hotels of their
    duty under the Civil Rights Law.
Congress and UN. Claim by the United States of the right to screen
    its citizens to be employed by the United Nations. Presbyter-
    ians take a stand on Congressional investigations.
Supreme Court decisions
"Jeffersonian Heritage"—a phonograph record available
Random reading remarks—
    The defense of everybody: The New Yorker on Roger N. Baldwin
    How to be a security risk; Sarah Lawrence vs. The Legion: The
        Humanist
Gagging information service—Frederick Kuh in Chicago Sun-Times
Then follow a dozen briefer items, of which less than half would
    cheer those devoted to civil liberties.[8]

By 1971 the affairs of Iowa took all the space of The Defender for March. Written while the General Assembly was in session, three sections discussed the proposal that tenure in the state universities be replaced by contracts running five years or less. Three sections urged a reform of the court system, particularly the abolition of justices of the peace—persons of whom little legal knowledge is required and who often have strong incentives to be biased. Further sections gave advance notice of the annual meeting, endorsed a bill that would authorize employment of conscientious objectors by municipalities, expressed interest in court action on abortion, called for good funding of the Iowa Civil Rights Commission, opposed sex discrimination in housing rules at the University of Iowa. One page was devoted to school rules about boys' hair styles. It was reported that the US Supreme Court refused to review the decision of the Iowa Supreme Court, according to which Grinnell College students were fined for undressing as an act of protest. (These two subjects are treated at some length in Chapter 9.) A final item noted that the refusal of the US Supreme Court to review another decision benefited a second Grinnell group—those whose underground Pterodactyl, while still in manuscript form, had been given by the printer to Attorney General Richard Turner.

Louise R. Noun, president of ICLU, is the author of Strong-Minded Women, a history of the woman-suffrage movement in Iowa, published in 1969. The author generously assigned all royalties from the sale of her book to ICLU. Since the right to vote is among the most important civil liberties, the writing of this work is strong testimony to Louise Noun's devotion to equality in all basic rights.[9]

Donald R. Murphy, of the editorial staff of Wallaces Farmer, joined the Union in its first years; he became one of the most effective chairmen of the Union and was a member of the Board of Directors as long as his health permitted. He was among the few Iowans elected to the Advisory Committee (successor of the National Committee) of ACLU. (Louise Noun received this honor in 1974.) In his honor a Donald Murphy Book Fund was established by ICLU. In 1972 the fund was used to enable ICLU to give copies of

Eternal Vigilance: The American Civil Liberties Union in Action by Barbara Habenstreit to high school libraries. The 23 schools receiving the book were chosen by the chapters of ICLU and, in Des Moines, by the central organization. (The librarian of Boone Senior High School, when offered the book, showed the copy he had already acquired and put in circulation.) This is the first book about the ACLU written especially for young persons but is also suitable for anyone who wants to understand the concepts of civil liberties.[11]

"WHAT'S DOING WITH THE ICLU?" is an activities report sent to members of the boards of ICLU and its chapters and others "in leadership position." It was initiated in the autumn of 1973 by Herbert D. Kelly, at that time executive secretary of ICLU. Appearing between issues of The Defender, it was intended to give more immediate—and at times more detailed—information than would appear in the long-established publication. The new bulletin's first issue stated that it would be published "more or less" regularly.

Finances

At the outset ICLU was, in both finances and membership, independent of ACLU. A person could be a member of either without belonging to the other. However, as early as December 1935 (the end of the Iowa Union's first year) there was a mutual agreement: if an Iowan contributed $3.00 or more to ACLU, ICLU would receive $1.00; likewise, if one gave $3.00 or more to ICLU as dues, ACLU would get $2.00 of it.

Dues for ICLU began at $1.00 a year, though most members contributed $2.00. Records from early years (largely from papers preserved and then transmitted by Esther Immer, former treasurer and secretary) show wide fluctuations in the amounts collected and spent. Usually the money passing through the treasurer's hands was small in amount; however, it was augmented substantially when there was special need.

From October 19, 1935, to November 7, 1936, income was $60.00, of which $10.00 went to the New York office. For the 15 months preceding July 1, 1940, $83.95 was paid out, of which $11.00 went to ACLU. (We have no record of dues paid by Iowans direct to New York.) A treasurer's report (by Esther Immer) shows that from December 1, 1943, to June 10, 1944, only $18.00 was collected and $12.60 spent—including $3.00 designated for ACLU. From November 18, 1947, to January 20, 1949, the bank statement shows deposits of $727.20. This was the period of the Coppock case, when money was frequently donated for this specific cause.

The financial quasi separation of ACLU and ICLU ended in June 1951, after long study as to just and feasible methods of integration. At that time about 150 persons in Iowa belonged to one or both of the Unions. For the twelve-month period ending January 31, 1951, the ACLU income from the Iowa area had been $575. From then on every Iowa member of one of the two organizations became an ipso facto member of the other. Other affiliates had preceded Iowa in

Organization   135

integration. The process was completed in the United States by 1972.

A complete account of the gradual increase of ICLU in membership and income would be tedious. The dimensions of the growth are shown by certain recent figures, furnished by Herbert Kelly, executive secretary.

Year	Membership	Income
1964		$13,062
1965		6,304
1966	773	10,969
1967	732	11,609
1968	980	15,488
1969	908	10,680
1970	1161	12,169
1971		11,148
1972	1221	12,307
1973	1726	13,586
1974	1600	17,313
1975	1700	27,973

To the income given above must be added, from 1970 on, that of the Iowa Civil Liberties Foundation. The contributors to this Foundation may deduct their gifts from taxable income; the resulting fund may not be used for influencing legislation. This income has been:

1970	$ 5,669
1971	5,683
1972	7,108
1973	10,010
1974	4,989
1975	13,218

From 1969 on, the membership figures do not tell the actual number of persons who belong to ICLU. A "Mr. and Mrs. membership" was then introduced; we have no record of how many of the memberships account for pairs.

Apportionment of dues and contributions originating in Iowa between ACLU and ICLU has been made according to various patterns; the assignment of 60 percent to the affiliate is typical.

Presidents and Staff

Dates of accession are given; in some cases they are slightly uncertain.

Presidents (or Chairmen)

1935 Edward S. Allen   Iowa State University (mathematics); also active in AAUP

Year	Name	Description
1938	Hortense N. Dillon	Lawyer; author of ICLU study on criminal syndicalism laws
1940	Willard Johnson	Plymouth Congregational Church; Drake University; National Council of Christians and Jews
1942	Luther W. Stalnaker	Drake University (Dean)
1944	Edward S. Allen	
1945	Grant Butler	Unitarian minister
1948	R. J. Blakely	Des Moines Register and Tribune (editorial staff)
1949	Edward S. Allen	
1951	Donald R. Murphy	Wallaces Farmer (editor)
1953	Charles F. Ransom	Des Moines Register and Tribune (editorial staff)
1954	Kenneth Everhart	Labor organizer, AFL/CIO
1962	Sydney Levine	Lawyer
1964	Louise R. Noun	Des Moines League of Women Voters (president); Des Moines Art Center (member, Board of Trustees); author of Strong-Minded Women
1972	John Chrystal	Banker; State Superintendent of Banking when he became president of ICLU
1974	Russell G. Pounds	Iowa State University (economics)
1975	Elizabeth Turner	Iowa School of Social Work; Des Moines Area Community College

All were residents of Des Moines except Allen and Pounds (Ames) and Chrystal (Coon Rapids).

Employed Staff

Katherine Bertin became secretary in 1958 and later (1965) was granted a salary as executive secretary. In this post she was succeeded by Oval Quist (1965), Herbert D. Kelly (1968), Claudia Morrissey (1974), and Howard Weinberg (1976). Soon after Morrissey's appointment the title of the office was changed to executive director.

Dan Johnston was counsel for ICLU, 1966-72; Gordon Allen became staff attorney in 1972. In 1975 Gordon Allen formed a legal firm together with Leslie Babich and Mark W. Bennett; this firm then signed a contract with ICLU for legal services. The contract replaced the previous form of relationship with Allen, who remained the one member of the firm most concerned with and knowledgeable about the ideals and practices of ICLU. At the same time Allen, Babich, and Bennett and ICLU moved to new quarters with adjoining offices (102 E. Grand Avenue) in Des Moines. This arrangement gave ICLU the advantage of direct access to the firm's law library and a shortened distance from the offices of state government—including its law library.

For the sake of readers who may wish to communicate with ICLU or ACLU (e.g., as to membership, offers of assistance) we give their respective addresses:

Iowa Civil Liberties Union
102 E. Grand
Des Moines, Iowa 50309

American Civil Liberties Union
22 E. 40th St.
New York, NY 10016

APPENDIX 1

Correspondence Relating to the 1940 Resolution

509 Welch Ave.
Ames, Iowa
18 June, 1952

Mr. Ernest Angell
156 E. 66th St.
New York, N.Y.

Dear Mr. Angell,

    Only today did I receive the minutes of the Board Meeting of June 4, and I must say that I am terribly depressed by the last item. The Board of Directors submitted to the representatives of the affiliates a draft of new by-laws which omitted the 1940 resolution—both the text and all reference to the text. In the affiliates' conference not a voice, I believe, was raised for such inclusion; in fact, there was only satisfaction that we could hope instead of it to have an all-inclusive insistence on positive demonstration of loyalty to freedom for all.
    Members of the Board of Directors, if they wished to speak for the insertion of the old resolution in the by-laws, might well have done so when there was an opportunity for us, who came from afar, to have our opinions heard—either in the first sessions of the conference or at the Board meeting on May 14. In fact, I was surprised that the whole document was not made part of the agenda at that time, but naturally assumed that nothing would be inserted which was neither in the draft submitted nor in the amendments proposed in the affiliates' conference.
    These considerations would apply to any charges which might be made after our departure, regardless of my own views on their merits. As to this particular one, I should like to state a few of the reasons why the resolution of 1940 has never had the approval of me or of the Iowa Civil Liberties Union.
    It overemphasizes just one criterion of loyalty to our principles—that of affiliation, which we generally recognize to be one

Appendix 1 139

of the least reliable tests—and does it in a purely negative way.

It puts us in the class of those who, gratuitously boasting of not being Communist, help create an atmosphere in which persecution threatens Communists, those who associate with them for any purpose, those who announce agreement with any of their stated goals, even those who would defend the rights of any of the foregoing classes.

It makes it difficult for others to believe in the sincerity with which we claim for Communists—for instance—the right to employment as teachers.

Not only the Iowa Civil Liberties Union but a large fraction of the other affiliates disapproved of the resolution when it was first adopted; their opinion, however, was not sought. Some, at least, of those more recently founded have affirmed it only because it was made a condition for their recognition. Insistence on that statement, verbatim, when its whole intent—and much more—are implicit in the text agreed to in the May conference this year, works grievously against that unity of spirit which we should have, and which the other changes made in the by-laws will, to our gratification, substantially promote.

What can be done now? I would urge that, when the new constitution and by-laws are submitted to the Corporation, the insertion made on June 4 be the subject of a separate vote, and that that vote not be requested until all the Corporation have had an opportunity to hear from those who differ with the Board of Directors. Will you be so good as to present those considerations to the Board as soon as possible?

Yours sincerely,

(Signed) Edward S. Allen

June 21, 1951

Mr. Edward S. Allen, Chairman
Iowa Civil Liberties Union
509 Welch Avenue
Ames, Iowa

Dear Ed:

Pat has given me your letter of June 18, addressed to Ernest Angell.

The draft of the new by-laws submitted to the delegates of the Conference, as you know, was tentative and was marked "Office Draft." It was presented to the delegates for suggestions and amendment, with the explanation that the draft which came out of the Conference would be submitted to the Board of Directors and the Corporation, as required by the old by-laws under which we still operate.

I recall the discussion on the 1940 Resolution, and I remember that Pat specifically told the Conference that he did not believe that the Board would repeal the 1940 Resolution, and that he thought the Board would be willing to continue the 1948 policy of seeing that it was applied in practice even though not formally adopted by some. The amendment to the by-laws, referred to in the minutes of June 4, item 6, should be interpreted that way. There was much discussion at the Board meeting concerning application of the 1940 Resolution to the affiliates, and after several motions, Norman Thomas suggested the wording which was approved for submission to the Corporation. I am sure that you will agree that the Board also has the privilege of amending statements submitted to it for its opinion before submission to the Corporation.

In your second paragraph, you express the opinion that members of the Board of Directors who were present during the Conference should have expressed opinions about the insertion of the Resolution in the by-laws. Board members attending the Conference could not speak for the whole body. The amendment you object to resulted from the review and discussion by the Board of the approved Conference draft. Dorothy Bromley, Walter Frank and William Fitelson on Thursday night clearly expressed the opinion that the Board would not repeal the 1940 Resolution. The hope was expressed by some of us that the wording of paragraph (b), on page 2 of the draft of the by-laws (approved by the Conference, May 10-14), would be satisfactory to the Board of Directors and that the action of the Board in 1948, reaffirming the 1940 Resolution as it applied to new affiliates, would only be brought up on such occasions as there were applications for affiliation.

The proposed by-laws, as amended, and sent to the Corporation, are subject to further amendment. Note Section 11, page 7, of the draft you have received, and Section 14, page 7, of the by-laws under which we are still operating, dated April 3, 1950.

You will note in the letter dated June 13 to the members of the Corporation concerning revision of the by-laws, that in the last paragraph it is noted that the affiliates may not be meeting during the summer months and no final action will be taken until all are heard from. We will, of course, bring to the attention of the Board any objections that are raised by the affiliates.

Concerning your reasons for disapproving the 1940 Resolution, the Board, in the past, has had the benefit of all of the arguments for and against the Resolution, but it is of the opinion that the Union must clearly state, particularly at this time, qualifications for membership on its governing bodies and staff.

Pat has let me see your letters of June 2 and 16, and if there are any questions unanswered, I'll see that the information is forwarded to you by the member of the staff best qualified to give you the facts.

With all good wishes, I am

Sincerely,

George E. Rundquist
Assistant Director

APPENDIX 2

Three Statements of ACLU Concerning the 1940 Resolution

May 8, 1953

STATEMENT ON: NATURE OF COMMUNIST PARTY
DEFENSE OF CIVIL LIBERTIES REGARDLESS OF ASSOCIATIONS
ALLOWABLE CONSIDERATION OF ASSOCIATIONS (IN GENERAL)

On February 5, 1940, the American Civil Liberties Union adopted a resolution barring from its governing bodies and staff any person "who is a member of any political organization which supports totalitarian dictatorship in any country (including the American Communist Party, the German-American Bund and any native organizations with obvious anti-democratic objectives or practices), or who by his public declarations indicates his support of such a principle." On January 17, 1949, the Union adopted a resolution reiterating its opposition to "any form of the police state or the single party state, or any movement in support of them, whether Fascist, Communist or known by any other name."

The ACLU holds that the American Communist Party is distinctively and essentially characterized both by extreme anti-democratic doctrine and practice and by obedience to the government of the Soviet Union, a despotic foreign power which dominates a world-wide revolutionary movement unprecedentedly threatening the national independence and individual civil liberties of all other countries. It is thus sharply differentiated from traditional American political parties, and all its present adherents are to some degree involved in its distinctive and essential character.

The ACLU does not hold that all persons who submit to the Communist Party's rigid totalitarian discipline (whether formal members or not), or even all those who are its leaders, are engaged in illegal secret conspiracy or illegal acts. And since the Union is opposed to any tendency by which American democracy might stoop to the level of Communist tyranny in withholding any civil liberties from Communists (or Fascists, Ku Kluxers or adherents of other totalitarian doctrines), including the Constitutional rights of due process, equal protection of the law, and freedom of speech, press and association, it will defend those rights regardless of the associations of individuals to whom they may be denied.

But: (1) It is not a violation of civil liberties to take into account a person's voluntary choice of association when that choice is relevant to a particular judgment—providing that such a judgment is not indiscriminate or automatic, but specific and comprehensive in weighing all relevant factors. (2) There are a number of judgments wherein it is relevant, just as there are judgments wherein it is not relevant, to discipline of the Communist Party. This is not to condone "guilt by association" in the reprehensible sense of holding a person guilty of believing or doing what someone else with whom he is (often remotely) connected believes or does. And, in taking a person's adherence to the Communist Party into account, weight must be given to the time and circumstance of such adherence and to its duration and, if terminated, the sincerity of its termination. It is particularly important that persons not be penalized because of an association which has been abandoned.

STATEMENT ON: ALLOWABLE CONSIDERATION OF ASSOCIATIONS
(IN EDUCATIONAL AND UNITED NATIONS EMPLOYMENT)

(a) Regarding educational employment: The ACLU reaffirms the two-fold position set forth in its April 1952 statement on "Academic Freedom and Academic Responsibility":

> It is [a teacher's] duty . . . not to advocate any opinions or convictions derived from a source other than his own free and unbiased pursuit of truth and understanding. Commitments of any kind which interfere with such pursuit are incompatible with the objectives of academic freedom. . . . The ACLU does not oppose the ouster or rejection of any teacher found lacking in professional integrity. . . . On the other hand, the ACLU steadfastly opposes any ban or regulation which would prohibit the educational employment of any person solely because of his personal views or associations (political, religious or otherwise). Even though a teacher may be linked with religious dogmatists or political authoritarians, the ACLU believes that he must nevertheless be appraised as an individual. . . . The ACLU will intervene in appropriate cases involving the discharge of a teacher when action is taken by administrative officials without a prior unfavorable judgment by the teacher's colleagues based on professional incompetence, immoral conduct, or perversion of academic process.

(b) Regarding the United Nations employment: The ACLU does not oppose the application by the United Nations to its employees of a program, aimed at promoting the integrity of the United Nations and the security of each of its member nations, and based on the following principles: (1) The program should be aimed, not at making United Nations' employees of any nationality the servants of their government instead of their employer the United Nations, which would be contrary to United Nations principles; but at preventing its employees of any nationality (or without any nationality) from wrongly serving the interests of any government instead of their employer the United Nations, and thus—among other things—preventing its employees of any nationality from wrongly serving the interests of any other government against their own. (2) The program should be framed and administered, not by any member government, but by the United Nations as a whole. (3) The program should honor the principles previously proposed by the ACLU for the American government's security and loyalty program for its employees, with due regard to recognized principles of due process.

STATEMENT ON: PROPRIETY OF QUESTIONS AND COMPETENCY OF AUTHORITY
REFUSALS TO ANSWER QUESTIONS ABOUT ASSOCIATIONS
ALLOWABLE CONSIDERATION OF SUCH REFUSALS (IN GOVERNMENT, UNITED NATIONS AND EDUCATIONAL EMPLOYMENT)

Questions concerning possible violation of any law may be asked by any authority legally responsible for upholding that law. Questions concerning any other matter may properly be asked only if information thereon is relevant to a purpose legally permissible to the authority asking the questions. For example, questions concerning Communist or other totalitarian associations which are not illegal should, in the case of a legislative committee, generally be limited to the purpose of possible legislation within its purview. But any authority legally responsible for employment to which information concerning Communist or other totalitarian associations is relevant may ask questions concerning such associations.

The ACLU heartily supports the rights guaranteed by the Fifth Amendment, and fully recognizes that a person, in availing himself of the privilege against self-incrimination guaranteed therein, does not thereby justify an imputation of guilt of any crime. But the exercise of that privilege does not challenge the propriety of the question to which answer is refused or the competency of the authority asking it, nor does it carry protection against any consequence of having exercised it except the imputation of criminal guilt. And the ACLU recognizes that there are certain situations in which a person's exercise of the privilege may be inconsistent with his duty of full disclosure toward an employer, whether public or private. For example, there are certain types of work with regard to which it is legitimate for an employer or prospective employer to consider whether a person has surrendered his judgment to control by some totalitarian organization—Ku Klux, Fascist, Communist, etc. Therefore, we believe that it is not a violation of civil liberties for employers in those types of work—including government, the United Nations, and educational authorities—to take into account the refusal of an employee or prospective employee, on the ground of possible self-incrimination, to answer questions asked by any duly constituted authority and relating to his present, recent or pertinently past membership in, or submission to the discipline of, the Communist Party or other totalitarian organizations, and to give such weight to the refusal as may be appropriate in the particular circumstances. This position is taken without prejudice to our examination of cases of such refusal which may present extenuating circumstances.

Although it should be emphasized that the proposition has not been judicially established, the ACLU will continue to maintain that a person, by refusing to answer on the ground of the First Amendment's protection of free association, may challenge the propriety of any question concerning his or another person's Communist or other totalitarian associations. And the ACLU will continue to maintain that he may also, on proper grounds, challenge the competency of any authority to ask such a question. But we believe that it is not a violation of civil liberties for authorities legally responsible for employment in certain areas—including government, the United Nations and education—to ask, before or after such a challenge, questions relating to an employee or prospective employee's present, recent or pertinently past membership in, or submission to the discipline of, the Communist Party or other totalitarian organizations, and—if he refuses to answer—to take into account that refusal and give it such weight as may be appropriate in the particular circumstances. This position is taken without prejudice to our examination of cases of such refusal which may present extenuating circumstances.

Any judgment on qualification for employment which takes into account either sort of refusal to answer questions concerning membership in or submission to the discipline of the Communist Party or other totalitarian organizations should be, like any judgment taking into account such associations themselves, not indiscriminate or automatic, but specific and comprehensive in weighing all relevant factors. And, as in all matters, due process appropriate to the particular employment should be scrupulously observed.

When an external investigation causes an employer to re-examine the fitness of an employee to hold his position, it is of vital importance that the employer give full consideration to the employee's entire record of past service, including appropriate recognition of any tenure rights the employee may have. Doubts in the employer's mind about an employee's continued fitness for his position as a result of the employee's conduct in an external investigation should not be allowed to outweigh or obscure an overall employment record of competent service and personal integrity.

As for employees of the United Nations, we recall the pledge of all member nations not to attempt to influence the conduct of the secretariat, and note that current inquiries have often the intent and effect of violating that pledge. Such an employee's refusal to speak may well express his protest against that violation.

We believe that a witness asked about personal beliefs, and associations relevant only as an index to beliefs, should have a right to refuse to answer on First Amendment grounds. We recognize that the courts have so far failed to uphold witnesses in this claim and that our attitude toward the Fifth Amendment must take into consideration the fact that rights more closely related to the First Amendment are being forced to seek the shelter of the Fifth.

APPENDIX 3

Statement of ICLU Relating to the 1940 Resolution

June 1, 1964

We, the Board of Directors of the Iowa Civil Liberties Union, are happy that we can participate in the coming Conference of the American Civil Liberties Union at Boulder, Colorado. We urge that, among the important matters to be discussed there, the Resolution of 1940 and later actions related to it be accorded a place on the agenda.

The Resolution was passed on February 5, 1940, and says in part:

> The Board of Directors and the National Committee of the American Civil Liberties Union hold it inappropriate for any person to serve on the governing committees of the Union or on its staff, who is a member of any political organization which supports totalitarian dictatorship in any country, or who by his public declarations indicates his support of such a principle.
> Within this category we include organizations in the United States supporting the totalitarian governments of the Soviet Union and of the Fascist and Nazi countries (such as the Communist Party, the German-American Bund and others); as well as native organizations with obvious anti-democratic objectives or practices.

The Resolution has had favorable effects—higher regard for the ACLU among the general public, probably greater financial support, heightened ability to defend Communists and persons accused of too close proximity to them.

In spite of this, we find grounds to regret the Resolution's passage. The affiliates were not consulted; this fact alone detracts from its moral force. It was passed against the opposition of many firm supporters of civil liberties and of the Union, and immediately caused the resignation of a number of them. They saw in the Resolution (as we do now) a violation of the basic principles of the American Civil Liberties Union—they saw in it a recognition of guilt by association, of punishment without proof of personal wrong-doing.

In one of the earliest conferences of affiliates with the American Civil Liberties Union in New York (about 1954) an agreement was reached that certain important statements of policy should have no specific reference to Communists (or other groups) but only to our devotion to the principles of freedom. Within a few weeks, however, the Board passed a motion that provisions in the By-Laws must be interpreted in accordance with the Resolution of 1940. Thus for the first time, the By-Laws explicitly named Communists (and members of the German-American Bund, long non-existent), even if only by reference.

In conformity with the Resolution in question, the Board of Directors has insisted that new affiliates incorporate it into their own Constitution or By-Laws. At least one has objected vigorously, but to no avail. Others may well have deprived themselves of firm advocates of civil liberties (and there are notable ones) who oppose the Resolution.

Yet another action of the Board of Directors in the same direction—again without sanction of the affiliates—was the insertion, on blanks of application for membership, of the sentence: "The ACLU needs and welcomes the support of all those and only those whose devotion to civil liberties is not qualified by adherence to Communist, Fascist, KKK or other totalitarian doctrine."

Our most important objection to the Resolution of 1940 and the related measures is that they support and encourage that undiscriminating anti-Communist public opinion which has made the maintenance of freedom of speech and assemblage so difficult. It leads people to say: "If the Civil Liberties Union itself excludes Communists, why should we not also deny them a voice, employment, housing, passports?" No argument of ours can alter the fact that we have definitely contributed to a biased atmosphere. The Resolution has narrowed the scope of those civil liberties which the American Civil Liberties Union is able and willing to defend.

We object, also, to the Resolution because of the disregard for the opinions of the affiliates in its passage and in later actions for its implementation.

The present is a particularly opportune time for a change on the part of the ACLU. More than ever, it is important not to treat Communism as a single, evil thing, but to distinguish among types of Communists and among acts of Communists. This is a time when uncritical anti-Communism has led the United States—e.g., in its policies as to China, Cuba, South Vietnam—to acts which excite an unusual degree of disapproval abroad, even in nations normally friendly to us.

George F. Kennan, in his foreword to "On dealing with the Communist world," says: "I think there could be no more useful innovation in the discussion, public and governmental, of the affairs of the 'Communist' orb, than a law which forbade all of us, including myself, to use the word 'Communist' at all, and forced us to treat the regimes and peoples of each of these countries specifically, for what they are." The same principle should require the ACLU to consider every person who is invited to membership or considered for appointment for what he is, not for the groups with which he is associated.

A member of the Communist Party, an outspoken admirer of a particular "Communist" country is no more certain to approve of the whole program of the party or of all policies of the country than an ACLU member is sure to approve of the Resolution of 1940.

What, then, is to be done? We would recommend the following actions:

1. Repeal of the 1940 Resolution.
2. Repeal of the reference to it in the interpretation of Constitution and By-Laws.
3. Abolition of the requirement that new affiliates subject their own staffs and committees on the restrictions of the Resolution.
4. Removal of reference to particular groups in the welcome to membership. The least drastic acceptable change would lead us to say: "The ACLU needs and welcomes the support of all those and only those whose devotion to civil liberties is not qualified by adherence to totalitarian doctrine."

This is being sent to the chief officers of the American Civil Liberties Union, of its Board of Directors, of the National Committee and to all affiliates. We hope there is still time for each to consider this matter before the Boulder Conference.

We shall welcome all comments, and will supply additional copies on request.

APPENDIX 4

Statement from the State Board of Regents, July 1970

In recent months this Board has given, and will continue to give, intensive consideration to campus unrest. We have noted that throughout the nation recent events, including campus disorders, have raised serious questions about the ability of universities to continue to serve as effective centers of learning. The conditions which have produced these events are national, and even international, in scope. The causes are multiple and the solutions not simple. While we work as a nation toward the solution of the underlying problems of our society, we must also insure that our universities remain open as centers of free inquiry. This Board, charged by law with the responsibility for the governance of the public universities of Iowa, reaffirms the following beliefs and intentions which will continue to serve as bases for the discharge of the Board's responsibilities.

1. The citizens of this State have established and supported the state universities in order to make higher education available at reasonable cost. It is the responsibility of this Board to insure that this purpose is not subverted.
2. Neither violence nor the threat of violence has any place in a university.
3. Freedom of inquiry and freedom of expression are indispensable elements of academic life.
4. The freedom to express dissent by lawful means, including peaceable assembly and petitions to authorities, is no less important on a university campus than elsewhere in our society.
5. The exercise of this freedom to dissent must not interfere with the rights of others.
6. Adaptation and change are necessary processes by which an institution renews and preserves itself.

In line with these beliefs, the Board adopted at its July 1970 meeting a Code of Personal Conduct and also two formal policy statements relating to (1) a prohibition against the universities' becoming instruments of political action and (2) university closings. These statements follow.

UNIFORM RULES OF PERSONAL CONDUCT AT UNIVERSITIES UNDER THE JURISDICTION OF THE STATE BOARD OF REGENTS
(Adopted by Board of Regents, July 1970)

(1) <u>Definitions</u>. For purposes of these rules, the following words shall have the meaning set forth unless the context requires otherwise:
   (a) . . .
   (k) "Suspension" of a student means that during the period of suspension, the student shall be denied admission to the university and as a condition precedent to admission following the period of suspension, the student must satisfy the president of the university that he is unlikely to disrupt the orderly processes of the university in the future.
(2) <u>Rules of Personal Conduct</u>. Any person—student, member of the faculty or staff, visitor—who commits or attempts to commit any of the following acts of misconduct shall be subject to disciplinary procedures by the university as hereinafter provided:
   (a) Intentional obstruction or disruption of teaching, research, administration, disciplinary procedures, or other university or university-authorized function or event.
   (b) Unauthorized occupation or use of or unauthorized entry into any university facility.
   (c) Physical abuse or the threat of physical abuse against any person on the campus or at any university-authorized function or event, or other conduct which threatens or endangers the health or safety of any such person.
   (d) Theft or damage to property of the university or of a person on the campus.
   (e) Intentional interference with the right of access to university facilities or with any other lawful right of any person on the campus.
   (f) Setting a fire on the campus without proper authority.
   (g) Use or possession on the campus of firearms, ammunition, or other dangerous weapons, substances, or materials (except as expressly authorized by the university), or of bombs, explosives, or explosive or incendiary devices prohibited by law.
   (h) Aid others in committing or incite others to commit any act of misconduct set forth in (a) through (g) above.
(3) <u>Sanctions</u>. Any person who, after appropriate hearing,* is found to have violated any of the foregoing rules of personal conduct shall be subject to the following sanctions:

---

*This means pursuant to existing hearing procedures in effect at the university for students and members of the faculty and staff.

Appendix 4   151

   (a) Any student or member of the faculty or staff who is found
       to have violated any of the rules of personal conduct set
       forth in (2) above may be sanctioned up to and including
       suspension, expulsion or dismissal. If the violation is
       found to be of a serious nature or to have contributed to a
       substantial disruption of the orderly processes of the uni-
       versity, then such student or member of the faculty or
       staff shall, at a minimum, be suspended or dismissed from
       the university immediately following such finding for one
       academic year. If a suspension or dismissal is ordered
       after the start of a semester or quarter, however, the
       time period of the suspension or dismissal shall be deemed
       to run from the beginning of the semester or quarter rather
       than from the actual date of the order. A faculty or staff
       member who is dismissed shall receive no salary during the
       period of his dismissal; provided, however, that he shall
       be paid for work done prior to the date of the dismissal
       order.
   (b) A visitor to the campus who is found to have violated any
       of the rules of personal conduct set forth in (2) above
       may be permanently denied admission to or employment by
       the university. If the violation is found to be of a seri-
       ous nature or to have contributed to a substantial dis-
       ruption of the orderly processes of the university, then
       such visitor shall, at a minimum, be denied admission or
       employment for twelve months immediately following the vi-
       olation.
   (c) Any sanction imposed under (a) or (b) above shall have op-
       erative effect at all universities, and a person not eli-
       gible for admission to or employment by one university
       shall be barred similarly at the other universities.
(4) Temporary Bar from Campus. The president of the university is
    authorized to bar from the campus any student or member of the
    faculty or staff who, in the president's judgment, has com-
    mitted an act of misconduct in violation of the rules of per-
    sonal conduct set forth in (2) above and whose continued pres-
    ence on the campus constitutes a clear and present danger to
    the orderly processes of the university.
   (a) The president's order barring such a person from the cam-
       pus may be made without prior hearing and may permit access
       to the campus for such limited purposes as attending or
       teaching classes, or preparing for and attending the hear-
       ing of the charges against him. In any case where the
       president's order permits a person access to the campus
       for limited purpose, the president may impose appropriate
       conditions in such right of access.
   (b) A member of the faculty or staff temporarily barred from
       the campus shall continue receiving his pay until the dis-
       position of the charges against him by the university and
       the board.
   (c) An appropriate hearing on the charges shall, if at all

practicable, be held within ten days after the date of the president's order barring the person from the campus but in no event more than twenty days thereafter.
(d) Despite a finding at the hearing that a person temporarily barred from the campus did not commit an act of misconduct in violation of the rules of personal conduct set forth in (2) above and, thus, is not subject to sanction on that basis, such person may be sanctioned up to and including expulsion or dismissal upon a finding that he violated the president's order barring him from the campus. Upon such a finding, such person shall, at a minimum, be suspended or dismissed from the university immediately following such a finding, for one academic year, as provided in (3) (a) above. This sanction shall have the operative effect provided in (3) (c) above.
(5) <u>Constitutional Rights</u>. The foregoing rules shall be construed so as not to abridge any person's constitutional right of free expression of thought or opinion, including the traditional American right to assemble peaceably and to petition authorities.

ICLU Statement on Regents' Uniform Rules of Personal Conduct

Disturbances on the campuses of Iowa's three state universities in the spring of 1970 resulted in the formulation by the Board of Regents of uniform rules of personal conduct at the universities. The process by which these rules were promulgated and the implications for the civil liberties of the citizens of this state and the students, staff and faculty of the universities are of great concern to the Iowa Civil Liberties Union. The ICLU is obligated to express its concern by raising the possibility that these rules and the method by which they came into existence may diminish the reputations of our state universities and endanger fundamental concepts of due process to which all citizens and residents of this state are entitled.

The question of whether such rules are needed at all is by no means settled. It has been argued that the civil statutes are adequate to cover the kinds of disturbances encountered by University administrators and civil authorities last spring. This question, as well as the substance of any rules governing behavior at these institutions, should have been considered by appropriate representatives of the staff, faculty and student bodies, in joint meeting with the Regents. This was not the case. The rules were approved by the Board during the summer without the consultation of any representatives of those persons most likely to be affected by them. The ICLU supports the recent statement by the American Civil Liberties Union on "Academic Freedom and Civil Liberties of Students in Colleges and Universities." This report urges that "students should participate fully and effectively in formulating and

Appendix 4

adjudicating college regulations governing student conduct" and further states that "regulations governing demonstrations should be made by a committee of administrators, representative faculty and democratically selected students." Failure of the Regents to seek participation of representatives of the various university constituents may seriously jeopardize relationships between the Regents and the persons they seek to govern.

Many sections of the rules are so vague as to be virtually unenforceable and are questionable with respect to preserving the civil liberties of persons affected by them. The ICLU wishes to focus on those portions of the rules which seem to clearly violate established legal principles and contractural relationships, and which in fact contradict the disclaimer found in Section 5 that the rules should not be construed as violating constitutional rights.

Section 4 authorizes the President of the university to temporarily bar from the campus any person who in the "president's judgment" has violated the rules of personal conduct. Aside from placing an extraordinary burden on the president, this rule dispenses with due process entirely in that none of the safeguards (such as confrontation of one's accuser, hearings at which evidence is presented, and a mechanism for appeal) usually afforded an accused violator are provided.

Section 4 (d) authorizes the expulsion or dismissal of a person who violates the President's order temporarily barring him from the campus, even if a hearing should determine that the individual is innocent of an act of misconduct. This rule allows for the possibility of a bizarre series of events in which an innocent person can lose access to his university for violation of what is subsequently found to be an erroneous or invalid order. The provision in Section 1 (k) that a suspended student must satisfy the president of the university that he is unlikely to disrupt the university in the future in order to be readmitted constitutes a disclaimer, and is as distasteful as a loyalty oath. Moreover, the provision places an impossible burden on the president. After serving his sentence of suspension, whatever its term, a student should be as admissible as anyone else; to allow extension of his sentence or resentencing at this point is not only unfair but also violates the humanitarian principle of rehabilitation. This principle is similarly violated in Section 3 (b) which provides that visitors to the campus (e.g., the citizens of this state) may be permanently denied admission to or employment by a university.

Serious concern must be expressed about the effect that the Regents' Rules may have upon established rules and procedures regarding academic tenure. Section (j) under Definitions and Sections 3 (a) and 4 (a) and (d) would appear to by-pass those procedures which have been formulated by the American Association of University Professors for the hearing of cases involving the dismissal of tenured faculty. These AAUP principles (1940 Statement on Academic Freedom) have been accepted by all three state universities and must be considered as part of the contractural relationship between the university and the individual professor on tenure. The establishment of new procedures and contractural arrangements raises serious questions about the continued accreditation of the universities. It is especially desirable that an early reexamination of rules be accomplished with the participation of representatives of the faculty and student body.

APPENDIX 5

Resolution Urging Return of Japanese-Americans

Studying in Iowa Colleges to Their Relocation Centers

Passed by Senate Feb. 23, 1943, by House Feb. 24, 1943

<u>Whereas</u>, Upon the shoulders of American boys, eighteen years of age or over, has been placed the responsibility of forming a part of the armed forces engaged in the present titanic struggle for world liberty, and

<u>Whereas</u>, Apart from the physical aspect of the sacrifice our younger men are thus called upon to make is the matter of their education. It is a serious and a momentous thing, to them and to their country, to interrupt, perhaps to prevent, their academic and professional training, and

<u>Whereas</u>, It now appears that it is the purpose of the War Relocation Authority of the United States to accord eligibility to some twenty-five hundred young Japanese-American students, located in war relocation centers, to leave such centers and enter any of the large number of colleges and universities—in other words, to accord the privileges of higher education to a group of young people, citizens by virtue of their birth in this country, whose loyalty and patriotism are rendered doubtful because of their racial extraction, thereby unfitting them to be soldiers while denying a similar opportunity to our own young men of unquestioned loyalty, and

<u>Whereas</u>, It is admitted that practically all of the Japanese-Americans to whom higher education is to be afforded are physically fit and capable of performing services which would be useful to the war effort, where their patriotism might be demonstrated without placing them in a position where possible disloyalty might be perilous,

<u>Therefore Be It Resolved by the Senate, the House Concurring</u>:
1. That no discrimination be shown in the matter of educational advantages, between America's young citizens, of whatever race or nationality—in short, while young men of undoubted loyalty and

Caucasian extraction are required to serve in the armed forces, that these young men of Japanese ancestry and less certain loyalty be given opportunity to serve the war effort in ways in which their racial extraction will prove no impediment.

    2. That steps be taken, through executive intervention or order, or by means of legislation if necessary, to prevent allowing Japanese-American youths the privilege of leaving concentration centers and securing an education in American colleges and universities, while the same privilege is denied to loyal American young men called to military service.

    3. That if any Japanese-American youths have already been given the privilege of attending colleges and universities, they be returned to their relocation camps, and

    <u>Be It Further Resolved</u>, That a copy of this resolution be sent to the President of the United States, also to the two Iowa senators, and to the eight Iowa members of the House of Representatives, and that they thus be petitioned to use their influence and best offices that the injustices mentioned may be avoided.

APPENDIX 6

ICLU Statement on Governmental Data Banks and Civil Liberties

The ICLU is concerned about the safeguards for privacy and due process of personally identifiable records in data banks, and supports the following principles regarding such records in governmental data banks:

COLLECTION OF INFORMATION

1. The determination of information to be collected in a governmental data bank should be made by legislation rather than by administrative rule.
2. The legislature should specifically exclude the collection for any reason of: information relating to lawful political activities, such as meetings, speeches, demonstrations, or membership; anonymous information.

RETENTION OF INFORMATION

A statute of limitations on the retention of information should be an integral part of the regulation of governmental data banks. The statute should provide for the removal of personal identification from records and the removal of certain specified information from an individual's personal record.

NOTICE OF PERSONAL RECORD

1. All documents filled out by individuals from which information is transferred into any governmental data bank must prominently identify each data bank into which information is transferred.
2. The state should seek to ensure that citizens are aware of governmental data banks, their contents, and the persons having custody of the data.
3. Each individual must have the right to demand and inspect any information about him in a governmental data bank.

DISSEMINATION OF INFORMATION

1. The determination of information to be disseminated and of the persons to whom it may be disseminated should be made by legislation rather than by administrative rule.
2. A full record should be kept of dissemination of information with each personal record in a governmental data bank.
3. Records from a governmental data bank should be disseminated only to governmental employees and governmental agencies which have restrictions on dissemination of information that are compatible to the Iowa restrictions.

CORRECTION OF INFORMATION

1. Each individual must have a right to: contest the accuracy of information; correct errors and remove erroneous material; have corrections recorded in the files and reported to prior recipients of the erroneous data.
2. Each individual must have the right to place explanatory information in the file.
3. An independent appeal board, with its findings subject to judicial review, shall be established to determine the need for, and to order, the correction of information in a record if the person having custody of the record disputes the claim of an individual requesting correction of records.

SANCTIONS

1. There should be appropriate penalties for illegal collection, release or acquisition of records from a governmental data bank and for each illegal use of individual records.
2. Individuals who have suffered damages from the illegal release, acquisition, or use of information from their personal records shall be entitled to civil action against the person or persons responsible and against the state.

AUDIT

There shall be an independent audit of each governmental data bank every year which shall, as a minimum, ensure:

Compliance with legislative definitions of collection and dissemination of information;

Compliance with an informational statute of limitations;

Correction of information agreed to by the custodian of the data bank or ordered by the independent appeal board or by the courts;

The existence of appropriate security measures with regard to physical security, casual observation of records, etc.

Appendix 6   159

CRIMINAL JUSTICE

1. In criminal data systems, all arrest records should be automatically expunged after final disposition not resulting in conviction, or after three years, unless there has been a conviction, whichever comes first.

2. Criminal allegations must be updated as to disposition and disseminated to previous recipients of the original allegations.

3. There ought to be a procedure for full restoration of civil rights and expungement of records after a certain number of years of good behavior following completion of sentence.

4. All convictions should be systematically recorded under the statute violated so that expunging is readily possible upon any determination of invalidity of the statute.

(Data banks, in the above statement, include all collections of data: computerized, microfilm, videotape, filing cabinets, etc.)

ABBREVIATIONS

Organizations

AAUP	American Association of University Professors
ACLU	American Civil Liberties Union
AFL	American Federation of Labor
AUAM	American Union against Militarism
CIO	Congress of Industrial Organizations
ICLU	Iowa Civil Liberties Union
ISEA	Iowa State Education Association
NCLB	National Civil Liberties Bureau
YMCA	Young Men's Christian Association

Persons

ESA	Edward Switzer Allen		PMM	Patrick Murphy Malin
RNB	Roger N. Baldwin		LBM	Lucille B. Milner
KB	Katherine Bertin		WN	Walter Nelles
CB	Carl Bogenrief		LRN	Louise R. Noun
JMB	J. M. Britchey		CFR	Charles F. Ransom
LMC	Laetitia Moon Conard		RR	Robert Root
GC	Gilbert Cranberg		GER	George E. Rundquist
EGF	Elizabeth Gurley Flynn		LWS	Luther W. Stalnaker
CF	Clifford Forster		FS	Forrest Spaulding
JEF	Jeffrey E. Fuller		DWVV	D. W. VanVliet
BBH	Bourke B. Hickenlooper		JFW	J. F. Wirds
REH	Ralph E. Himstead			

NOTES

Chapter 1

1. Most of the records of AUAM are in the Peace Collection of the Swarthmore College Library; we rely largely on them.
2. <u>Detroit Times</u>, July 11, 1917.
3. AUAM Board Minutes, June 15, 1917.
4. Berle D. Eastman, Sept, 27, 1917. AUAM Papers.
5. Minutes cited in Donald Johnston, <u>The Challenge to American Freedoms: World War I and the Rise of the American Civil Liberties Union</u>, University Press of Kentucky, Lexington, 1963. This book gives an admirable account of the organizations we have been considering, as they were related to issues of the First World War.
6. Dated May 4, 1918. Unfortunately, I found no earlier bulletins in the AUAM Papers where this one is preserved.
7. Letters from Campbell, Aug. 6, 1917, Jan. 30, 1918; letters to him Aug. 8, 1917, Feb. 2, 1918. ACLU Archives, vol. 20.
8. LMC to RNB, Mar. 18, 1918; RNB to LMC, Mar. 20, 1920. ACLU Archives, vol. 20. A letter from Henry Conard, husband of Laetitia, says that Baldwin's caution was ignored. Correspondence with the three inmates continued; one of them later studied at Grinnell and had a very successful career as a botanist.
9. 245 US 366.
10. Letter, Nov. 12, 1917. ACLU Archives, vol. 6.
11. RNB to Oswald G. Villard, Dec. 10, 1917. ACLU Archives, vol. 6.
12. Mrs. Blodgett to RNB, Feb. 6, 1918. ACLU Archives, vol. 32.
13. Mrs. Blodgett to WN (NCLB), Feb. 20, Mar. 22, 26, 1918. ACLU Archives, vol. 32.
14. WN to Mrs. Blodgett, Apr. 2, 1918. ACLU Archives, vol. 32.
15. WN to Utterback and others, Feb. 25, 1918. Utterback to WN, Mar. 2, 1918. Mason to WN, Mar. 2, 21, 1918. ACLU Archives, vol. 32.
16. Blodgett to Wilson, June 10, July 27, 1918. Mason to WN, Mar. 21, 1918.

17. Mason to WN, Mar. 21, 1918. ACLU Archives, vol. 32.
18. Brammer, Lehman, and Seevers to RNB, Mar. 14, 1918. ACLU Archives, vol. 32.
19. Horack to WN, Mar. 8, 1918. ACLU Archives, vol. 32.
20. Des Moines Register, Dec. 24, 1921.
21. Kendall to ACLU, Nov. 18, 1921. ACLU Archives, vol. 182.
22. Case to ACLU, Nov. 24, 1921. ACLU Archives, vol. 182.
23. ESA to LBM, Dec. 3, 1921; LBM to ESA, Dec. 15, 1921. ACLU Archives, vol. 182.
24. ACLU news release, Dec. 8, 1921. ACLU Archives, vol. 182.
25. AFL, Jan. 20, 1923. ACLU Archives, vol. 237.
26. AFL, Aug. 4, 1923. ACLU Archives, vol. 237.
27. ACLU Archives, vol. 373.
28. New York Telegram, Oct. 17, 1929. Denison to ACLU, Oct. 29, 1929. ACLU Archives, vol. 373.
29. ACLU Archives, vol. 549, Aug. 15, 1932.
30. Daily Worker, Nov. 6-7, 1933.
31. New York Times, Aug. 29, 1932. Bruce Bliven had articles on the Farmers Union—sympathetic but with restricted optimism—in New Republic, Nov. 22, 29, 1933.
32. New York Herald-Tribune, May 6, 1933. Actually the law (45 GA, HF 193) does not mention sale of the property; presumably there were to be no forced sales. A continuance of a mortgage could last until Mar. 1, 1935; in the meantime the court granting continuance would set a fair rental on the property.

This act, which expired in 1935, was replaced in 1939 by a similar one. It provides for a continuance until the following Mar. 1—in exceptional cases for an extra year, if failure to make mortgage installment payments is due to one of several natural causes "or when the governor of the state of Iowa shall have by reason of a depression declared a state of emergency." Such an emergency had been declared by the governor in 1933, with concurrence of the legislature.

The 1939 law differs from that of 1933 in having no time limit and in providing that rental payments, after meeting specified costs, should be credited against the mortgage.

33. New York Times, Apr. 29, 1933.
34. Milwaukee Leader, Apr. 28, 1933.
35. New York Times, May 2, 1933.
36. New York Herald-Tribune, May 2, 1933.
37. Buffalo (N.Y.) Times, May 3, 1933.
38. ESA to LBM, June 3, 1933. ACLU Archives, vol. 658.
39. LBM to Whitfield, July 21, 1933. ACLU Archives, vol. 658.
40. John L. Shover, Corn Belt Rebellion, University of Illinois Press, Urbana, 1965; Everett O. Luoma, The Farmer Takes a Holiday, Exposition Press, New York, 1967.
41. Powers Hapgood, An Experiment in Industrial Democracy, privately printed, 1931.
42. ACLU Archives, vol. 482-C. Powers Hapgood, Kidnapping in Council Bluffs, The Nation, Dec. 16, 1933.
43. Report of Papcun to ESA, June, 1966.

44. *New York Herald-Tribune*, Mar. 25, 1933.
45. ESA to LBM. ACLU Archives, vol. 658.

Chapter 2

1. This information is from the files of the American Union against Militarism, the original organizer of the National Civil Liberties Bureau. These documents are part of the Swarthmore College Peace Collection.
2. South Dakota Code, Chapter 12.08.
3. State v. Tonn, 195 Iowa 94 (1923).
4. *Daily Worker*, Aug. 25, 1934. Letter from Newell to ESA, June 6, 1934. ACLU Archives, vol. 745. Letter from ESA to LBM, Mar. 4, 1934. ACLU Archives, vol. 745.
5. *Des Moines Register*, Jan. 16, 1935.
6. State v. Gibson, 189 Iowa 1212 (1919).
7. Woodward to RNB, Dec. 22, 1917; RNB to Woodward, Dec. 31, 1917.
8. ESA to LBM, Mar. 10, 1935. ACLU Archives, vol. 838.
9. ACLU Archives, vol. 745.
10. *Des Moines Register*, Jan. 17, 1935.
11. ACLU Archives, vol. 838.
12. Wilbert Allison to Hortense N. Dillon (ICLU), June 18, 1938. ACLU Archives, vol. 2033. Allison was president of the local.
13. *New York Herald Tribune*, July 7, 1938.
14. *New York Times*, July 9, 1938.
15. *Dubuque Telegraph Herald*, July 13, 1938.
16. *Newton News*, July 22, 1938.
17. *New York Times*, Aug. 6, 1938.
18. *Christian Century*, Aug. 24, Sept. 21, 1938.
19. ACLU press release, Nov. 25, 1939.
20. Rosemont to Wulf, Apr. 14, 1964; Wulf to Rosemont, Apr. 24, 1964. ACLU Archives, vol. 24.

Chapter 3

1. ESA to Frank Miles, editor of *Iowa Legionnaire*, Mar. 28, 1935. ACLU Archives, vol. 838.
2. ESA to LBM, Apr. 14, 1935. ACLU Archives, vol. 838.
3. H. S. Conard to Mrs. C. C. Pendray, Iowa Senate, Apr. 22, 1935. ACLU Archives, vol. 838.
4. ACLU Archives, vol. 935.
5. ESA to LBM, May 25, 1935. ACLU Archives, vol. 807.
6. ESA to Herbert M. Levy, Mar. 16, 1951. ACLU Archives, 1951, Gen. Corr., vol. 37. *ACLU Weekly Bulletin*, Apr. 23, 1951. Arnold A. Rogow, The Loyalty Oath Issue in Iowa, 1951, *American Political Science Review*, 55:861 (Dec. 1961).
7. *The Defender*, Jan. 1960.
8. ICLU Board Minutes, May 8, 1959. ACLU Archives, 1959, vol. 2.

9. The Defender, June 1965.
10. The Defender, Feb. 1970.
11. The Defender, Apr. 1970.
12. Board Minutes, Dec. 20, 1973, Jan. 24, 1974.

Chapter 4

1. In The Trial of Elizabeth Gurley Flynn by the American Civil Liberties Union (Horizon Press, 1968) Corliss Lamont gives as appendices Ward's letter of resignation and protests by 17 men including Franz Boas, Theodore Dreiser, Henry Pratt Fairchild, Robert Morse Lovett, Robert S. Lynd, Carey McWilliams, and I. F. Stone; by Alexander Meiklejohn and two other members of the National Committee; by A. F. Whitney, president of the Brotherhood of Railroad Trainmen and member of the National Committee.
2. ESA to LBM. ACLU Archives, vol. 2230.
3. ACLU Archives, vol. 2230, Feb. 27, 1940.
4. ICLU Bulletin, Apr. 9, 1940. ACLU Archives, vol. 2230.
5. The Trial of Elizabeth Gurley Flynn, p. 97.
6. Quoted in The Trial of Elizabeth Gurley Flynn, p. 181.
7. Full transcript of this session in The Trial of Elizabeth Gurley Flynn.
8. Nation, July 3-10, 1976.
9. LWS to RMB, July 25, 1942. ACLU Archives, vol. 2410.
10. LBM to LWS, July 29, 1942. ACLU Archives, vol. 2410.
11. ESA to RNB, Dec. 20, 1942. ACLU Archives, vol. 2476.
12. ACLU Board Minutes, Feb. 16, May 24, June 7, July 11, Oct. 25, Dec. 6, Dec. 20, 1948. ACLU Archives, 1948, Gen. Corr., vol. 3.
13. ACLU Board Minutes, July 11, 1949. ACLU Archives, Gen. Corr., vol. 5.
14. ACLU Report of Conference of Affiliates, Des Moines, Iowa, Jan. 14-15, 1950.
15. Report of meeting of Committee on Affiliates.
16. GER to ESA, Aug. 16, 1950. ACLU Archives, Gen. Corr., vol. 7.
17. ACLU Board Minutes, May 14, 1951. ACLU Archives, Gen. Corr., vol. 1.
18. Corliss Lamont, Freedom Is as Freedom Does (Horizon Press, 1956), p. 281.
19. ACLU Board Minutes, Oct. 27, Nov. 13, 1953. ACLU Archives, Gen. Corr., vol. 1.
20. ACLU Board Minutes, Feb. 15, 1954. ACLU Archives, Gen. Corr., vol. 1.
21. ACLU Board Minutes, Aug. 2, 1954. ACLU Archives, Gen. Corr., vol. 1.
22. ACLU Board Minutes, Nov. 22, 1954.
23. ACLU Board Minutes, Jan. 29-30, 1966.
24. ICLU Board Minutes, Dec. 15, 1967.
25. The Trial of Elizabeth Gurley Flynn, pp. 26-28.
26. Civil Liberties, Nov. 1973.

Chapter 5

1. DWVV to Gov. Bourke B. Hickenlooper, Sept. 22, 1943. ACLU Archives, vol. 2544.
2. DWVV to BBH, Oct. 1, 1943. ACLU Archives, vol. 2544.
3. DWVV to Iowa State Board of Education, Nov. 5, 1943. ACLU Archives, vol. 2544.
4. DWVV to CF (ACLU), Nov. 30, 1943. ACLU Archives, vol. 2544.
5. CF to LWS, Mar. 7, 1944. ACLU Archives, vol. 2544.
6. RNB to R. E. Buchanan, June 21, 1944. ACLU Archives, vol. 2544.
7. DWVV to REH, Nov. 19, 1943. ACLU Archives, vol. 2544.
8. CF to REH, Jan. 5, 1944. ACLU Archives, vol. 2544.
9. Minutes of Committee on Academic Freedom, Apr. 5, 1944. ACLU Archives, vol. 2544.
10. LBM to Hoyt, June 16, 1944. ACLU Archives, vol. 2544.
11. T. W. Schultz to ESA, Dec. 17, 1970.
12. Valuable information on this period is contained in Earle D. Ross, The Land-Grant Idea at Iowa State College, Iowa State College Press, Ames, 1958, pp. 217-20.
13. New Republic, May 1, 1944. Buchanan to RNB, June 12, 1944. ACLU Archives, vol. 2544.
14. ICLU Board Minutes, Oct. 20, 1967.
15. The report was filed with the clerk of the district court Dec. 27, 1968. Copies were offered for sale at 80 cents; the whole text was reproduced in the Ames Daily Tribune, Jan. 7, 1969.
16. Comment on Portage County (Ohio) Grand Jury report concerning disorder and killing at Kent State University. Jan. 30, 1971.
17. Ames Daily Tribune, Jan. 9, 1969.
18. Des Moines Register, Nov. 12, 1969.

Chapter 6

1. Iowa Code 279.24.
2. Iowa Code 279.13.
3. Bergstrom to LBM. ACLU Archives, vol. 838.
4. Chicago New World, May 18, 1951. ACLU Archives, Clippings, vol. 1.
5. ICLU Statement, July 2, 1951. ACLU Archives, 1951. Gen. Corr., vol. 2.
6. "Teacher Quits in Dispute on Red Charges," Des Moines Register, Oct. 29, 1950.
7. ACLU Archives, 1951, Gen. Corr.
8. Reporter for Conscience' Sake, July 1958.
9. ACLU Archives, 1953, Gen. Corr., vol. 2.
10. Des Moines Register, Apr. 23, 1971.

Chapter 7

1. For most details I am indebted to letters from Bruce L. Fishwild, city editor, Cedar Rapids Gazette, Dec. 16 and 21, 1970. He in turn had helpful information from William Walter, who had been the model for some of the figures.
2. ICLU Board Minutes, May 8, 1968.
3. ICLU Board Minutes, Aug. 16, 1968.
4. The Defender, Dec. 10, 1968.
5. ALA Bulletin, Jan. 1939. ACLU Archives, vol. 2062.
6. ESA to RNB, Oct. 5, 1940. ACLU Archives, vol. 2230.
7. ICLU Bulletin, Sept. 1959. ACLU Archives, 1959, vol. 2.
8. Watts to Markman, Dec. 7, 1959. ACLU Archives, 1960, vol. 11.
9. ACLU Bulletin 2061. ACLU Archives, 1960, vol. 11.
10. The Defender, Oct. 1962. ACLU Archives, 1962, vol. 82.
11. Des Moines Register, May 3, 8, 1967.
12. Des Moines Register, July 10, 1948.
13. The Defender, Mar. 10, 1971.
14. The Defender, Dec. 21, 1971.
15. Florence Stiles, Public Information Director, Iowa State Traveling Library, to ESA, Aug. 25, 1972.
16. ICLU Board Minutes, May 25, 1972.
17. Letters to Katherine Lucchini from Paul Cunningham and George A. Wilson, Feb. 27, 1947; from B. B. Hickenlooper, Feb. 25, 1947. Immer Papers, G 15, 18, 19.

Chapter 8

1. Des Moines Register, July 25, 1921.
2. W. G. Daniel to RNB, Oct. 1, 1921. AUAM Papers, vol. 216. New York Call, Aug. 25, 1921.
3. Des Moines Tribune, Sept. 1939.
4. ESA to RNB, Mar. 15, 1937. ACLU Archives, vol. 1041.
5. CFR to Jerome S. Machlin, Dec. 26, 1939. ACLU Archives, vol. 2127.
6. CFR, report to ICLU. ACLU Archives, 1950, Gen. Corr., vol. 48.
7. ACLU Annual Report, 1959-60, pp. 64-65.
8. ICLU Board Minutes, Oct. 20, 1961. ACLU Archives, 1961, vol. 47.
9. ICLU Board Minutes, Nov. 20, 1959. ACLU Archives, 1959, vol. 2.
10. ICLU Board Minutes, Feb. 19, 1960. ACLU Archives, 1960, vol. 1.
11. Smith to ESA, July 3, 1969.
12. The Defender, Mar. 1965.
13. The Defender, Mar. 1965.
14. Des Moines Register, Aug. 23, 1970.

Notes to Pages 66-80   169

Chapter 9

1. ICLU Board Minutes, Dec. 17, 1965.
2. The whole case was well summarized in the Des Moines Register, Feb. 25, 1969.
3. ICLU Board Minutes, July 21, 1967.
4. ICLU Board Minutes, Sept. 15, 1967.
5. The Defender, Sept. 15, 1969.
6. Des Moines Register, Sept. 6, 1970.
7. Report of Oval Quist, executive secretary, ICLU, to annual membership meeting, Apr. 20, 1968.
8. The Defender, June 8, 1971.
9. Ibid.
10. Cited in a letter from President Glenn Leggett to alumni, parents, and friends, Apr. 1969.
11. ICLU Board Minutes, Feb. 21, 1969.
12. Des Moines Register, May 27, 1969.
13. Des Moines Register, May 29, 1969.
14. Washington (Iowa) Journal, June 21, 1969.
15. Des Moines Register, June 24, 1970.
16. Des Moines Register, Sept. 23, Nov. 13, 1970.
17. Des Moines Register, Feb. 23, 1971.
18. ICLU Board Minutes, Apr. 17, 1971.

Chapter 10

1. ACLU: memorandum from office to the Board of Directors, Aug. 10, 1966.
2. ICLU Board Minutes, Feb. 16, 1966.
3. ICLU Board Minutes, Mar. 16, 1966.
4. ICLU Board Minutes, Sept. 16, 1966.
5. Des Moines Register, Feb. 28, 1966.
6. Des Moines Register, Nov. 2, 1966.
7. Des Moines Register, Aug. 15, 1968.
8. Des Moines Register, Aug. 18, 1968.
9. The Defender, Jan. 8, 1973.
10. Civil Liberties, May 1973. Des Moines Register, Mar. 19, 24, 1974; Nov. 13, 18, 1974.

Chapter 11

1. William Card (AFL organizer) to RNB, June 23, 1938. ACLU Archives, vol. 2033.
2. "I am found guilty." ACLU Archives, vol. 2033.
3. Dubuque Leader, Oct. 28, Nov. 4, 1938.
4. Des Moines Register, July 22, 1938.
5. JFW to William Evjue, Capital Times, Madison, Wis., July 5, 1938. ACLU Archives, vol. 2033.

6. RR to ESA, June 14, 1944. Immer Papers, G 36.
7. *Dubuque Leader*, July 29, 1938.
8. ACLU Board Minutes, Aug. 23, 1938. JFW to JMB (ACLU), Aug. 27, 1938. ACLU Archives, vol. 2033.
9. JFW to JMB, Oct. 22, 1938. ACLU Archives, vol. 2033.
10. JFW to CFR, Mar. 12, 1940. ACLU Archives, vol. 2230.
11. Carter to RR, ICLU. July 12, 1944. Immer Papers, I 31.
12. KB to Melvin Wolf, Nov. 1, 1962. ACLU Archives, 1962. vol. 25; *The Defender*, Oct. 1962. ACLU Archives, 1962, vol. 82.
13. ICLU Board Minutes, Mar. 16, 1966.
14. Ashby v. Haugh, 260 Iowa 1047.
15. ICLU Board Minutes, Jan. 19, 1968.
16. ICLU news release, "Beginning Of Court Action."
17. *The Defender*, Apr. 15, 1966.
18. 384 US 1000; 385 US 804.
19. Kenney v. Haugh, 163 NW 2d 428.
20. *The Reporter*, July 14, 1966; ICLU Board Minutes, Jan. 20, 1967.
21. ICLU Board Minutes, Oct. 23, 1969. Melvin H. Wolf to ESA, Aug. 2, 1972.
22. *Des Moines Tribune*, May 8, 1972.
23. *The Defender*, Mar. 22, 1974.

Chapter 12

1. CFR to ACLU, June 16, 1940. ACLU Archives, vol. 2230.
2. Cynthia Lucas to ACLU, July 8, 1940. ACLU Archives, vol. 2230.
3. J. T. Erickson to Francis Biddle, Solicitor General, July 17, 1940. ACLU Archives, vol. 2230.
4. Dale C. Whitmer to Biddle, May 5, 1941. ACLU Archives, vol. 2329.
5. Sworn affidavit of George Sullivan, May 3, 1941. ACLU Archives, vol. 2329.
6. *ICLU Bulletin*, Nov. 29, 1941.
7. The whole case was summarized in the *Des Moines Register*, Jan. 13, 1948.
8. *ICLU Bulletin*, Sept. 1959.
9. *ACLU Bulletin*, Apr. 1959.
10. *Des Moines Register*, Nov. 25, 1962.
11. *Des Moines Register*, Dec. 29, 1965.
12. *Des Moines Register*, Nov. 11, 1962, Aug. 18, 1967.
13. *Des Moines Register*, Oct. 12, 1965.
14. *Des Moines Register*, Oct. 29, 1965.
15. *The Defender*, Apr. 11, 1967.
16. *Des Moines Register*, Feb. 23, 1966.
17. *Des Moines Register*, May 10, 1966.
18. *Des Moines Register*, Feb. 23, 1967.
19. *Des Moines Register*, July 31, 1971.
20. Elmer and Dorothy Schwieder, *A Peculiar People: Iowa's Old Order Amish*, Iowa State University Press, Ames, 1975.

Notes to Pages 92-102

21. ICLU Board Minutes, Dec. 18, 1959.
22. Donald E. Boles, The Bible, Religion, and the Public Schools, 3rd ed., Iowa State University Press, Ames, 1965, pp. 169-86.
23. Marie Loomis to JEF, Dec. 4, 1957. ACLU Archives, Gen. Corr., vol. 9.
24. ICLU Board Minutes, Sept. 21, 1962.
25. Letters dated March 6, 18, 21, 1964. ACLU Archives, vol. 15, p. 42.
26. Boles, Bible; The Two Swords: Commentaries and Cases in Religion and Education, Iowa State University Press, Ames, 1967.

Chapter 13

1. ESA to LBM, Mar. 2, 1938. ACLU Archives, vol. 2033.
2. LBM to ESA, Mar. 7, 1938. ACLU Archives, vol. 2033.
3. GC to Melvin Wulf, July 7, 1962. ACLU Archives, 1962, vol. 45. There was promised a full-time physician within a year.
4. The Defender, June 1965.
5. James Polson and Randall Bezanson, Contemporary Studies Project: Facts and Fallacies about Iowa Civil Commitment, Iowa Law Review, Apr. 1970, 55(4):895-980.
6. The Defender, Aug. 12, 1970.
7. The Defender, July 12, 1972.
8. ICLU Bulletin, Mar. 1943. ACLU Archives, vol. 2476.
9. Ibid.
10. ACLU Archives, 1947, Gen. Corr., vol. 4.
11. ICLU Bulletin, Sept. 1948. ACLU Archives, Gen. Corr., vol. 3.
12. ICLU Bulletin, Dec. 1949. ACLU Archives, vol. 6.
13. ICLU Bulletin, Oct. 1952. ACLU Archives, Gen. Corr., vol. 2.
14. ICLU Bulletin, 1954. ACLU Archives, Gen. Corr., vol. 3. ACLU Annual Report, 1953-54.
15. ACLU Archives, vol. 2618.
16. Marcus Lamoreux to ACLU. ACLU Archives, Gen. Corr., vol. 24.
17. ESA to CF, Jan. 15, 1948. ACLU Archives, Gen. Corr., vol. 24.
18. Des Moines Register, Nov. 13, 1947.
19. Des Moines Register, Mar. 24, 26, 27, 1948.
20. Des Moines Register, Apr. 4, 1948.
21. ACLU Bulletin 1624. ACLU Archives, 1953, Gen. Corr., vol. 37.
22. Des Moines Tribune, Oct. 31, 1941.
23. ICLU Bulletin, Jan. 30, 1942. ACLU Archives, vol. 2410.
24. ICLU Bulletin, Mar. 1943. ACLU Archives, vol. 2476.
25. Des Moines Register, Mar. 26, 1948.
26. ESA to RNB, Mar. 13, 1947. ACLU Archives, Box 4, vol. 10.
27. ICLU Board Minutes, Sept. 24, 1958. ACLU Archives, Gen. Corr., vol. 2.

28. ICLU Board Minutes, Nov. 20, 1959. ACLU Archives, vol. 2.
29. ACLU Archives, 1961, vol. 21.
30. ICLU Board Minutes, Aug. 13, 1961. ACLU Archives, vol. 23, No. 82.
31. *Iowa Civil Rights Reporter*, July 1970.
32. *The Defender*, May 9, 1972.
33. AUAM Papers, vol. 16.
34. AUAM Papers, vol. 25.
35. NCLB Papers, vol. 14.
36. ACLU Archives, vol. 2476.
37. Immer Papers, G 41, B 1 (Annual Report of ICLU, 1943-44).
38. ICLU Board Minutes, Aug. 21, 1943. Immer Papers, G 41.
39. ACLU Archives, 1947, vol. 7.
40. ESA to CF, Nov. 21, 1948. ACLU Archives, 1948, Gen. Corr., vol. 96.
41. *ICLU Bulletin*, Mar. 1950. ACLU Archives, Gen. Corr., vol. 9.
42. ESA to Carl Vinson, Feb. 14, 1950. ACLU Archives, Gen. Corr., vol. 20.
43. ESA to ACLU and affiliates, Dec. 21, 1950. ACLU Archives, 1951, Gen. Corr., vol. 2.
44. ESA to PMM, Jan. 12, 1951. ACLU Archives, Gen. Corr., vol. 2.
45. *ACLU Bulletin*, Sept. 12, 1955. ACLU Archives, Gen. Corr., vol. 20.
46. *The Reporter*, May-June, 1959. ACLU Archives, vol. 50.
47. War Victims: Five for Amnesty, *Civil Liberties*, Jan. 1974. The article describes widely varying examples of war resistance.
48. McMichael to ESA, Mar. 15, 1937. ACLU Archives, vol. 1041.
49. *ICLU Bulletin* 3, 1937. ACLU Archives, vol. 1041. Information Service, Feb. 15, 1938, ACLU Archives, vol. 2018.
50. Horace E. Williams to ACLU, Mar. 22, 1945; CF to Williams, Apr. 2, 1945. ACLU Archives, vol. 2697.
51. *Civil Liberties*, Oct. 1961.
52. ICLU Board Minutes, Feb. 16, 1966. Irwin Wolkstein, Deputy Director, Program Policy, Bureau of Health Insurance, HEW, to ESA, Aug. 21, 1972.
53. ICLU Board Minutes, May 25, 1972.
54. *The Defender*, June 8, 1971.
55. *The Defender*, Feb. 1, 1972.
56. *The Defender*, July 12, 1972.
57. ICLU Board Minutes, July 27, Aug. 24, 1972.
58. ICLU Board Minutes, Aug. 24, 1972.
59. ICLU Board Minutes, May 25, 1972.
60. ICLU Board Minutes, June 22, Aug. 24, Dec. 21, 1972; Mar. 22, 1973.
61. *The Defender*, Apr. 23, 1974.
62. Ibid.
63. *The Defender*, Sept. 1, 1973.

Chapter 14

1. ICLU Bulletin, 1951. ACLU Archives, Gen. Corr., vol. 2.
2. ICLU Bulletin, Apr. 1953. ACLU Archives, Gen. Corr., vol. 2.

Chapter 15

1. Gaebler to JEF, Jan. 9, 1950; GER to Gaebler and ESA, Jan. 19, 1950; ESA to Gaebler, Jan. 24, 1950. ACLU Archives, Gen. Corr., vol. 9.
2. ICLU Board Minutes, Nov. 2, 1969; Jan. 15, 1970.
3. ICLU Board Minutes, Oct. 26, 1972.
4. The Defender, Nov. 22, 1972.
5. ICLU Board Minutes, Dec. 15, 1961. ACLU Archives, 1961, vol. 47.
6. Daily Iowan, Jan. 26, 1962. ACLU Archives, vol. 72.
7. ICLU Board Minutes, Aug. 18, 1967.
8. ICLU Board Minutes, Nov. 22, 1968.
9. John Ely, chapter vice-president, to HDK, May 23, 1970.
10. Hawkeye Area Board Minutes, Jan. 16, 1971.
11. ICLU Board Minutes, July 29, 1971.
12. ICLU Board Minutes, Jan. 20, 1972.
13. Report on meeting of Apr. 16, 1962. ACLU Archives, vol. 82.
14. ICLU Board Minutes, Oct. 19, 1962; Mar. 15, 1963. ACLU Archives, 1963, vol. 79.
15. Joseph F. Wall to ESA, Oct. 13, 1971.
16. ACLU Archives, 1962, vol. 82.
17. ICLU Board Minutes, June 14, 1963. ACLU Archives, 1963, vol. 79.
18. John Neith to Leanna Golden (ACLU), July 31, 1963. ACLU Archives, 1963, vol. 79.
19. Melvin H. Wolf to city clerk, Dubuque, Sept. 21, 1970.
20. ICLU Board Minutes, June 22, 1972.
21. Sioux City Journal, May 21, 1970.
22. ICLU Board Minutes, Feb. 16, 1962. ACLU Archives, 1962, vol. 82.
23. ICLU Board Minutes, Sept. 15, 1967.
24. Sid Shapiro, chapter secretary, to Harold Stevens, principal of Central High School, Mar. 11, 1970; William A. Anderson, superintendent, to Shapiro, Mar. 23, 1970.
25. ICLU Board Minutes, Sept. 15, 1967.
26. The Defender, July 12, 1972.
27. The Defender, Nov. 22, 1972.

Chapter 16

1. ACLU Archives, 1954, Gen. Corr., vol. 3.

2. ACLU Archives, 1955, Gen. Corr., vol. 2.
3. The Defender, Oct. 1962.
4. The Defender, June, 1965.
5. ICLU Report of Annual Membership Meeting, Apr. 11, 1969.
6. The Defender, June 25, 1970.
7. The Defender, May 9, 1972.
8. ACLU Archives, 1953, Gen. Corr., vol. 2.
9. The Defender, Jan. 14, 1970.
10. Barbara Habenstreit, Eternal Vigilance: The American Civil Liberties Union in Action, Julius Messner, New York, 1971.
11. The Defender, Feb. 1, 1972.

NAME INDEX

Addams, Jane, xv, 3-4, 105
Alesch, Gus, 15
Ali, Mohammed, 85
Allen, Edward S., ix, 14-15, 20, 28, 32, 34-35, 46, 52, 116-18, 130, 135-36, 138-39
Allen, Gordon, 76-77, 115, 132, 136
Allen, Irving L., 119
Allen, Minne Müller-Liebenwalde, ix, xii, xiv, xv
Allison, Wilbert, 17
Alsager, Darlene and Charles, 75-76
Alsager, George, 78
Anderson, Judge F. L., 10
Anderson, Ruth, 104
Anderson, William A., 124
Andre, Floyd, 45
Angell, Ernest, 4, 34, 138-39
Angell, Norman, 4
Apfel, Dr. Kurt, 117
Ashby, Dennis, 81, 82

Babich, Leslie, 136
Backensten, Paul, 55
Bailey, Genevieve, 118-19
Baker, Newton, 3-4
Balch, Emily Greene, 4-5
Baldwin, Roger N., xi, xv, 4-7, 11-13, 15, 17-18, 30, 32-33, 39, 117, 133
Bannister, Dwight and Margaret, 73, 75

Bartels, Robert, 98
Becker, Justice Francis H., 72, 82, 131
Belin, David, 83
Benedict, Pope XV, 4
Bennett, Mark, 85, 136
Bergstrom, Ralph, 51
Berle, A. A., 6
Berry, Dr. Kenneth, 76
Bertin, Katherine, 136
Besig, Ernest, 35
Bezanson, Randall, 97-98
Biddle, Francis, 170
Black, Justice Hugo, 66-68
Blakely, R. J., 136
Blodgett, David T., 8
Blodgett, Mrs. David T., 8
Boas, Granz, 166
Bogenrief, Carl, 17, 81
Bohlen, Joe, 53
Boles, Donald E., 47, 92-93, 95, 102, 131
Bonfield, Arthur, 132
Boulding, Kenneth, 106
Bourne, Reginald, 86
Bowen, Howard R., 23, 46, 91, 131
Bradley, Judge C. C., 11
Britchey, J. M., 17, 80
Broderick, Jack, 118, 119
Brody, Joseph I., 15
Bromley, Dorothy, 140
Brookhart, Sen. Smith Wildman, 10

Brown, Clarence Ray, 12
Brown, H. Charles, 41
Brownlee, Oswald Harvey, 40, 43
Buchanan, R. E., 40-41, 43
Bundy, E. O., 14
Burdell, Mary, 104
Burling, Edward, Jr., 74
Buss, William, 122
Butler, Grant, 136

Caldwell, Erskine, 57
Campbell, Duane, 123
Campbell, George, 18
Campbell, H. E., 7, 163
Card, William, 169
Carlson, Douglas, 58
Carlson, Ronald, 122
Carr, Luther, 17
Carter, Archie, 79-81
Case, Clarence N., 9
Cassill, Mary E., 52
Chermley, Hugh, 60
Chidester, Walter, 128
Chrystal, John, 38-39, 129, 136
Ciardi, John, 58
Clark, Alexander P., xii
Clark, Susan, 99
Clay, Price, 82
Clemens, Dick J., 63
Coak, Nanette, 114
Coleman, John S., 102
Conard, Henry, 163, 165
Conard, Laetitia Moon, 7, 14, 111, 163
Conlin, Roxanne, 132
Connolly, John, 80
Cooley, Wayne, 114
Cooper, Judge, 20
Coppock, Russell, 101, 134
Cornell, Julien, 106
Covert, George F., 126
Covington, J. Henry, 74
Cranberg, Gilbert, 39, 62, 82, 130
Crouch-Hazlett, Ida, 60
Cunningham, L. B., 55
Cunningham, Rep. Paul, 168

Daniel, W. G., 168
Danielson, Allen L., 129
Davis, Charles, 119

Davis, Lane, 121
Debs, Eugene, 9
DeKoster, Lucas, 47
Denison, John D., 10, 14, 20, 124
DeSilver, Albert, 6-7
Dewey, Judge Charles A., 88
Dillon, Hortense, 15, 17, 136
Dingwell, Judge E. W., 11
Douds, Sen. Alden L., 23
Douglas, Justice William O., 72
Draper, Brice, 70
Dreiser, Theodore, 166
Dresser, Mary, 97
Dunn, George, 130
Dunn, Paul F., 63
Durham, Leona, 112, 121-22

Eads, Judge William R., 120-21
Eastman, Berle D., 163
Eastman, Crystal, 6
Eckhards, Christopher, 65
Eckhards, Mrs. William, 65
Ellis, Jimmy, 85
Ely, John M., Jr., 120-21
Emerson, Donald, 79-80
Emerson, Cecilia, 80
Enich, Michael, 71
Ennis, Edward J., 37
Ensley, Rev. F. Gerald, 131
Entsminger, Harvey, 82, 120
Erbe, Norman, 57
Erickson, J. T., 170
Estes, John, 102
Everhart, Kenneth, 35, 124, 130, 136
Evjue, William, 169

Faches, William, 132
Fairchild, Henry Pratt, 166
Farbstein, Rep. Leonard, 110
Farrar, Ralph, 127
Fay, Michael, 121
Ferguson, Rev. H. A., 88
Fischer, H. William, 119
Fishwild, Bruce L., 168
Fitelson, William, 140
Flatt, Joseph, 47
Flyger, Douglas, 53-54
Flynn, Elizabeth Gurley, 30-31, 166

Name Index

Follett, Roy Wilson, xiii-xiv
Forster, Clifford, 42
Fortas, Justice Abe, 66
Fraenkel, Osmond, 29, 32
Frank, Walter, 18, 140
Freeman, Dennis, 124
Friley, Charles E., 40-41, 43
Frizzell, Charles, 92
Fuller, Jeffrey, 118
Futrell, Gene, 44

Gaebler, Max D., 118
Gardner, Orrington Spencer, 82
Garretson, William, 72
Gasper, Lawrence, 11
Genung, I. T., 101
George, Thomas, 81-82
Gillon, Judge Frank, 57
Gilmartin, Aron S., 14-15
Glanton, Judge Luther, 68
Glanton, Willie, 102
Glassel, Don, 55
Goldman, David, 129
Goodpaster, Gary, 69
Gordin, George, 24
Gore, Warren, 52
Gormly, Walter, 81, 96
Graven, Judge Henry N., 56
Griffin, Edna, 102
Grimes, James W., 99
Groos, Beverly, 26

Haas, Herbert, 122
Habenstreit, Barbara, 134
Hacker, Sally, 113-14
Hall, Earl, 41
Hall, Hollis, 18
Hallinan, Charles T., 4, 105
Hanson, Robert, 27
Hanson, Judge William C., 69, 76-77, 94
Hapgood, Powers, 12
Harlan, Justice John M., 66
Hawkes, Glen R., 74
Hayes, Alvin, Jr., 112
Hays, Arthur Garfield, 14, 16, 18
Heady, Earl O., 45
Heifner, Richard, 44
Herring, Gov. Clyde, 11
Heslop, John, 10

Hickenlooper, Sen. Bourke B., 22, 92, 168
Higgins, Malcolm, 102
High, Jesse, 104
Hillgardner, J., 9
Hilton, James H., 44-45
Himstead, Ralph E., 42
Hitler, Adolf, 29, 86
Hoegh, Atty. Gen. Leo, 92, 101, 133
Hoffmans, Edward, 46
Holly, C. O., 8
Holmes, John Haynes, 32
Horach, H. C., 8
Howard, Lawrence, 102
Hoyt, Elizabeth E., 42
Huebsch, B. W., 4
Hughes, Alfred, 57
Hughes, Gov. Harold, 90
Hukill, Craig, 26

Immer, Esther, xii, 134

James, Paul, 101
Javits, Sen. Jacob, 110
Jefferson, Thomas, 128
Jeffries, Everett, 55
Jesse, Norman, 21, 24, 62, 81, 97
Johnson, Donald E., 53
Johnson, Howard, 55
Johnson, Oliver, 104
Johnson, Vernon, 101
Johnson, Willard, 87, 136
Johnston, Dan, 26, 39, 62, 65-66, 68, 71-72, 83, 122, 131, 136
Johnston, Donald, 163
Jones, Harry, 55
Jones, John Paul, 33
Jones, Marita, 111
Jumper, Will C., xii

Kaldor, Don, 44
Kazan, Elia, 58
Kelly, Herbert D., xii, 134-36
Kendall, Gov. Nathan, 9, 60
Kenline, Judge Karl, 23
Kennan, George F., 147
Kennedy, President John F., 83
Kenyon, Dorothy, 111
Kerensky, Alexander, 4

Kilmer, Carl, 122
Kilmer, Harry J., 122-23
Kilmer, Paul, 26
King, Sen., 13
Kinnamon, Jon, 121
Kirkwood, Robert, 18
Kirschbaum, Ray and Kathryn, 113
Kittleman, Judge H. J., 81
Klahn, Richard P., 63
Knock, Joseph R., 131
Kraschel, Gov. Nelson, 17-19
Kugel, Dr. Robert, 76
Kuh, Frederick, 133
Kutish, Francis, 44

Ladejinsky, Wolf, 130
Laird, Melvin, 108
Lamont, Corliss, 36, 132
Lamoreux, Marcus, 171
Lane, Stoddard, 14
Lannon, Sharp, 71
Latimer, T. E., 7-8
Laughlin, Donald E., 53
Lawrence, Sarah, 133
Lechner, Rosemarie, xi
Le Tourneau, L. K., 71
Levine, Sidney, 81, 136
Levy, Herbert M., 165
Levy, Robert J., 94
Lewis, J. C., 14
Lewisohn, Alice, 3
Ligutti, Msgr. Luigi, 23
Lincoln, Edwin, 71
Lippmann, Walter, xiii
Long, Ronald, 97
Longren, William, 18
Loomis, Marie, 171
Loveless, Gov. Herschel C., 24
Lovett, Robert Morse, 166
Lubbers, I. J., 91
Lucas, Cynthia, 87
Lucchini, Katherine, 59
Lumpkins, Rev. Clay, 75
Luoma, Everett O., 164
Lutter, John, 100-101
Lynd, Robert S., 166

McCarthy, Sen. Joseph, 117, 132
McCormally, John, 122
McManus, Judge Edward J., 70

McMichael, Ethel F., 109
McNair, Jerome, 33
McSwiggin, Judge John J., 58
McWilliams, Carey, 166
Machlin, Jerome S., 168
Malcolm, Mary, 71
Malin, Patrick Murphy, 33-35, 139-40
Mannheimer, Rabbi Eugene, 61
Mannheimer, Robert E., 26, 61, 81, 106
Maple, Clair, 126
Markman, Sherwin, 57, 110
Markt, Vera, xii
Martin, James, 68
Mason, E. R., 8
Matias, Robert, 120
Maucker, William, 41
Maxwell, Judge, 97
Maytag, E. H., 19
Meiklejohn, Alexander, 166
Messerly, Francis, 47-48
Meyerding, Ed, 61
Miles, Frank, 18, 29
Miles, Gen. Nelson A., 3
Miller, Sen. Jack, 92, 112
Milner, Lucille B., 9, 29, 42
Mollenhoff, Clark, 130
Monroe, Eason, 35
Morgan, Charles, 38
Morris, James, 101
Morrissey, Claudia, 132, 136
Murphy, Donald R., 5, 28, 34, 130, 133, 136
Murray, John S., 98, 128
Murray, Pauli, 111
Murray, William G., 43-44
Myron, Julius, 57

Needham, Judge Dring, 110
Neibur, Richard, 18
Neith, John, 123
Nelles, Walter, 8
Newell, E. C., 14
Nicholle, William, 40
Nixon, President Richard, 37, 39, 48, 104, 119
Norris, David A., 46
Noun, Louise, xi-xii, 39, 82, 97, 108, 110-12, 122, 124, 130-31, 133, 136

Name Index

Nueborne, Burt, 76

Oberbillig, Robert C., 98
Oliver, Lawrence, 102
O'Neill, James, 42-43
Osmundson, Judge Robert, 121
Oxberger, Judge Leo, 85

Painter, Harold, 73-75
Painter, Jeanne, 73
Painter, Mark, 73, 75
Painter, Marylyn, 73
Papcun, George, 11-12
Paradise, Judge George M., 83
Parker, Addison, 23, 106
Parks, W. Robert, 46-47, 130
Patterson, Isadore, 100
Paulsen, Arnold, 44
Payer, Donald R., 74-75
Peck, George J., 12
Pemberton, John de. J., Jr., 108
Pendleton, Judge Donald, 83
Pendray, Mrs. C. C., 165
Pierce, James M., 5
Platt, John, 121
Pollard, R. H., 19
Polson, James, 97
Pounds, Russell G., 38, 102, 136
Proudfoot, A. U., 12

Quist, Oval, 24, 110, 136

Railsbach, Rep. Tom, 119
Rampona, Dr. Joseph and Mrs. Ruth, xi
Ransom, Charles F., xii, 60, 102, 130, 136
Ray, Gov. Robert, 26, 91, 121, 126, 131
Reed, Rev. J. W., 12
Reitman, Alan, 20
Remige, Rev. E. A., 19-20
Reno, Milo, 10-11
Rhodes, Don, 55
Roberts, Earl, 62
Robinson, William, 93
Rockefeller, Nelson, 83
Rogo, Arnold A., 165
Roosevelt, President Franklin, 55

Root, Robert, 161
Rosemont, Franklin, 20
Ross, Earle D., 167
Rugg, Harold, 57
Rundquist, George E., 33-34, 118, 140
Rupe, W. B., 41
Ryan, Rep. Bryce, 41, 110

Sawyer, Craig, 65, 82, 107
Saylor, Eugene, 58
Scalise, Atty. Gen. Lawrence, 89
Schantz, Mark, 26, 104
Schoenthal, Val, 26, 35, 74, 82
Schultz, Theodore W., 40-43
Schumann, Rev. Wilhelm, 9
Schwarzschild, Henry, 109
Schweitzer, Jay, 85
Schwieder, Elmer and Dorothy, 170
Scism, Robert, 56
Scott, Judge George C., 10
Selden, Lauren, 108
Sellers, Charles E., 87, 88
Semple, Alfred, 85
Sendlinger, W. W., 90
Sentner, William, 17-18, 20
Serson, George F., 92
Shadduck, Ione, 85, 115
Shapiro, Sid, 173
Shepherd, Geoffrey, 44
Shields, Earl, 18
Shorb, Robert, 52
Shover, John L., 164
Shull, Henry C., 41
Shuman, Charles R., 44-45
Sieverding, V. F., 60
Slycord, William, 62
Smith, Rev. Gordon, 91
Smith, James R., 61
Smith, Rep. Neal, 92
Smith, Stephen, 107
Smith, Theron, 57
Soth, Lauren, 53
Spaulding, Forrest, 31, 57
Spaulding, J. Lloyd, 105
Stalnaker, Luther W., 31, 136
Steffen, Judge Philip, 118-19
Stein, David J., 124

Stephenson, Richard, 92, 96
Stephenson, Judge Roy, 66, 94
Stevens, Harold, 173
Stiles, Florence, 168
Stone, I. F., 166
Stuart, Judge William C., 94
Sullivan, George, 87
Synhorst, Melvin, 58

Tatum, Lyle, 61, 105
Terrell, Harry, 12
Thomas, Donald E., 120-21
Thomas, Rev. James, 91
Thomas, Norman, 3, 105, 131
Thomas, William K., 47
Thompson, Edna, 81
Thompson, Leon, 45
Thompson, Ronald E., 50
Tidrich, Judge Don T., 75
Tinker, John F., 65
Tinker, Leonard, 65
Tinker, Mary Beth, 65
Tonn, Henry, 14
Treuhaft, Robert, 75
Truman, President Harry, 132
Turner, Elizabeth, 111, 136
Turner, Atty. Gen. Richard C., 58, 114, 133
Twitty, Alfred, 100-101

Uhlenhopp, Justice Harvey, 72
Utterback, Hubert, 8
Uviller, Rena K., 76

Van Vliet, D. W., 41-42
Vernon, David, 26, 119
Vieg, John, 40
Villard, Oswald G., 163
Vinson, Carl, 172

Wald, Lillian D., xv, 3, 105
Walker, Kenneth, 60, 61

Walker, Max, 61
Wall, Beatrice, 26
Wall, Joseph F., 46, 130
Walter, William, 168
Wangerin, Otto, 7
Ward, Harry F., 29
Watts, Rowland, 57
Waymack, W. W., 28
Webber, Robert, 111
Webster, Daniel, 105
Weinberg, Howard, 136
Weinberger, Casper, 114
Welch, William, 122
Welk, Barbara, 59
Weston, Hanna, 39, 126
Wheeler, Lewis Stephen, 62, 104
White, John K., 12
White, Robert, 55
Whitfield, Allen, 11
Whitmer, Dale C., 170
Whitney, A. F., 166
Wilhelm, Henry, 58
Williams, Horace E., 172
Willoughby, George, 52, 61
Wilson, Sen. George A., 168
Wilson, James F., 99
Wilson, Robert, 120
Wilson, President Woodrow, 4, 8, 13
Wirds, J. F., 80
Wolf, Melvin H., 84, 123
Wolkstein, Irwin, 172
Woodward, W. Theo, 15
Wooters, Dr. R. C., 62
Wulf, Melvin L., 20

Yates, Stanley M., 126

Zahradnik, Miriam, 116
Ziwet, Alexander, xiv, xv, xvi